Women
of
Letters

Selected Letters of

Elizabeth Barrett Browning
&
Mary Russell Mitford

Elizabeth Barrett Browning
(1806–1861)

Drawn at Swallowfield
April 12ᵗʰ 1852
John Lucas
To Mrs Acton Tindal, with Mr Lucas's respectful compliments

Mary Russell Mitford
(1787–1855)

Women
of
Letters

Selected Letters of

Elizabeth Barrett Browning

&

Mary Russell Mitford

Edited and Introduced by

Meredith B. Raymond and
Mary Rose Sullivan

TWAYNE PUBLISHERS • BOSTON
A Division of G.K. Hall & Co

LIBRARY OF CONGRESS CATALOGING-IN-PUBLICATION DATA

Browning, Elizabeth Barrett, 1806–1861.
  Women of letters.

  Includes index.
    1. Browning, Elizabeth Barrett, 1806–1861—
Correspondence.   2. Mitford, Mary Russell, 1787–1855—
Correspondence.   3. Poets, English—19th century—
Correspondence.   4. Authors, English—19th century—
Correspondence.   I. Mitford, Mary Russell, 1787–1855.
II. Raymond, Meredith B.   III. Sullivan, Mary Rose.
IV. Title.
PR4193.A46   1987   821'.8 [B]   87-28136
ISBN 0-8057-9023-3

This publication is printed on permanent/durable acid-free paper
MANUFACTURED IN THE UNITED STATES OF AMERICA

CONTENTS

Contents

FLORENCE, BAGNI DI LUCCA, AND ROME
Conclusion—Late Successes and Last Words,
1853–54 *253*

INTRODUCTION

Publication in 1983 of *The Letters of Elizabeth Barrett Browning to Mary Russell Mitford 1836–1854* made clear that Elizabeth Barrett Browning's correspondence with her friend and fellow writer provides both an attractive introduction to the career and personality of one of the century's best letter writers and an enlightening view of relationships between women writers in nineteenth-century England. It also offers important commentary on social history. The complete three-volume edition, however—containing almost 500 extensively annotated letters—is inaccessible to the larger public, which has become increasingly interested in women of letters and, in particular, in Elizabeth Barrett Browning, whose *Aurora Leigh* is the age's major statement about the woman artist. Hence the decision to select from the complete edition some 100 representative letters, or excerpts of letters, for reprinting, with minimal annotation, and to add some examples of Mary Russell Mitford's side of the correspondence.

The rationale for selecting the Elizabeth Barrett Browning letters was twofold. First, these letters provide the reader with a narrative thread of significant events in the almost twenty-year span of the correspondence—events which explain the interests, personal and literary, which propelled the friendship and encompassed EBB's serious illness and long confinement, her release into marriage and motherhood, and her rise to international acclaim as a poet. Second, they illustrate her theories and opinions on a range of topics of general interest, such as literature, politics, marriage, and the place of woman in society, especially that of the woman artist. Choice of the Mary Russell Mitford letters, on the other hand, was dictated largely by their availability and relevance. Her correspondence has so far appeared only in some early collections that suffer from editorial excisions and inaccuracies of transcription. Limited and incomplete as these token selections included here must be—making MRM's voice simply an obbligato to EBB's solo—they serve to give the reader a sense of her brisk, unpretentious style, her wide-ranging interests and forthright views, and her abiding affection for her one-time protégée.

When the correspondence began in 1836, EBB (as she signed

herself, for Elizabeth Barrett Barrett) was a thirty-year-old aspiring poet, and MRM (who remained throughout the correspondence "ever dearest Miss Mitford" to EBB) was forty-nine and famous for her mastery of the prose idyl. Introduced by the genial literary dilettante John Kenyon, EBB and MRM visited the British Gallery and the Chiswick gardens and, on MRM's return to her home at Three Mile Cross near Reading, immediately began to correspond—about their work, reading, families, health, and friends. After EBB contributed to a series of annuals MRM was editing, the initial footing of mentor and protégée shifted to that of collaborators. Over the years it was to shift many more times, with EBB eventually assuming on various occasions the roles of confidante, advisor, critic, and consoler. A modern reader is struck by the obvious differences between the two friends—not only of age but of background, temperament, and character—but what makes the strength and durability of the friendship surprising to us made it the more satisfying to them.

Just a generation the elder, MRM was more a child of the eighteenth century than the nineteenth. Born 16 December 1787 at Alresford, Hampshire, she was the only surviving child of Mary Russell, a descendant of the ducal Bedfords, and George Mitford, a doctor who preferred cards and coursing to practicing medicine and who ran with equal speed through his wife's fortune and his daughter's childhood lottery winnings. Although in her early years MRM lived in the stately Bertram House and attended a school in Chelsea, which gave her a firm grounding in English literature and the French language as well as a certain cosmopolitan ambience, at the time she met EBB she and her father had been reduced to renting the cottage at Three Mile Cross. In the 1820s she made a name, and some little money, by writing a series of historical dramas, the most famous of which was *Rienzi* (1828), but she was and remains most widely known and loved for the idyllic sketches of country life originally appearing in the *Ladies Magazine* and collected under the title *Our Village*.

By the time of her meeting with EBB, MRM's productive professional life was essentially over. There were to be no further stage triumphs and, despite the urgings of EBB and others, few tales after the publication of *Country Stories* in 1837. She chose to devote herself to her aged father and her prize-winning geraniums, to entertaining visitors at tea and enjoying books and country walks with her dog. Her only writing—except for a book of fiction (*Atherton and Other Tales*) and one of literary reminiscences (*Recollections of a Literary Life*) in the last two years of her life—was an occasional editing task taken on to pay debts, like that for *Findens' Tableaux* to which EBB had contributed between 1837 and 1840. After Dr. Mitford's death in 1842, MRM's life was beset with frustrations—failure of publishing expectations, declining health exacerbated by several accidents, and domestic crises. Various schemes for a change of residence did not materialize until conditions at the cottage forced her to move to nearby Swallowfield in 1851. Here her last years were brightened by a more comfortable dwelling, correspondence with such new friends as John Ruskin and James T. Fields, and the constant, affectionate letters of EBB as, by slow degrees but sure, her world shrank from countryside and garden to house and chair and bed. Still an indomitable letter writer, she continued her correspondence virtually to the day of her death in January 1855.

Forced by Dr. Mitford's extravagances to provide an income for them both, MRM came to regard writing as a craft to be mastered and to be exercised pragmatically. Clarity and precision of concrete detail were hallmarks of her best work, often compared to fine etching, and were the characteristics she valued in others' work. She read memoirs, letters, and novels not, like EBB, for revelations of inner life, but for reflections of the manners and style of a society. Her own manners and appearance were as unadorned as her writing style. Short and stout in figure, she ignored fashion and, surprisingly, scorned bluestockings and "Pen and Ink" types—pretentious amateur women writers. Nevertheless, she was accepted among the lions of literary London and her calendar on her infrequent visits to the city was a crowded one.

By contrast EBB was, by her own admission, introspective and sensitive, a dreamer, and a worshiper of Romantic poets, especially Byron. From earliest childhood she was convinced of her own vocation as poet. Despite its evangelical coloring, her background fostered this romanticism. Born 6 March 1806 at Coxhoe Hall, Durham, eldest of eleven surviving children of Edward Barrett Moulton-Barrett (known as "Edward Barrett"), whose wealth originated in his family's Jamaican trade and plantations, and Mary Graham-Clarke, daughter of a lawyer and successful businessman, she spent her early years at a palatial estate built by her father at Hope End near the Malvern Hills in Herefordshire. Here she wrote family birthday odes, an epic poem at age twelve, taught herself Hebrew, and translated Greek. Her mother died in 1828 and, after financial reverses in the Jamaican interests forced the sale of Hope End, the family moved first to Sidmouth in 1832 and three years later to London, eventually settling at 50 Wimpole Street in 1838. Their comfortable, upper-middle-class existence buttressed by a staff of servants and somewhat distanced by Mr. Barrett's aversion to society, allowed EBB a reclusive life, especially after recurrence of a lung disease, first diagnosed at age fifteen. The outing with MRM in May 1836 was a rare occurrence and EBB describes her anxieties in the retrospective paragraphs of her letter of 1 April 1842. For the next decade her energy was given to reading and writing poetry, including the *Findens' Tableaux* contributions for MRM. In 1838, at the time her volume *The Seraphim, and Other Poems* received favorable notice, a lung hemorrhage forced her removal to the milder climate of Torquay in Devon where in 1840 her brother "Bro" was drowned in a boating accident. Prostrated with shock, EBB was unable to rejoin her family in Wimpole Street until the following year. Eventually she was able to resume her writing, including some critical essays, and in 1844 published *Poems*, a collection that established her poetic reputation at home and abroad. This event also brought a letter from an admirer of her work, the poet Robert Browning. Their correspondence led to courtship and in September 1846, to the surprise of family and friends—including MRM—EBB and Browning married—secretly, to avoid a confrontation with her father,—and left for a new life in Italy, where her health improved dramatically. After the first winter in Pisa, they moved to Florence and ultimately established themselves in Casa Guidi, the fifteenth-century palazzo that became their principal residence until EBB's death in 1861. Here their child Robert Wiedemann (or "Pen") was born in 1849 and here both poets continued their writing careers. In 1851 and 1852, when the Brownings returned to England for a visit, MRM was in failing health; by the time of their next return in 1856 she had died, without again seeing EBB or her crowning poetic achievement, *Aurora Leigh*, completed that year.

Thus the friendship between EBB and MRM was one conducted essentially on paper. Illnesses and geographical separations prevented their meeting scarcely more than a half-dozen times in eighteen years. In the early years MRM periodically made the forty-mile journey to London, but for three years EBB was at some distance in Torquay, and after her marriage, only a visitor to England. MRM came to see EBB and her husband and child on their London visit in 1851, but the next year EBB's illness prevented a planned trip to Swallowfield.

Necessary or not, visiting by way of letters seemed to have been, for both, the more satisfactory form of contact. For MRM, a natural, spirited talker, the dark and airless sickroom at Wimpole Street must have had a sobering effect. For EBB, on the other hand, shy and nervous, her voice weakened by disease, the excitement of entertaining callers brought about sleepless nights before and after. Barely audible, her small, pale face almost hidden by the dark curls hanging on either side, she seemed to callers like MRM an almost disembodied spirit. But when she took pen in hand, she reveled in the opportunity to participate on her own terms in a lively give-and-take; she lost her shyness and became, in John Kenyon's words, "perverse" or "obstinate," always articulate and often eloquent.

Their correspondence filled a void in the lives of both women. At the outset, EBB was hungry, in the midst of a large and doting family, for someone with whom she could share her poetic aspirations and her passion for books. "How delightful to be able to write so heart to heart to you!" she wrote after one satisfying exchange. "There is no one in the world whom I w^d or c^d write so to except yourself!" Although surrounded by chatting visitors, MRM felt the same urge for a companionship that was intellectually and emotionally congenial. Mutual needs overrode disparities of temperament and background and made likenesses more apparent. Both, after precocious childhoods marked by literary ambitions, had matured into independent-minded women who remained, nevertheless, under the strong influence of dominating fathers. Both were, moreover, because of uncertain health, unusually dependent on medical men and the services of maids. Both were omnivorous readers, with a fondness for Shakespeare, seventeenth-century playwrights, eighteenth-century letter-writers, and nineteenth-century memoirists and novelists. Both were also actively curious about their contemporary world. They exchanged reading lists, political opinions, and news of friends and public figures, and had lengthy discussions about symptoms, medical diagnoses, and cures of major and minor ailments. They subscribed to the same foreign-book catalog, and traded gossip obtained from MRM's informant at court and EBB's brother George on the legal circuit. Both women were correspondents of the painter Benjamin Haydon and the journalist-author Richard H. Horne. They particularly enjoyed any information on the peripatetic and eminently marriageable John Kenyon, who first brought them together. A genial widower whose wife had been MRM's friend, he was also a distant cousin of

EBB's father, and as generous with his society as with his fortune (and later was to become a faithful benefactor of EBB in her married life). A special link between the two friends was Flush, offspring of MRM's spaniel, sent to Torquay in 1841 to divert the despondent EBB—which he did, with spectacular success, from then until his death only months before MRM's.

It was a solid basis for friendship, a meeting of minds and hearts, but not one dependent on seeing eye to eye on every topic. EBB enjoyed "quarreling" over such subjects as the respective merits of a Frederika Bremer and a Jane Austen; such debates illustrated a "singular *sympathy in dyspathy*" between her and MRM that was far more stimulating than mere agreement. Sometimes the disagreements ran deeper: EBB's exalted view of the poet's moral function, for example, was never shared by MRM who demanded a certain clarity of expression and who held a less romantic view of poetry than EBB. EBB vigorously defended her views, not only of Browning (who perfectly matched her idea of a "true poet"), but of her own taste for religious subjects, holding, with Burns, that "An irreligious poet is a Monster." The marked move away from mystical themes in her *Poems* (1844), however, probably owed something to MRM's influence. The most popular poem in that collection, "Lady Geraldine's Courtship," was written, she admitted to MRM, "more on your principle than mine." And it was the favorable reception of this poem, weaving topical allusions into a romantic narrative, that encouraged EBB to write her long verse-novel about modern life, *Aurora Leigh*. Mainly, MRM provided a sounding board for EBB's ideas and a sympathetic ear for confiding emotions too intimate to disclose to anyone else. To no other correspondent does she tell so much about her remorse over Bro's death and its effect on her already complex relationship with her father; her fascination with George Sand as a writer and a woman; her curiosity about Harriet Martineau's mesmeric "cure"; her chafing at the overbearing behavior of a visitor, and hopeful suitor, Rev. George B. Hunter; and her appetite for sensational French novels and for gossip about the marriage prospects of Horne, Kenyon, and Tennyson.

In return, EBB provided help to MRM in a variety of forms: gifts of food, drink, medicines, and household items during the protracted illness of Dr. Mitford, and practical advice on a range of topics from the investing of MRM's subscription to ship schedules for a neighbor's trip. For all her down-to-earth attitude toward writing, MRM was surprisingly impractical in managing her affairs and the reclusive

EBB found herself called on for advice on dealing with publishers, rental agents, and feckless servants. Her counsel—to treat the mischief-makers fairly but firmly—may not always have been followed by MRM but was gratefully received. The image of EBB, at almost literally the last moment before leaving Wimpole Street forever, sending her maid out to renew MRM's foreign-book subscription, and again, of her taking time out from her poetry to copy out the entire list of Balzac's works for MRM's benefit, proves that the relationship was grounded in affection as well as gratitude.

Certain parallels in EBB's and MRM's experience, despite their differing backgrounds, carry implications about the lives of women in general in nineteenth-century England. EBB's domination by her father seems to have been matched by MRM's almost slavish devotion to Dr. Mitford, even though that sports-loving country gentleman had neither the moral nor the economic power of a paterfamilias like Edward Barrett. Both women, despite their mature age and professional status, seemed acutely sensitive to other expressions of masculine opinion: MRM of Henry Chorley's "looking grave" at their choice of a friend and EBB of the Rev. Hunter's criticism of her poetry. Both were victims of primitive medical practice. MRM's attendant Mr. May seems to have been able to offer little help for her physical ailments but sympathy, and EBB—whose doctors included a court physician—benefited scarcely more from the medically approved treatment of tuberculosis, which included prescribing of blisters and opium and confinement to airless rooms. Although their religious views differed, MRM belonging at least nominally to the Church of England, and EBB being quite determinedly evangelical, they were both attracted to parapsychology and the occult—clairvoyance, mesmerism, and spiritualism—interests which perhaps reflected a feeling in both women that institutionalized religion left questions about the mysteries of existence not fully answered. Even their experiences with servants show a similarity of emotional turmoil when a favorite maid left service, suggesting that habits of dependency—perhaps exacerbated by their physical frailties—carried over into the most intimate sphere.

In the sphere of the professional woman, the relationship of EBB and MRM seems, except for its intensity, characteristic of the way many women writers interacted. Of those mentioned in these letters—poets like Joanna Baillie and Felicia Hemans, novelists like

Frances Trollope and Ellen Pickering, travel writers and historians like Julia Pardoe and Jane Porter—all were friends or correspondents of MRM—a fact which suggests a kind of informal "networking" system among women writers was operating during the first half of the century. The astonishing number of women authors mentioned, whether experienced professionals like Mary Howitt and Harriet Martineau or rank amateurs like MRM's neighbors Henrietta Tindal and Lucy Partridge, suggests the openness of the literary marketplace, but the contacts between these women indicate a felt need to band together in a market run by male publishers, editors, and reviewers (women's editing being largely confined to the kind of ladies' magazines and giftbooks MRM worked on). Frequent mention by both EBB and MRM of writers seeking pensions, subscriptions, better publishing terms, or copyright protection reflects the profession's financial insecurity (not of course restricted to women) and the cultivation of friendships among publishing women allowed for newcomers to the profession to receive advice, criticism, helpful introductions, or simply encouragement in a competitive field. Hence, even a painfully shy EBB could, like a long line of aspiring writers before her, initiate a correspondence with the famous Miss Mitford, confident of an encouraging reply; hence, too, a young Dinah Mulock could dedicate a novel to the celebrated Elizabeth Barrett Browning and be sure of a gracious response. It was not a matter of blind favoritism toward their own sex—MRM scorned women celebrity hunters and EBB dismissed much of the ladies' magazine writing as "trash'—but rather an unspoken assumption that successful women, like themselves, in the profession owed something to those who followed after.

More specifically, the established woman writer served as a role model for younger women seeking exemplars. EBB, for example, was always intensely interested in other women poets, almost as much in their private lives as in their work. Feeling the lack of women's tradition in poetry, she allied herself for a time with minor talents like Felicia Hemans and Letitia Landon, perhaps because of her sympathy for their melancholy personal histories rather than for a sense of poetic kinship. She quickly moved beyond them, however, when introduced to women of more substantive achievement, like Anna Jameson, Harriet Martineau, and George Sand—all of whom were successful within, but independent of, the male establishment. She took to measuring herself against them, contrasting, for example, Harriet Martineau's courage in enduring public ridicule for a principle with her own position of shrinking from a public stand on controversial Corn Laws. But, motivated by love and courage, she did not shrink from the extraordinary decision to marry without parental consent or knowledge and thereby to free herself from the familial dependence that had governed her entire life. Thus she joined a significant group of women of that time who defied social conventions and chose a course of action based on its own merits.

As these letters show, for women seeking mutual support, letter writing was a natural medium. Even the busiest professional writer could find time to correspond at a frequency and length quite foreign to present-day letter writers. Further, letters were saved, even when not planned for publication, although the idea of publication may often have been a latent hope. MRM admitted, for example, that she might publish her letters from Bath and EBB accepted that some of her own letters might eventually be published—but only posthumously. Aware of Victorian publishing practices, she probably assumed that nineteenth-century editors would liberally excise personal details. Judging by the EBB-MRM correspondence, however, neither spontaneity nor candor seems to have been affected by the possibility of a wider audience.

For MRM, often harried by requests for help, letter writing was often simply a necessary chore, to be done on whatever scrap of paper was at hand, and her large loose handwriting, often crossing over her own lines, indicates haste as well as vigor. She writes to communicate rather than to ruminate, but occasionally a letter, such as her report in [January 1845] of the neighborhood children's party for the Queen, conveys a real pleasure at recreating a memorable moment not only for the shut-in EBB but for herself and, quite possibly, for posterity.

For EBB, on the contrary, letters played a very different role. She rapturously describes her feelings: "For now, I will confess to you. I like letters per se . . & as letters! I like the abstract idea of a letter—I like the postman's rap at the door—I like the queen's head upon the paper—and with a negation of queen's heads (which doesn't mean treason) I like the sealing wax under the seal and the postmark on the envelope." The appearance of her letters conveys a similar delight in the act of writing: abbreviations and expressive dashes and ellipses reflect exuberance and rapidity of thought and postscripts and lines running onto margins and the flap of the envelope show a reluctance to "make an end." For her, writing a letter was an opportunity not only to share thoughts and feelings but to apprehend experience more fully as it took form for her reader.

EBB's best letters are, in fact, the fine art of conversation on paper, and even the conventional Victorian expressions of affection, effusive by modern standards, cannot obscure the originality, grace, and flexibility of EBB's style. Once she recovered from her initial self-conscious literary manner evident in the early letters to the celebrated Miss Mitford, she fell into her natural easy expression marked by clarity and nuanced precision. It is a style that conveys her individual quality of thought, experience, and emotion sincerely and completely, yet fuses tact with honesty. The reader senses the evaluative element and quite naturally begins to form a profile of her personality. Her passion for truth even when narrating a dramatic and emotional episode is illustrated in the breathless account of Flush's dramatic rescue from the dog-stealers, as she pauses for a qualification: "I never slept (or scarcely) for the second night." The description of her visit to George Sand, in its detailed rendering of dress, gesture, and dialogue, its sense of immediacy and its narrative pace, is more akin to imaginative literature than mere reporting. It is a way to savor the relived moment and to let MRM experience it vicariously. EBB can be self-deprecatingly witty and adept at the unobtrusive literary allusion: "I have taken a great gasp of courage and sent a copy [of her poems] to Carlyle. I pray all the heroes that he may not devote the entrails of my votive sacrifice to make endpapers for Mrs. Carlyle." She can turn a neat image: "the spiders have grown tame—and their webs are a part of our own domestic œconomy"; a departed visitor has "gone into solitude at the back of the Isle of Wight . . by a tether of ten days." She can be subtle or forthright as the occasion demands, slyly teasing or grave, reticent or expansive, but never devious or self-pitying. And, finally, her wide reading is reflected in the numerous quotations and allusions she weaves into her paragraphs for emphasis, clarification, or humor; thus, "The letters . . . will stand confessed in the yet unopen eyes of 'Prince Posterity;' " or "here . . . some two hundred yards from Regent's Park which opens out to 'Hampstead's breezy heath' it is all imagination to cry out for 'air' "; or "We tried to make the monks of Vallombrosa let us stay with them for two months—but their new abbot implied that Wilson and I stank in his nostrils, being women." Writing from the heart, she often betrays her turmoil ("I have thrown down the paper, and taken it up again"), but she will destroy a "moaning" letter—"you might have heard it moan in your hand"—rather than inflict it on MRM. It is this combination of grace of spirit and grace of expression that makes her letters so rewarding to the reader, whether a Mary Russell Mitford responding to the emotion of the moment or a modern reader responding after the passage of a century.

Beyond the intrinsic value of EBB's letters, a major reward of reading her correspondence with MRM is the opportunity to watch history unfolding from a highly personal angle. Most of the major events of the mid-century touched their lives to some degree: the end of the slave trade, for example, reflected in the Barretts' loss of Hope End. We see Victoria as young wife and mother—as well as beleaguered monarch, in the Lady Flora Hastings affair—in MRM's reports from her court informant, along with such humanizing touches as the queenly preference for lion tamers over Shakespeare and the Duke of Wellington's role of parsimonious host to royalty. Legislative reform takes on a personal significance when EBB agonizes over writing for the Anti-Corn Law League. The Irish political question comes down to the controversial personality of Daniel O'Connell. Expansion of the Great Western Railroad means for MRM the possibility of a train trip to Bath; replacement of franking with the penny postage system means that letters will reach Three Mile Cross or Wimpole Street within a day. On a grander scale, celebration of the Florentine Grand Duke's reforms and of Louis Napoleon's triumphal entrance into Paris are events reported by EBB as eyewitness. And literary stars of the age appear in unfamiliar or informal poses: Robert Browning strolling in the park with George Sand, Margaret Fuller Ossoli presenting EBB's child with a Bible; Ruskin bringing his bride to meet MRM.

Against this crowded background, the personal story of crises and successes reads like plot and subplot of an engrossing novel. Early traumas—Bro's sudden death and Dr. Mitford's long final illness—are followed by other losses, many shocking: Benjamin Haydon's suicide, the shipwreck of the Ossolis, the Story child's death of fever in Rome. The triumphant drama of Robert Browning's entrance into EBB's life, their courtship, flight to Italy, and their child's birth are counterpointed by sorrows: EBB's miscarriages and continuing estrangement from her father; the death of Robert's mother; MRM's mishaps and declining health. Throughout there are diverting adventures—Flush's rescue from dog thieves, Horne's dalliances with heiresses at Three Mile Cross—and deep satisfactions, like the proposal that EBB be made laureate and the popularity of MRM's late publications. The final triumph is in the way the friendship withstands all the strains imposed by the passage of time, geographical separation, and difference of opinion, with mutual respect and affection enduring to the end. Here is a record of friendship between "women of letters" that simultaneously presents a biographical, social, and historical record. Finally, this correspondence reveals insights into the creative process—the labor, aspirations, failures, and successes attendant upon the efforts of two women writers whose achievements won them, and continue to win them, deserved recognition.

A Note on This Edition

The text of Elizabeth Barrett Browning's letters is taken from *The Letters of Elizabeth Barrett Browning to Mary Russell Mitford 1836–1854*, 3 vols., ed. Meredith B. Raymond and Mary Rose Sullivan (Winfield, Kansas: Armstrong Browning Library of Baylor University, The Browning Institute, Wedgestone Press, and Wellesley College, 1983). The format of dates has been standardized, with conjectured dates in square brackets. A question mark follows a doubtful element—for example, in [4? June 1842] the day is subject to question while the month and year are based on firm evidence. The day of the week is supplied in square brackets when omitted by EBB. Where she did not supply an address it has been omitted, as the headnotes indicate changes of location. Words or letters in ⟨ ⟩ are illegible in the manuscript because of blots or tears. Words or letters enclosed in [ ] do not appear in the manuscript and are inserted for clarity of meaning.

The main body of manuscripts for the letters of Elizabeth Barrett Browning to Mary Russell Mitford is in the English Poetry Collection at Wellesley College, Wellesley, Massachusetts, and we gratefully acknowledge permission for their use. A complete list of the letters taken from this collection appears in Appendix C at the end of this volume.

We also acknowledge permission granted by the Folger Shakespeare Library, Washington, D.C., to use fragments of a few letters bound in Folger MS W.6.47; by the Syndics of the Fitzwilliam Museum, Cambridge, England, to use five letters plus some fragments; by Edward R. Moulton-Barrett, Platt, England, to use several fragments (many on envelopes) from his private collection; by the British

Library, British Museum, London, to use the letter dated 20 August [1847]; and by the Beinecke Rare Book and Manuscript Library of Yale University, New Haven, Connecticut, for the letter dated 24 September [1851].

Further comments on the history of the collection may be found in the preface to the 1983 edition of the letters.

Acknowledgment is also made to John Murray Publishers, London, for arranging copyright permission with Twayne Publishers, Boston, Massachusetts.

A special note of appreciation is due Philip Kelley, who bore the main responsibility for the genesis and completion of the three-volume edition. For the present edition, we acknowledge the editorial and production staff of G. K. Hall and Co. Among those to whom we are indebted are: John Amburg, Athenaide Dallett, Lewis DeSimone, Michael Sims, Elizabeth B. Todesco.

The text of the selections from Mary Russell Mitford's letters is taken from *The Life of Mary Russell Mitford, Told by Herself in Letters to Her Friends*, 3 vols., ed. A. G. K. L'Estrange (New York, 1870) and *The Friendships of Mary Russell Mitford as Recorded in Letters From Her Literary Correspondents*, 2 vols., ed. A. G. L'Estrange (London, 1882). Some obvious errors in transcription have been silently corrected. The dates, except where our correction is indicated by a *sic*, are those of L'Estrange. Other elements in the headings, as well as ellipses, are also those of these editions.

A word about EBB's idiosyncrasies of spelling and punctuation is necessary. Because EBB fairly frequently misspelled words, not always consistently, no attempt has been made to call attention to each misspelling by a *sic* or to normalize the spelling. She was also inconsistent in the use of apostrophes, accent marks, quotation marks, and capital letters. Her most common punctuation mark, the dash (used usually as the full stop), often, by its length, denotes degrees of emotion, as does the number of exclamation points. We have retained these inconsistencies and idiosyncrasies as an integral part of her style. The spaced periods, usually two in number, are EBB's and, it should be emphasized, do not indicate editorial excision, which we have chosen to note by three bullets.

MEREDITH B. RAYMOND
MARY ROSE SULLIVAN

LONDON

Meeting and Collaboration
1836–38

EBB was living at 74 Gloucester Place in London with her father, sisters Henrietta and Arabel, and younger brothers Charles ("Stormy"), George, Henry, Alfred ("Daisy"), Septimus ("Sette"), and Octavius ("Occy"), when their mutual friend, the genial philanthropist John Kenyon (1784–1856), introduced her to MRM in 1836. EBB was thirty years old, but her life of semiretirement—caused by uncertain health and a protective family—made her seem much younger. (MRM described her at their meeting as "a delightful young creature; shy and timid and modest.") MRM was almost twenty years her senior, famous as a dramatist and fiction writer, feted by such luminaries as Wordsworth and Landor on her visit to London. Nevertheless, EBB began the correspondence by venturing to send to Three Mile Cross a copy of her 1833 translation of *Prometheus Bound* and some early poems ("the little book"). MRM responded with critical advice, an introduction to the influential literary critic of the *Athenæum*, Henry Chorley (1808–72), and, in June 1837, a request for a contribution to *Findens' Tableaux*, the fashionable gift-book annual she was editing for the publisher Charles Tilt. EBB sent a long ballad, "The Romance of the Ganges," and the relationship was firmly established on a professional as well as personal footing. EBB's initially self-conscious literary style gave way to her natural, easy manner as she eagerly shared enthusiasm for eighteenth-century writers like William Hayley (1745–

1

1820), author of *The Triumphs of Temper* (1781) and *Life of Cowper* (1803), and Anna Seward (1747–1809), poetess and author of six volumes of letters. She participated vicariously in MRM's country life of raising dogs and prize-winning geraniums as well as in her frustrating attempts to have a drama (*Otto*) produced in London. By the spring of 1838, the Barretts were settled into their permanent London home at 50 Wimpole Street. From here EBB wrote a poem for the 1839 *Findens' Tableaux* ("The Romaunt of the Page") and brought out her first volume of poetry under her own name, *The Seraphim, and Other Poems*, published by Saunders and Otley.

74 GLOUCESTER PLACE
FRIDAY MORNING. [3 JUNE 1836]

My dear Miss Mitford,

I send you the little book. I have been disappointed in not being able to have it bound in time: but I wish that its worst fault were on its outside!

In ending these happy days, you must let me thank you for allowing me to join together two ideas, each of them precious in its kind . . of an admired writer . . and a dear friend: & for allowing me to call them *Miss Mitford*. I thank you for this rather than for your personal & touching kindness to me—because it is easier.

May God bless you & make you happy in your re-union to those dearest to you. You were so kind—I sh^d not have dared to ask it—as to speak of writing to me. Will you write to me dear Miss Mitford, BEFORE I write to you: and will you do so as soon as you can spare a thought from the nature & affection to which you go, for the *least* important things of London?——

Your affectionate & obliged
E B Barrett.

Three-mile Cross
August 16, 1836.

My dear Friend—Did Henry Chorley call himself? He told me that his heart had failed him. The nosegay was a very shabby one—I was myself in all the grief of parting from this same Henry Chorley, one of the most affable companions I have ever known, and I was besides *befraddled* by the eternal visitors, morning and evening visitors, who make this cottage during the summer and autumn months a sort of tea-garden, or rural Beulah Spa[1]—then, John, the lad who manages my geraniums, was, on his part, in the joyful agony of preparing for the Reading Horticultural Show. For my own part, my vanity goes rather to the beauty of the flowers in a mass, or in that great nosegay my garden, than to the mere points of growth, and bloom, and sorts, by which the judges at flower-shows decide their merit. Nevertheless, as John loves to get prizes, and I have no objection, why we take the thing in very good part; only it certainly (joined with my grief at losing a pet visitor) spoilt your posy; at least made that shabby which ought to have been splendid.

You should take my venturing to criticise your verses as a proof of the perfect truth of my praise. I do not think there can be a better test of the sincerity of applause than the venturing to blame. It is also the fault, the one single fault, found by persons more accustomed to judge of poetry than myself; by Mr. Dilke,[2] for instance (the proprietor of the "Athenæum"), and Mr. Chorley (one of its principal writers). Charles Kemble[3] once said to me, with regard to the drama: "Think of the stupidest person of your acquaintance, and, when you have made your play so clear that you are sure that he would comprehend it, then you may venture to hope that it will be understood by your audience." And really I think the rule would hold good with regard to poetry in general, as well as tragedies. My Dash sends his respects to your doves; faithful and gentle they are both. Ever, my dear friend, most affectionately yours,

M. R. M.

1. The Royal Beulah Spa was a London tea-garden that could be rented for parties.
2. Charles Wentworth Dilke (1789–1864). EBB subscribed to the *Athenæum* (from 1836 to 1846) and occasionally contributed poems and essays to it.
3. Charles Kemble (1775–1854), actor-manager who appeared in MRM's *Foscari* in 1826.

74 GLOUCESTER PLACE.

WEDNESDAY. [24? AUGUST 1836]

·   ·   ·

I am sure dear Miss Mitford, I need not tell you that I thank you with grateful thoughts for both praise & criticism—& that I hope neither may be *more* thrown away than is made necessary by a good deal of unworthiness. Of course you are very right in the censuring part; and I will try to put more clearness & distinctness into my language as I go on attempting to write it. At the same time, & putting aside my own case as an indefensible one,—I mean to be bold enough to say to you that I do not & cannot see the force of M.ʳ Kemble's observation even with regard to tragedy unless you w.ᵈ apply it exclusively to the body or mechanism of tragedy—to the plot & management of the dialogue—& that I am quite sceptical as to the fact of any poet tragic or otherwise, writing poetry dramatic or otherwise, with the ideas of his creating faculty in eternal vicinity to the prescribed idea of "the stupidest person of his acquaintance".

"Oh! who *could* hold a fire in his hand
In thinking of that frosty Caucasus!"

Shakespeare w.ᵈ have bayed the moon till it was black in the face before he did such a thing! And above all—Æschylus! who wrote sublime riddles! What would *he* have said to M.ʳ Charles Kem⟨ble!⟩ Dear Miss Mitford! whatever YOU said, I am quite sure & you see I am mischievous enough to say it, that you never did his bidding—*whether you thought you did or not.*

You have not read all Tennyson's poems—neither have I—but did you see his 'mermaid' at the end of Leigh Hunt's paper on mermaids in the New Monthly Magazine? There is a tone in the poetry—in the very extravagance of the poetry & language—an abandonment & wildness—which seemed to me to accord beautifully with the subject, & stayed with me afterwards—a true sign of true poetry—whether I would or not. And if there are, as in far inferior writers, occasional perplexities & obscurations in the meaning—still, no one could complain of them *there*—seeing that the language seems to have caught its strangeness with its music from the Mermaid's tongue. Do read the poem & tell me that you like it.

I am very anxious to read something besides—having seen in Saunders & Ottley's catalogue of new publications—*A new novel by Miss Mitford*. How long are people to stand on tiptoe waiting for it?

Perhaps M.ʳ Chorley did not call here after all. My only reason for supposing that he did, was the sight of his card, & the hearing that a gentleman had brought it.

Somebody says that human nature loves to be envied, but when you told me of your "troops of friends" & compared your dwelling to Beulah Spa you proved yourself too virtuous for the pleasure. If my envy had begun, it ceased that moment—& I became miraculously contented with my *solitude* IN LONDON!

My hope for this presumptuous letter—I am afraid of reading it over for fear of confirming my own impression of it—is that you will forget its offences in M.ʳ Kenyon's conversation. You see he is going away from us for some time!!! but I am driven into the corner!

Your affec.ᵗᵉ
E B Barrett.

74 GLOUCESTER PLACE.
THURSDAY. [29? SEPTEMBER 1836]

· · ·

For all the kindness, the far far too much kindness of your words to me, how can I thank you enough? Let me be silent, & love you! And as to what you say that others say, I am much obliged—of course I am—to everybody! but not too obtuse to understand that your kind words have been the seeds of those kind words from those other people. And so I persist in thanking your's for their's, & M.ʳ Kenyon's for your's: yes! & your own generous affectionate spirit for your's, *as well as* M.ʳ Kenyon. He does deserve *me* to speak of him gratefully—& so I do! but he is at the Land's End by this time & cannot hear me. Before he went for the new six weeks tour, he told me about you & the dahlias, for the *thought* of which, receive my thanks. *It* is fresher than *they* could have been, had you done your kind will & sent them to me; for as nothing but withered stalks could I have seen them, after such a long pilgrimage without their roots. The letter (unlike the flowers—tho' the vanity chose to settle on *them*!) remained in that perpetual freshness which is the privelege of all Miss Mitford's written words (not of her flowers!) & which will stand confessed in the yet unopen eyes of "Prince Posterity", "when the landscape round he measures" about the Village, & debates the meaning of certain phrases relating to the obsolete game of cricket, at some new Roxburgh club. Now forgive the daring of predicting such obsoletism to *you*! Certainly no chief batter ever did so much to make it immortal as *you*! I have eight brothers—all of them cricketers,—even Occyta—who can *run*! and yet I do confess my infirmity of never standing to see a whole game in its beginning middle & end . . except at the Village. And as my brothers forgive me, *you* must (they put it down I dare say to the [']'natural inferiority''. of womankind!)—you must forgive me: & indeed dear Miss Mitford it is quite as well for me that you should have a little practice in forgiving before you come to the full sight of all the many many faults which your short knowledge of me & much kindness to me now hide from your discernment. You *frighten* me by praising me! May those [']'evils which you know not of'' find you expert in forgiving—& not repentant of loving. How sh^d I bear to lose every shred of *your* love, when I dont like to lose anybody's? It is very seldom perhaps never, that I wish those to love me who do not,—but if ever the love comes & goes—I *must* have a regret for it,—if not for the person's sake yet for the *abstraction's*. But not to walk in my obscure ways,—or into melancholy ways which are worse! let me enquire after your garden! and that is dark & melancholy too just now—is it not? or growing so? It must be well nigh shorn of its rays, & its vision—departed! a vision departing, I do trust, to make room for one brighter to dwellers in London. Do you know I cant help hoping—notwithstanding Mr Kenyon's ominous looks, & your ominous silence—I cant help hoping with my own *indigenous* sanguineness, that when there are no flowers to keep you in the country, you may help to carry the MSS into the city, & not leave the conveyance of them to Dr Mitford alone, as sadly "I heard sain" you thought of doing! I heard from the same tongue (Mr Kenyon's) something about this work I long so to read—how he heard from you the analysis of it, & how he liked it for its simplicity of story & consequent susceptiveness of the unfolding of individual character, & how the last touches of that hand which is "so fine a finisher," w^d secure for it the liking of everybody whose liking was worth securing. Will it be of the usual three volume length?——

Mrs Lenox Conyngham's[1] name had come to my ears but it was not familiar to them,—& your brief account of her w^d have interested me even if you had not said that she thought kindly of me. I am going to read her poems, & to go on reading Mr Chorley's Memorials.^{2} Shame upon me you may think, for not having finished reading *them* long ago! Indeed my not doing so was far from being caused by a want of respect for the biographer, or of love & admiration for that pure hearted & nobly gifted woman whose body & whose genius have gone each to its 'own place' —the earth & the memory of her country. Mr Chorley seems to have done his task in a spirit she w^d herself have chosen for such a task. You knew her—did you not? dear Miss Mitford⟨.⟩ We think the same of *her*,—if we do not of another. And perhaps we do of that other—beside⟨—⟩of Miss Landon.^{3} You *said* that we did. I am sure that you do think admiring thoughts, as I do, of her very brilliant imagination & her *nature turned towards music,*—altho they might have been brighter & stronger & more harmonious with that music which is in the Chief Intellect, than now they are. I admire & have often been touched by much in her poetry. But like the "toujours perdrix", the toujours tourterelle (not to say anything disrespectful in the presence of my doves) is a little wearisome—& sets us a[-]wishing for

> "WHATEVER tones of melancholy pleasures
> The things of nature utter!"

The striking of one note does not make a melody. And besides, is it not true that the strength of our *feelings*, often rises up out of our *thoughts*—out of our bare intellectuality,—hard & cold thing as it is, of itself?– It seems so to *me*; & that if she had been more intellectual she w^d have been more pathetic. Of her personal history I know nothing at all. There is a lovely tender closing passage in her Improvisatrice which went to your heart *I know* when you read it, as it did to mine. Are you acquainted with her? My idea in connection with her poetry is, that she is capable of something *above it*. But even as it is,—tho' I wish for the vanishing of a page here & a page there, & for the presence of a strength which is not visible on many pages—it *is* poetry,— & long may her crown be green!

You found out my name! my ugly name! You will find out all my faults I am afraid ⟨in⟩ time, & then you wont care for me! As to that name of mine, I might almost forget it myself & have to sit down, as you did, on some tripod & find it out by an afflatus, so very very sel-

dom—so never—do I hear it from mortal lips. Everybody calls me—
(now I defy you, with an afflatus like a whirlwind) to find out *that*
name → Ba! When I was a ba—by, I used to call myself 'Ba' abreviat-
ingly, & straightway everybody followed my good example & called
me Ba. And I do believe that to this day, the name with its etymology
& all, is sufficiently applicable. Is not this an harmonious "household
word" to send you! Dᵣ Mitford is sure to laugh! but do you defend it
dearest Miss Mitford! for it is a name associated with the love of all
my beloved—& besides it really does sound quite as well as *Dash*, if
he puts up his ears disdainfully when he hears you say so, or not! Do
tell me how the picture is going on. Is Mᵣ Lucas[4] in London again,
or still with you?

I tremble to confess that you are likely to see initials of mine in
the next New Monthly Mag⟨azine.⟩ I conclude, as they sent me a
proof two days ago, that it will be there on the first. It was half written
when the *criticisms* came upon me,—& my trembling is not, because
I fear your want of indulgence, but because I fear my own want of
deserving any better thing than such criticisms renewed. But tell
me—DO—your exact thoughts, even the severest. Yes! you must see
Papa & *I* must see Dᵣ Mitford! that is, if he will let me. Forgive this
long hurried letter! It deserves both epithets & worse ones beside.
May God ever bless you & all dear to you.

> Your affectionate
> E B Barrett.

Do write to me *whenever* you can. Am I not shameless?

1. Elizabeth Emmet Lenox Conyngham published *Hella, and Other Poems* in 1836.
2. *Memorials of Mrs. Hemans* (1836) by Henry Chorley. Felicia Browne Hemans
   (1795–1835) was the author of several books of verse, including *Songs of the
   Affections* (1830).
3. Letitia Elizabeth Landon (1802–38), known as "LEL," popular minor poet and
   novelist.
4. John Lucas (1807–74), artist, who was painting Dr. Mitford's portrait. He
   exhibited regularly at the Royal Academy and did two portraits of MRM, one in
   1829 and one in 1852.

74 GLOUCESTER PLACE
MONDAY. [LATE FEBRUARY OR EARLY MARCH 1837]

Dearest Miss Mitford,

Mꞁ Kenyon was here on Saturday, & then & before then I was longing to write to you to tell you how your mournful letter was responded to by my mournful thoughts,—& how sadly they dwelt upon your being ill & out of spirits, & disappointed in persons (worse than any disappointment in *things*) to whom you had granted the *praise* of your confidence. It is difficult to know what Mꞁ Forrest[1] can mean by his strange inconsistent proceeding. I suppose the whole resolves itself into another echo of the ancient words "Arise & depart hence—this is not thy rest—it is POLLUTED—" or into another manifestation of the Recklessness & heartlessness which "strew about" in the wide world their coldnesses & their cruelties,—& most thickly beneath the feet of those who are fearless & unguarded *because* they are generous & true. I confine myself to such sympathy,—not knowing & not daring anything beyond. Mꞁ Kenyon may write something better. I am sure he will put his head, as his heart put itself, into the subject. My own hope is, that the *very* end, as far as concerns it, will *not* be sheer disappointment: & I *do persist* in hoping besides that you will come to London before our London summer is quite smoked away. Can you not hope my dear friend, that, after all, everything may terminate happily,—& that what justice & honor failed to extort, self interest when it has had time to be better considered, *may*. At any rate my imagination fails me, when I attempt to think of a work of *yours* thrown by as waste paper. I could as soon, in idea, separate Mꞁ Forrest's Niagara (but it *shant* be Mꞁ *Forrest*'s Niagara!) from its sound, as a work of yours from its result. It is the prerogative of some minds, that no labour of theirs, beneath the sun or, beneath the rain, can be unproductive first & last; & their consolation under all difficult & disappointing circumstances ought to be, a recurrence to this consciousness.

And so, I do entreat you dearest Miss Mitford not to despond, & above all things not to injure your health with too much labour. Now ought you not—just now when you are not well—to put by the papers, & go to bed early, & think of nothing as far as the earth is concerned, except Dash's ears, or the flowers which *shall* be in another two months? Now ought you not—if it were but for a touching motive—for your father's sake? The earthly good of this world is its happiness; & its happiness, like its sorrow, issues from its affections—&

if you make him unhappy by making or keeping yourself ill, what other good c^d you find, with all your seeking, which w^d *be* a good to *him*? How impertinent all this is! Do I deserve ever to be written or spoken to again? But then again, have you not "adopted" me? Am I not your very own relation?—your '*niece*'? or at least your friend? And so have I not a right to be just as impertinent as I please, without the reproach of a word or a thought? At any rate I have . . to be forgiven.

Of course the knowledge of your kind permission to read Otto in MS, makes me very anxious to do it—but Mr Chorley is gone to Liverpool, as Mr Kenyon made out when, some days ago, he called upon him. Mr Kenyon is looking very well, & happy in the prospect of seeing his brother in London this summer!–

May God bless you my dear friend! When this troublesome letter is put out of sight, you must still remember the sympathy & affection of

E B Barrett

Do give to Dr Mitford my very kind remembranc⟨e⟩ & receive yourself whatever you will accept.

1. Edwin Forrest (1806–72), American-born actor, who withdrew from MRM's *Otto* after a quarrel with the actor-manager Macready.

Three-mile Cross,
June 28, 1837.

My Sweet Love—I want you to write me a poem in illustration of a very charming group of Hindoo girls floating their lamps upon the Ganges—launching them, I should say. You know that pretty superstition. I want a poem in stanzas. It must be long enough for two large pages and may be as much longer as you choose. It is for "Finden's Tableaux," of which I have undertaken the editorship; and I must entreat it within a fortnight or three weeks if possible, because I am limited to time, and have only till the end of next month to send up the whole copy cut and dry. I do entreat you, my sweet young friend, not to refuse me this favor. I could not think of going to press without your assistance, and have chosen for you the very prettiest subject and, I think, the prettiest plate of the whole twelve. I am quite sure that, if you favor me with a poem, it will be the gem of the collection. Now to less pretty considerations. My proprietor, Mr. Tilt,[1] has put into my hands £30; that is to say, £5 each for my six poets (I am to do all the prose and dramatic scenes myself); and with this £5, which is, I believe, the usual price, I shall have the honor of sending a copy of the work, which will be all the prettier and more valuable for your assistance. I will not contemplate a refusal, and have only to request that I may receive one line to tell me that you consent, as speedily as may be. If you like I will send you the engraving, or rather an unfinished proof of it in my possession. Heaven bless you! Ever yours,

M. R. MITFORD.

If you can give me time and thought enough to write one of those ballad-stories, it would give an inexpressible grace and value to my volume. Depend upon it that the time will come when those verses of yours will have a money value.

1. Charles Tilt (1797–1861), London publisher who controlled the lithograph trade at this time.

LONDON
THURSDAY, JUNE 29th.– [1837]

Will dearest Miss Mitford believe me when I tell her that the first sentence in her note, seeming to express that it was in my power to do her a "favor", surprised me with a new feeling of pleasure? Would that I could indeed do anything for her!– But it soon turned out that the favor was not to be done to *her*, but to myself—& that I have only to thank her (which is *not* a new pleasure) instead of obliging her.

Of course my dear friend, I shall be both pleased & proud, if I find myself conjoined in any way under the same book cover, with you—& in order to [do] it, I will do what I can & as quickly—pushing more terrestrial matters out of the way as much as possible: but I must beg of you for friendship's sake & *adoption's*, that if after all I do not appear to you to succeed, you will not have one scruple or uncomfortable feeling in sending back my MS & rescuing your fair Hindoos. Now do let this be a promise. Because if I feel it to be one, I shall both write & give to you what I write, with more freedom & pleasure. There shall not be a blotted leaf in a book edited by you—a leaf blotted by *me*!—no! not for the world!——

I was going to accept your proposal of sending me the engraving—but I have thought—& I believe now, that the picture from which it is taken, is one by Daniel,[1] in the Royal Academy this year. I remember that the subject is exactly the one you mention—moonlight & all. If this conjecture is a wrong one, I will ask you to correct me by a line, & a sight of the engraving—if you can conveniently; but should I *not* hear from you, I will put my faith in Daniel, & look at him again in the Exhibition.

You know of course that M.ʳ Kenyon & his brother are in Devonshire just now, on their tour in search of 'happy faces' instead of the picturesque. I heard OF them yesterday in the *juste milieu* between Axminster & Honiton. M.ʳ Edward Kenyon is a remarkable man—a deep & original thinker without any straining after originality—which indeed is the surest & dreariest mark of a mind utterly commonplace. I have seen & heard him two or three times, & liked his conversation very much,—& the under stream of benevolence which ran thro' it,— but after all, *our* M.ʳ Kenyon is unapproachable—for poetry of mind & vivacity of association—even when the auld lang syne & auld gramercies, are put out of the question. I envy them the sight they are to have of you on their way back to London. It will lighten the anticipation of a return to prison.

I am sure you must have much more to do than to read a longer letter from me . . But do think of me sometimes dearest Miss Mitford as

Your obliged & affectionate
E B Barrett

•   •   •

1. EBB's assignment was to write a poem for William Daniell's (1769–1837) illustration of Hindoo girls launching boats containing tiny flames which, according to the superstition, if they continued to burn, proved their lovers were faithful. The resulting poem was "A Romance of the Ganges."

[THURSDAY] OCT.ʳ 26.ᵗʰ 1837.

I thank you my dearest Miss Mitford for the beautiful annual, & together with it & more than for it, for your kindest accompanying letter. The kindness of its various expressions has been gratefully felt—& there is within me a deep response to all its affectionateness. I hope you will continue to love me, whatever & however many faults & inconsistencies and incoherences you may find in me. One can afford to lose a great deal on this earth when the sun shines on it, & not feel any the worse for the loss: but a single shred of human affection, one CANT afford to lose,—tho' the sun & moon & stars shone all at once!——

As to my ballad, even if it were as good as I wish it were, it would have its ends fulfilled,—(for *you* are kindly satisfied—& M.ʳ Kenyon too liked it!) yes, and its honor besides—for is it not under a cover bearing your name, and in association with honor-giving as well as honor-taking poetry & prose—?

> "Cloth of freize be not too bold,
> Tho' thou'rt matched with cloth of gold"!

THAT sh.ᵈ have been my motto, when you sent for one:– Thank you for all your indulgence.

·   ·   ·

The engravings are beautifully executed—the effect of light & shadow so expressive & picture like! I like M.ʳ Kenyon's, & Georgia & mine (as in duty bound) the best—but then the falconry is very lovely–I am so glad that the beauty of his longer poem is recognized in the Athenæum– It is not classical & cold as the pseudo-classical-ism—but classical and tender. I admire it much—too much to refer to Crabbe's lyrics as the critic does. You know I have a *pathy* about Crabbe which is not, whatever else it may be, a *sym*pathy. I never could praise anything in poetry, by connecting it in similitude with his!——

I have written a note containing your message to M.ʳ Boyd[1]—feeling sure that it would please him–

This is a terrible time of year, dearest Miss Mitford, to unroof yourself in! Could'nt it be put off to the spring? And could'nt you come to London during the operation? *That* is as good a *plan*, as M.ʳ Bang's!

Is the novel doing you harm, that you should be unwell? I am so glad that I shall hear from M̲ꞁ Kenyon all about you!—so glad too to hear of his near return to London. In a letter from a relative of ours & a stranger to him, dated Torquay & addressed to my sister, we had just heard that "M̲ꞟ Trollope![2] and M̲ꞟ Kenyon, a very literary man, were about to *spend the winter* there".

All prosperity to the Jackdaw!—but what does Dash say? Does he look like Othello?—— My poor little dove is very thoughtful or sad . . I wont call him *stupid* as my brothers do! He is probably in a deep puzzle between his innate ideas of trees & hills, & these ceilings & carpets—& being in a puzzle is the surest proof of philosophy!——

Talking of philosophy, I have seen in the papers the marriage of Miss Shepherd.[3] May it be a happy event for her! I cannot lose my interest in her!–

One is ungrateful here below even against one's will,—but I must mention late instead of never that I recognized the graceful song full of suggestions, "Lady &c["]–

God bless you my very dear friend—& keep us all from all greater sins than "the love of geraniums". Were *that* the only sin or the chief, what a lovely garden this earth would be—& these hearts would be!——I believe that some religious people, from the purest motives & (if the truth were known) from a want of *natural* sensibility to the beautiful, make a pitiable mistake in endeavouring to put it away from th⟨em⟩ that they may look at the face of God!– As if the beautiful were not an indication of the Chief Beauty!—or as if the whole fair universe were not one transparency—with a Great Light beyond!——

Ever & most affectionately your
E B Barrett

•   •   •

1. Hugh Stuart Boyd (1781–1848), blind scholar who tutored EBB in Greek at Hope End.
2. Mrs. Frances Trollope (1780–1863), prolific Victorian novelist and friend of MRM.
3. Mary, daughter of Lady Mary, author of philosophical essays, and Henry J. Shepherd, poet and dramatist, and contributor to *Findens' Tableaux* (1838).

Three Mile Cross
Dec. 15, 1837.

My dear Love,—I have only a moment in which to thank you most heartily for your very comfortable bulletin,[1] and to beg you to continue to send good news. We are in the agony of moving ourselves and our goods and chattels to a cottage still smaller than this, two doors off, whilst this house proper is repaired and painted—the two ends which have been taken down and built up again being to be roofed in on Saturday night, which drives the saws and hammers forward to the interior, and we find that in these closets (by courtesy called rooms) the workmen and we cannot co-exist, manage how we will. You may comprehend the capacity of our new mansion when I tell you that we are to pay £2 10s. for the quarter. Dash can't abide it; he sticks to me as if stitched to my gown-skirts.

Mrs. Hofland[2] writes to me about a young American poet (Mr. Thackeray), who came to England partly to see Miss Edgeworth and myself.[3] Miss E. was very kind to him, but what I shall do about him, in the present state of our house, heaven only knows! Did I tell you that I shall have a pretty up-stairs sitting-room, thirteen feet square, with a little ante-room, lined with books, both looking to the garden? I am only grieved at the expense, for though the building is done by our landlady, there must be incidental expenses—carpets, bells, stoves, etc., etc. However, it is less than moving, unless we had gone into Wales, to the house which a dear friend offered.

[M.R.M.]

1. Regarding the recovery of EBB's cousin and MRM's friend, John Kenyon.
2. Barbara Hoole Hofland (1770–1844), popular writer of tales and domestic novels.
3. Probably William Thackwray (also known as William T. Walworth) who published *The Ten Commandments in Verse* in 1819; Maria Edgeworth (1767–1849), English essayist and novelist who, with her father, Richard Edgeworth, wrote *Practical Education* (1798).

74 GLOUCESTER PLACE—
TUESDAY. [19? DECEMBER 1837]

Do write one line to me my dearest Miss Mitford, just to say how you are— I might have asked as much as this before—but felt unwilling to be in your way when so much else was there. One line—I must ask for now!—— It haunts me that you are suffering. May God grant that such a thought be one of my many vain ones!—& that the amendment you spoke of be not vain at all.

This is the first day of my release from prison—for during this terrible weather which held daggers for all weak chests, I was not permitted to get up before it was *deep* in the afternoon,—& so have scarcely had a pen in my hand for a fortnight past. I was glad to be able to breakfast as usual with Papa this morning—& feel an early-rising-vain-gloriousness almost as "thick upon me" as M.ʳ Boyd's is upon him—when (& he always does it) he gets up at four or five o clock in the morning & looks down upon the rest of the world. You cant think how much scorn I and my half past nine o clock breakfasts have met with from him. *You* would meet with no mercy. He has intimated to me again & again, that it was both a moral & religious sin not to get up before the second cock crowing– And that Peter's repentance, besides a good deal of sackcloth, sh.ᵈ wait upon the third– I believe I inferred the last—being logical: but the "moral & religious sin" was just his own expression.

How high you bribe dearest Miss Mitford! To *stand alone by your side* in praising Hayley & his contemporaries—or in doing anything else! That *is* a bribe,—& when I have read the essays on Scu[l]pture Painting & epic poetry,—anything more than the Triumphs of Temper,—I will make a desperate effort towards admiration. I admire him now as a *man*—and as Cowper's friend! I admire Miss Seward, not as a letter writer or a poet or a critic,—but as a kindly, generous hearted woman who loved poetical literature "not wisely" but very well,—who loved her friends still better than her vanities,—& who was not frozen to her pedestal! (she had one in her day!)—as many are apt to be in all days. When Sir Walter Scott edited her poems he cancelled such praise as he had given them in his own letters to her– It was an ungenerous act! The poor poetess could no more have committed it than she c.ᵈ have written Waverley!——

My dear friend! as you have changed your mind about the season of application for increase of pension, I have not said a word to M.ʳ Gosset.[1] If I am wrong, tell me immediately.

Finden is a triumph for you!– I am so glad of it. Dearest Miss Mitford, whenever I am able to do anything, or you fancy so & like me to try, by making me do it pray remember that you make me obliged–

The poor little dove, weak for the last three weeks, perished one cold night a fortnight since. I mean the poor little cockney dove. The others, I took up to my bedroom & kept very warm—& after some spiritless songless days, they revived & are perfectly well now. If I were to lose either of them, I should name it as a grief–

Goodbye—God bless you, dearest Miss Mitford. Do tell me that you are better. D.ʳ Chambers says that I shall lose my cough in the warm weather—April or May—& not before. So there is nothing for it but patience. And nothing makes one so patient, as knowing that patience is not needed for those one loves!—

Your ever affectionate
E B Barrett.

I have not yet seen M.ʳ Kenyon. He sent me M.ʳ Landor's last most exquisite book of which I have no time to speak–

The kind regards of all the house—do accept them!——

1. Ralph Allen Gossett, married to a first cousin of EBB's, was son of Sir William Gossett, serjeant-at-arms in the House of Commons.

74 GLOUCESTER PLACE,
MONDAY [MARCH 1838]

•   •   •

Thank you for your most interesting remarks upon the drama; Victor Hugo's plays I never read, but will do so. His poems seem to me not very striking, more bare of genius than such of his prose writings as I have happened to see. And little have I seen of the new school of French literature, and must see and know more of it. De Lamartine's "Pilgrimage" is the only traveller's book, except "Sindbad the Sailor" and "Robinson Crusoe," that ever pleased me much; and his poetry is holy and beautiful, though deficient, as it appears to me, in concentration of expression and grasp of thought. To speak generally, my abstract idea of a Frenchman is the antithesis of a poet, but pray do not, if the prayer does not come too late, think me quite a bigot. There is nothing, as you say, like the Greeks, *our* Greeks let them be for the future, and although I can scarcely consent to crowning Philoctetes over all, it would still be more difficult to take a word away from your just praise. The defect of that play is that it is founded upon physical suffering, and its glory is that from the physical suffering is deduced so much moral pathos and purifying energy. The "Œdipus" is wonderful; the sublime truth which pierces through it to your soul like lightning seems to me to be the humiliating effect of guilt, even when unconsciously incurred. The abasement, the self-abasement, of the proud, high-minded king before the mean, mediocre Creon, not because he is wretched, not because he is blind, but because he is criminal, appears to me a wonderful and most affecting conception. And there is Euripides, with his abandon to the pathetic, and Æschylus, who sheds tears like a strong man, and moves you to more because you know that his struggle is to restrain them.

But if the Greeks once begin to be talked of, they will be talked of too much. I should have told you, when I wrote last, that Mr. Kenyon lent me Mr. Harness's play,[1] which abounds in gentle and tender touches, and not, I think, might I say so, in much concentration and dramatic *power*. As to its being a domestic tragedy, I do not object to it on that account, and really believe that I don't share your preference for imperial tragedies. Do not passion and suffering pervade Nature? Tragedies are everywhere, are they not? Or at least their elements are, or is this the pathos of radicalism? My book is almost decided upon being, and thanks for your kind encouragement, dearest Miss Mitford, you, who are always kind. There is a principal poem, called the "Seraphim," which is rather a dramatic lyric than a lyrical drama, and as long, within twenty or thirty lines, as my translation, "The Prometheus of Æschylus," and in two parts. I can hardly hope that you will thoroughly like it, but know well that you will try to do so. Other poems, longer or shorter, will make up the volume, not a word of which is yet printed. Would not "by E. B. B." stand very well for a name? I have been reading the "Exile," from Marion Campbell, with much interest and delight; besides, she made me forget Dr. Chambers, and feel how near you were. A pleasant feeling to everybody, but how very pleasant to your affectionate and grateful

E. B. Barrett.

P.S.—My kind regards to Dr. Mitford, and Papa's and my sister's to you. Our house in Wimpole Street is not yet finished, but we hope to see the beginning of April in it. You must not think I am very bad, only not very brisk, and really feeling more comfortable than I did a fortnight since.

1. *Welcome and Farewell, A Tragedy* (1837) by William Harness (1790–1869), MRM's clergyman friend and mentor.

74 GLOUCESTER PLACE
MONDAY. [EARLY APRIL 1838]

My dear friend, I am going to put one question into as few words as possible,—being in great haste. Have you the least shadow of preference for my NOT comprizing the Ganges ballad, written for your Tableaux, in my little volume of poems? Do answer me quite plainly. I have not any wish about it, believe me; and even if I had, the stronger one would still be to attend to *your* wish–

Some of the MSS have actually *gone* to press. So now, there is room for only "the *late* remorse of *fear*". The Ganges is not wanted, even to fill up–

Are you quite well? Would that I could hear you say 'yes'—but I suppose there is no hope of that pleasant sound coming, actually & sensibly, to supersede my coughing. I am rather better I think, & do 'honor due' to a blister which I submitted to so reluctantly a few days ago–

Occy is a great *Murpheist*,[1] notwithstanding all the proved frailty of the prophecies,—& when Sette & I laugh at him for it, the retort is that *we* both believe in animal magnetism—which is much worse!— —'*Alice or the mysteries*'[2] is magnetizing me just now! I have read one volume.

Dearest Miss Mitford, I must say goodbye! You will readily forgive a short post[s]cript to my long letter of last week.

Your affectionate
EBB–

1. A believer in the predictions published in *Weather Almanack* (1837) by Patrick Murphy (1782–1847), a meteorologist.
2. A novel by Edward Lytton Bulwer (1803–73), later Lord Bulwer-Lytton, published in February 1838 as sequel to *Ernest Maltravers*.

LONDON AND TORQUAY

Illness and Literary Topics
1838–40

The *Seraphim* volume received generally favorable reviews (although Chorley found it somewhat "Port Royal," that is, excessively devotional). By late summer of 1838, however, EBB's lung disease required a move to a warmer climate. Only the responsibility of an aging father kept MRM from going with her; instead Henrietta and Edward ("Bro"), the oldest Barrett son just returned from Jamaica, accompanied EBB in August on the brief sea voyage to Torquay on the Devon coast. Her poetic production curtailed by the strict regimen prescribed by Drs. Barry and Scully, who succeeded her London physician Dr. Chambers, EBB nevertheless continued to read avidly in authors ranging from Tennyson to German dramatists to contemporary minor novelists like Catherine Gore (1799–1861) and MRM's friend Frances Trollope (1780–1863). Two characteristic concerns of EBB emerge in these letters: her sympathy with the artist in domestic scandals—reflected in her [16 May 1839] complaints about the roman à clef *Chevely* (1839) by Lady Bulwer (1802–88), estranged wife of the novelist Edward Bulwer-Lytton—and her conviction of the importance of the poet's moral function, reflected in her 3 August 1839 defense of religious themes in poetry after MRM had expressed dismay at her choice of religious subjects. EBB began a correspondence with Richard H. Horne (1802–84), the editor-journalist recently introduced to her by her former governess, Mrs. Orme. She admired his dramas

Cosmo de' Medici (1837) and *Gregory VII* (1840) and persuaded him to join her in contributing to MRM's 1840 *Findens' Tableaux*. By March 1840 EBB was enthusiastically encouraging the publication ("the PLAN"), never realized, of MRM's early letters to Sir William Elford (1746–1837), an M.P. from Plymouth.

FRIDAY [–SATURDAY]. [10–11 AUGUST 1838]

Ever dearest Miss Mitford,
    With the parcel of reviews which your kindness makes you care to see, I venture to put up a little memorial of the object of it—who although she w^d trust without any memorial to the pleasant likelihood of remaining unforgotten by you, yet feels that she cannot hold your memory of her (that being so precious!) by too many knotted threads!——

"And *She* must be
A *sterner* than thee,
Who would break a thread of mine".

    I am going away dearest Miss Mitford, possibly in a very few days & certainly as soon as the weather will let me, to Devonshire— to Torquay —there to remain over the winter. The plan involves a sadness of heart to me—for we cannot all go; but it is one which is to be submitted to, Dr Chambers having used very strong language as to its necessity. Indeed he told me plainly that my recovery *depended* upon its adoption. I am therefore going—with the *cold* hope of seeing Papa *sometimes*. My aunt & uncle Hedley who have resided at Torquay for the last two or three years under Dr Chambers's jurisdiction, on account of my uncle's being affected in some similar way to myself— are kind enough to receive me very gladly & to wish to keep me with them; but after a while & in the case of the climate agreeing tolerably with me, I shall remove to another house & to the companionship of another aunt, Miss Clarke, a dear favorite relative, who has promised to leave Gloucestershire for Devonshire just for that purpose. Here you see, is plenty of kindness. I ought not to talk of "cold" hopes in the midst of it. But I cannot help the pang with which I think of those who must be left—altho' it would, I know all the time, be unkind to

them & a wrong thing in itself, to risk my life by staying. As it is,—
that is, if I go—D! Chambers seems to be hopeful.– He believes that
there is not at present, any ulceration of the lungs—only a too great
fulness of the bloodvessels upon them; & he told me a fortnight ago,
that he had grounds for hoping in the affected lung's eventually recovering itself altogether. And it may please God, that I sh^d return
next spring to rejoice in better health & a less helpless condition—&
to rejoice in seeing *you* dearest Miss Mitford besides!

This is Saturday—& I began the letter I am writing, yesterday—
& yesterday, too, I received yours. Thank you for letting me see M!
Hughes's gratifying note which I *shall* thank you for allowing me to
keep in order to confront it with the proof. It shall be returned to you
afterwards. But perhaps now that I am going to Torquay, I must not
expect the proof? Must I not? Yet I hope I may. Do get it sent to me
if you can. I have no corrected copy of the ballad by me.

There was some sort of reason for my alteration of the line in
Margaret[1] —though what it was, has quite escaped my memory. My
impression however is, that I had detected the counterpart of the idea
in some other person's writings—& took refuge from a possible charge
of plagiarism, of which I always have a nervous dread,—in the flow of
the universe. I do not say that this was so—but that this is my impression & that a very faint one it is.

Keep the reviews which are sent to you—at least do not return
them to us. The Metropolitan, M! Kenyon says, I certainly wrote myself. Blackwood pleased me very much. It is something to be in a
cave with Professor Wilson & M! Milnes[2]—without being praised
there. But you see, opinion runs almost everywhere—even in the
Metropolitan article which I wrote myself!—*against* the Seraphim, &
in favor comparatively, of the shorter poems– The extracts from M!
Milnes's poems in Blackwood, will deeply delight you. The lay of the
humble—The Long Ago—Familiar Love—Youth . . . they are sur-
passingly exquisite!——

Your praise of my 'candour', my beloved friend, tells more of
your own warm affections than of my praise! And let it be so!

But was M! Henry Chorley really surprised that "Sister Seraphina-
Angelica" did not fly into the tempest of a passion without any manner of reason for it?– Now it seems to *me*, that we of the Port Royal
may very well keep our tempers——until we are are provoked to lose
them. Our saintship may prove itself so far! –

What you tell me of him is very interesting, & makes me respond to your wish that I knew him personally. Does he write for the Tableaux this year? And does M.̄ Proctor?

M.̄ Kenyon I saw yesterday. His continental plans are deferred as to the execution of them, until after the 15.̄th̄ before which day M.̄ Southey cannot come to London. In the meanwhile M.̄ Landor is coming.

Dearest Miss Mitford's
EBB—

•   •   •

1. For *The Seraphim, and Other Poems* EBB had altered several lines from "The Romaunt of Margret," which first appeared in the *New Monthly Magazine* for July 1836.

2. John Wilson (1785–1854), editor of *Blackwood's Edinburgh Magazine*, wrote under the pseudonym Christopher North; his article "Christopher in His Cave" in the August issue quoted from *Poems of Many Years* (1838) by Richard Monckton Milnes (1809–85), M.P., as well as from EBB's *The Seraphim, and Other Poems*.

[TUESDAY] OC.̄ᵗ 30.̄th̄ [1838]

•   •   •

I did not receive Finden immediately. I had desired Papa to unpack & take possession of it—because I fancied (you will think 'What an immense deal of vanity there is in all her fancies'!) it might be a pleasure to him. From this arrangement I have scarcely finished my own vision of the beautiful volume, while you may well be wondering at the apparent unthankfulness of my silence. And indeed if silence means any harm I confess to having suffered a *coup de silence* from one of the first pages—only the kind of *harm* cant be unthankfulness, for I was indeed my dearest kindest Miss Mitford, at once surprised & pleased & touched by the manner in which you named my ballad— there! I do not presume to tell you that it was too much for you to say—but I must feel that it w.̄d̄ have been enough for *me*, if *either* my ambition or affections had been gratified—without this gratification of both at once!——

\`

•   •   •

The volume is a very splendid one! As to your stories they are delightful. You cut away the 'pound of flesh' in vain—they *would not die*. Nor is it likely that they would for all your cruelty– –being works of yours!– I dare say I helped with my fellow-poets & sinners to whet the knife—and yet it does console me to observe in the very passion of my remorse that *my* poem is NOT *the longest*!

•   •   •

Your tales should be spoken of when I write next. The Buccaneer & the Cartel mentioned in the Athenæum, I pass over, not with an indifferent love, but because I care more for the Baron's daughter. Is it right or wrong to *do* so?– It is right to be very sure of the loss which all who care for beauty, sustained, by the cutting away you spoke of—and yet you are as surely wrong in imagining any substitution of "baldness for beauty" in consequence of anything!—you *are* surely. When I read your account it sounded bad & sad. It sounded as if your stories must be spoilt in such a process—& I never felt so cross with poets before—"A poet! oh! base". And then too, the crossness was not improved by a consciousness of utter powerlessness as to critics—by a certainty of not being able to *"explain"* a word of the matter to any critic much greater than Sette. I dont know one of them—not one. Nor do I know a person who knows one—except your own self & M! Kenyon the wanderer—& as to my "friend of the sunbeam", altho' he *has* been friendly to a wonderful degree, & altho' he *has* a name I suppose, I cannot guess what it is. Well! but reading the stories put out of my head all the bad & sad thoughts. They have enough in them to propitiate the critics, without explanations—& for my own part I prefer them to those of last year. Do you observe that M! Fo[r]ster[1] who found fault with you then for not keeping among the lanes, cant help being pleased now in meeting you anywhere? Indeed the whole volume seems to take a higher place than the former one. The literal *Tableaux* are very very beautiful—I congratulate you my beloved friend.

•   •   •

There remains so much to say. I *cant* say it. May D! Mitford like the cream—& may you be able to give me a good account of him. I am better—& what is better than being so, *Papa is with me*. Your letter was enclosed to me from London by those who knew that tho' I could wait for books & seeds, I could not for *that*. Thank you dearest Miss Mitford for the seeds– So kind it is in you!——

Ever your attached
EBB——

1. In the *Examiner* for 28 October 1838, John Forster (1812–76), editor and biographer, praised MRM's editorial choices.

3. BEACON TERRACE
WEDNESDAY. [7 NOVEMBER 1838]

Ever dearest Miss Mitford,

I wanted to write to you very very soon in reply to your last welcome note. I wanted to say to you very soon some words which it suggested. But I have been exceedingly unwell—confined to my bed nearly a week by a sudden return of bad symptoms & so weak since as scarcely to bear without fainting even the passive fatigue of being carried from this bed to the sofa down stairs, by all the gentleness of my brother's love for me. The prevalency of the east wind & sudden coldness of weather connected with it, are considered the causes of the attack– I was not suffered to write—& have only by mainforce written two post[s]cripts to two of Henrietta's many letters to London,—which I insisted upon doing because I knew that my writing & my *living* were ideas very closely associated in Wimpole Street. But *you*—I hope my beloved friend that another silence simply made you a *little cross* with me—& not uneasy. It is a disagreeable kind of hope—& I *indulge* in it (on the principle of a rustic friend of Papa's who always used to respond to his enquiry by—("Why Sir, I *enjoys* very bad health indeed") because almost anything is better than making you anxious, at a time too when you may be anxious enough without *me*. Henrietta proposed writing to you– I would not let her do it just to sadden you—& the physician here being very sure of my being better again, I dared making you think "she is not worth a thought" rather than the worse risk. The pulse is quiet now, & I can *sleep*— indeed the attack itself has quite passed away– And as to the weakness it is passing. From two days to two days I can perceive an increase of strength—and if it pleases God,—He has been so merciful!—in two or three weeks more I may be as strong as I was previous to the last pulling down.

My sister & brother & I removed to our present residence just in time—the very day before this illness. Since it, I could not have removed—and the difference between the Braddons & Beacon Terrace is all the difference between the coldest situation in Torquay & the warmest—& my *body* was so ungrateful as to require another sun besides that of kind looks & words.

Here, we are immediately *upon* the lovely bay—a few paces dividing our door from its waves—& nothing but the "sweet south" & congenial west wind can reach us—and *they* must first soften their footsteps upon the waters. Behind us—so close as to darken the back windows—rises an abrupt rock crowned with the slant woods of Beacon hill! and thus though the North & East wind blow their fiercest, we are in an awful silence & only guess at their doings.

The wind has changed now—and the gulf between autumn & winter or at least between the summer-part & winter-part of autumn is surely passed, & therefore no longer to be feared.

One thing I fear– Indeed I do—and so I will speak to you at once about it. In the first place my very dearest Miss Mitford, names that are worth gold & names that are worth nought cant be weighed in the same balance. Therefore the exclusive dedication of your name to the Tableaux could be no example to the nameless unless they were also modesty-less!– And then again there is a distinction between the office of an Editor & a contributor. I understand these two differences far too well to fancy even, that you meant a *word* in reference to *me* of what you said respecting your own resolve. But still when I had finished your note, I did fancy that you would—for some reason & perhaps for the simple one that you loved me—have preferred my having *not* written for M.ʳ Hervey's annual.[1] Now this might just have been a fancy of mine—I am given to be tormented by such. But it has helped to make me restless, more restless than usual, in wishing to write to you.

I need not tell you my beloved & kindest friend that if the very shadow of a like fancy had crossed my mind before, my *no* sh.ᵈ have been said civilly to M.ʳ Hervey. He wrote two letters—which in consequence of the difficulty he had had in finding my address reached me the same day,—to ask me, (not given you know to write for annuals) to send something to him for his. His request was made so very courteously & the making it seemed to have given him so much trouble, that I wrote down for him some stanzas, before floating about in my head, & sent them just for goodnature's sake—–thinking no more of it, than if I had sent such to magazine or journal. Now if by a straw's breadth you had *rather* that I had not sent them, I shall most assuredly wish all the annuals—always excepting the great one—with M.ʳ Hervey's ancestors! Not that I regard *them*—the ancestors—with *much* malice!

Do let me hear from you when you can write—*whenever* you can. I have so few pleasures!—and a few words from you bring many!– A true one to me was, that D.ʳ Mitford liked the cream. He shall have some more. How is he? How are you? *Do* go on caring for me!——

Did Papa send you the last Sunbeam?[2] I hope so. They are "friendly beams" indeed,—& everybody who happens to see them, will be sure to think that we made them up among us in Wimpole Street. The editor wrote to me before I left London, begging to have the Prometheus & Seraphim sent to him for reviewing purposes– He had seen extracts from the latter & intended an '*important essay upon my genius*'. We had a good deal of laughing about it—and little did I anticipate being made such a "Sun's Darling" of!——

Nothing yet of dear M.ʳ Kenyon. I know nobody here– –but the people seem very kind–M.ʳ & M.ʳˢ Bezzi[3] have ceased to live here, & are I believe on the continent.

May God bless you! Do you write now—& what?—or are you resting from the Tableaux? Was M.ʳ Chorley well or tolerably well, when you heard from him?——

Your always affectionate & grateful
E B Barrett.

•　　•　　•

Is anything *decided* about Martha?

1. In October, EBB's poem "A Sabbath on the Sea" appeared in the *Amaranth: A Miscellany of Original Prose and Verse Contributed by Distinguished Writers* (1839), edited by Thomas K. Hervey (1799–1859). Like *Findens' Tableaux* it was a predated annual.

2. *The Sunbeam*, a "Journal devoted to Polite Literature and Music," reviewed *The Seraphim, and Other Poems* in a series of laudatory articles beginning in the issue of 1 September 1838.

3. Giovanni Aubrey Bezzi (?–1879?), an Italian exile, translator, and friend of Kenyon, and his English wife.

[THURSDAY–TUESDAY] 7 [– 12] MARCH [1839]

Ever dearest Miss Mitford,

I must say so at the first word, though it may seem so contradictory to the long silence & neglect of which you have or surely *may* have (making every allowance for your tried kindness) judged somewhat severely. To explain it all, my beloved friend, I have been very ill—& your two last delightful letters were received by me when I was *quite* confined to my bed, & in such a state of debility as rendered writing a thing impossible. Even at this time, altho' more than a month has passed since this *laying up* began, the extent of my strength is to bear being lifted to the sofa for three hours a day—& I have not left my bedroom for six weeks. The cold weather at the end of January irritated the chest a good deal—& then most unaccountably—I never suffered from such a thing my whole life before—I had for ten days a kind of *bilious fever* which necessitated the use of stronger medecines than my state c^d very well bear—& then came on a terrible state of debility—the stomach out of sheer weakness, rejecting all sustenance except wine & water—& the chest, seeming to grudge the exercise of respiration. I felt oftener than once inclined to believe that the whole machine was giving way everywhere! But God has not willed it so! I am much better, & stronger—& growing with my strength has been the wish of assuring you—that indeed indeed I have *not* forgotten you, I am *not* ungrateful to you–

. . .

I am sure you were polishing your dagger just when you asked me to agree with you in giving Goëthe's laurel to Schiller. You might as well ask our young Queen to prefer Shakespeare to Mr Van Amburgh.[1] My doxy is that there is (now you know what my doxy must be) that there is more essential genius in Goethe's mysterious Faustic growlings than in Schiller's most eloquent eloquence. He is of the schools. He lights his lamp like any common man—& I am quite sure not only that he wrote with a pen, but that it might very possibly have been a steel one. Now Goëthe's poetry comes like the wind—we cannot tell whence it cometh —& what is more, never think of asking—and if *you* asked *me* I sh^d be obliged to shake my head & put on quite as mystic a face as his own.

Now you must forgive all this foolish criticism. Foolishness & criticism are so apt, do so naturally go together! and I am, for a critic, even unnaturally consistent, for I like Schiller's Robbers better than any other play of his I have read.

I had in my hands (not of course for my reading) for a part of an evening years ago & at a party Lord Francis Gower[']s translation of the Faust.[2] It was the only time I ever saw any translation of that untranslateable wonder—I never even saw the one you refer to. On the other hand, the time I have given to German literature has been but little—none at all until the summer before last—and so you must find some good excuse for me if I have written anything *very*, more than critically, foolish.

Do mention poor Lady Dacre.[3]

Thank you for all your encouraging kindnesses (how they multiply) about my poetry. But dearest Miss Mitford, if it were really the fashion to like it, w^dnt it be a little so to buy it! And Messrs Saunders & Otley gave bad accounts in the early part of the winter. Do you think there sh^d be more advertisements?

•   •   •

Your hurried but most
affectionate EBB.

Mr Kenyon is quite well—but very seldom seen in Wimpole Street.

1. Isaac A. Van Amburg (1811–65), American lion tamer who performed at Drury Lane, where Queen Victoria attended several of his performances.
2. Francis L. Gower (1800–57), first Earl of Ellesmere, whose translations had appeared in 1823 and 1825.
3. Barbarina Brand (1768–1854), a relative of MRM, was the wife of Lord Dacre and had published poetry and translations from the Italian. She had recently lost her daughter.

Three-mile Cross
May [*sic* for March] 28, 1839.

My Dear Friend,—I should always doubt any preference of mine when opposed to yours, always, even if my ignorance of languages did not make my writing about foreign poetry a very great presumption. French I read just like English, and always shall, and I have a tendency toward the comedies and memoirs, that makes me open a French book with real gusto. And little as I know of Italian, I like the gem-like bits of Ariosto. But after all to be English, with our boundless vistas in verse and in prose, is a privilege and a glory; and *you* are born among those who make it such, be sure of that. I do not believe, my sweetest, that the very highest poetry does sell at once. Look at Wordsworth! The hour will arrive, and all the sooner if to poetry unmatched in truth and beauty and feeling you condescend to add story and a happy ending, that being among the conditions of recurrence to every book with the mass even of cultivated readers—I do not mean the few.

I once remember puzzling an epicure by adding to an apple tart, in the making, the remains of a pot of preserved pine, syrup and all, a most unexpected luxury in our cottage; such would a bit of your writing be in a book of mine—flavor, sweetness, perfume, and unexpectedness . . . Yes, for one year, from eight and a half to nine and a half—I lived—*we* lived, at Lyme Regis. Our abode was a fine old house in the middle of the chief street; a porch and great gables with spread-eagles distinguish it. It was built round a quadrangle, and the back looked into a garden, which descended by terraces to a small stream, a descent so abrupt that a grotto with its basin and spring formed a natural shelter under the hilly bank, planted with strawberries. Arbutus, passion-flowers, myrtles, and moss-roses abounded in that lovely garden and covered the front of the house; and the drawing-room chimney-piece was a copy of the monument to Shakespeare in Westminster Abbey. How I loved that house! There is an account of a visit to Lyme in Miss Austen's exquisite "Persuasion." Some of the scenery in the back of the Isle of Wight resembles Pinny, but it is inferior.

I shall tell dear Lady Dacre of your sympathy. Heaven bless you, my own sweet love. Ever yours,

M. R. MITFORD.

TORQUAY.
THURSDAY. [16 MAY 1839]

•   •   •

I am glad you have looked at Cheveley. *Now* I can confess with
one blush less that I have just read it through. People obliged to be
dumb like me, & under a medical disciplinarian like Dr Barry have as
good an excuse as any can have for reading it—but after all, my *curiosity* & "not my will consented". I do believe, if it had not been for
you, I sh^d have looked about for some large Harpocratic cabbage
rose —very large—large enough & red enough to cover my offence
immediately after its perpetration. The book, if not the reader, is
without excuse. It is wonderful in unwomanliness—one thing being
easy & clear to see—that GRIEF NEVER MADE IT. My dearest Miss Mitford, if her children had all been rolled to Mount Taygetus in wheel-
barrows, grief would never have brought to pass such a book as
Cheveley. Wounded vanity might—never, wounded affections! The
book is a hard cold coarse book—a bold impudent book—& she who
wrote it may have COUNTED many stripes but has *felt* none—*not one*—
not even the worst & keenest which hardens after it has agonized.
    And so I can scarcely agree with you that any possible circum-
stances c^d have made—a *woman* of her! I cannot, cannot think it.
There is indelicacy of intellect & heart, from the root upward. Her
very learning has a flippancy in it, & a coarse-coloured blueism in the
display of of [*sic*] it—nothing of the scholar's polish & reserve & depth
& "signs of meditation" —& everything of the assumption & superfi-
cialness of third-form acquirement. Your words "clever & shrewd" are
just the right words– Dearest Miss Mitford, Mrs Gore is not a woman
of *genius*—at least I think not—but she is a *woman*—& is this Lady
Bulwer either?–
    Forgive me for being so cross—or laugh, which will be better. I
believe I feel a little angry for Bulwer's sake as well as for our womanhood's—& you *know* that *you* are angry simply for the latter cause. He
may have acted "without excuse" *as she* has written—but not (I very
much suspect) without provocation. That *he can feel*, I am as sure, as
that *she cannot*. And it is as fixed in my creed as it is repudiated from
hers, that no human being can write with passion & pathos to whom
those *things* are mere *words*. *That* (the supposition of such possibility)
is the cant of the world & of the Lady Byrons & the Lady Bulwers in

it—& whenever I hear that cant I shrink from the canter as from one
unsound at heart. Suppose *me* to write a treatise upon the Corn laws! or
a disquisition on Jereny [*sic*] Bentham's panopticon![1] A fine business I
sh.ᵈ make of it! And is the heart's ignorance less impotent than the
head's—?– Oh, DO agree with me–

You made me laugh with your report (upon Mʳ Chorley's authority) of the process of Mʳ Tennyson's inspiration. If I were a Miss
Tennyson I shᵈ be so inclined to retort––"Let the brother be taken
away & the writing desk" —only I conclude that writing desks are far
too sublunary for the inspired. I never shᵈ have expected the affectations of a "gentleman-parcel-poet" from HIM, & do trust that he may
smoke them into 'thin air' as soon as may be. It wᵈ be the best use
of tobacco, since Phillips's![2]

I was speaking of Mʳ May to Dʳ Barry—& he said "I think I have
heard of him." Dʳ Barry is a very intelligent physician—devoted to
his profession.

No plan fixed about my removal to London! I LONG to be at
home—but am none the nearer for *that*. God's mercies are very very
undeservedly great to me,—& for *me* to be *patient* under any little
trial, shᵈ be called rather *gratitude* than patience—but I DO HOPE to be
at home this summer.

· · ·

Tell me all you can about *yourself*. Mʳ Tilt's silence, if it continue
silence, becomes ominous. Mʳ Kenyon is quite well again (so Arabel
says) & Mʳ Wordsworth either is or has been staying with him, & Mʳ
Southey has been *asked, in vain*—being about, you know, to marry a
wife. Think of Mʳ Rogers doing the like?[3] —I mean as to marrying
the wife–"Deities, are you all agreed?" You will forgive the Queen
now for going to see the Lions! She deserves it of you!—and you deserve of me, that I shᵈ not weary you to death! Goodbye dearest
dearest Miss Mitford. Love to Dʳ Mitford—he shall have more fish—
& how cᵈ you fancy that it was a trouble or anything except a pleasure, for me to send it!–

Thank you again & again, though so late, for your valued letter.
May the next speak more blythely of you both!—that it may, *so* do
the part of all your writings, letters & all––"bring delight & *hurt not*"–

Most affect.ᵗˡʸ
Your EBB.

I hear that Ld Methuen has had a letter from Sir John C Hob-house in wh. he says that the Queen is in the utmost indignation—declaring that as long as she sits on the throne of England Sir R Peel shall never be reinvited to pass her palace gates.[4] Hic jacet Toryism – I am so glad Tait & Blackwood pleased D.r Mitford—& I will not forget to please him again when the opportunity arises.

• • •

1. Jeremy Bentham (1748–1832), English philosopher and jurist, advocated a "Panopticon," a prison built on a radial plan with guards at the center. It was a controversial subject as was the complicated debate on eliminating or reducing the "Corn Law" taxes on grain.

2. John Philips (1676–1709), minor English poet, who eulogized tobacco.

3. Samuel Rogers (1763–1855), banker-poet and art collector. The rumor of his marriage was false.

4. Paul Methuen (1779–1849), created Baron Methuen of Corsham, Wiltshire in 1838, lived in Torquay at this time, as did the politician John Cam Hobhouse (1786–1869), later Baron Broughton. Sir Robert Peel (1788–1850) had recently refused to serve as prime minister after the queen rejected his choices for the Ladies of the Bedchamber.

MONDAY. JUNE 17.th [1839]

• • •

I hear of M.r Kenyon's having given an immense party the other evening—a desert full of lions & lionesses, among whom M.r Charles Dickens stood rampant. My brother was "there to see".

By the way—talking of brothers—I mean to make an extract of your legal admirations and send them to my brother George who begins his circuits next year as a BARRISTER!! I shall be curious to observe how his enthusiasm for his profession, which actually set him down to read Coke among this exquisite scenery, when he came down with me last year, & his very high esteem for *your* opinions will bear up under the infliction. Oh yes! I *must*. I have a malignity about the law, & a particular pleasure in teazing him about it. I am always teazing him about it, & telling him that in time he will be worth an old bit of parchment, *ready* to be made a will but not made yet. And he, dear fellow, laughs very goodhumourdly, & goes on sitting up night after night, & sitting in chambers day after day—just as if he liked it—& I

cant believe that anybody really *can*. He is too good for the woolsack
& you sh.^d give him a seat in your summerhouse. Well! I wont abuse
his tastes any more today– He cares for mine, & sent me in the winter
Barry Cornwall's Ben Jonson.[1] By the way, Ben says somewhere that
there is no difference between law & poetry,—"it is all reading &
writing".

I meant to have written six words. It is always so.

May success attend your applications my dearest Miss Mitford to
the Landors Procters & Talfourds,[2] but I shall suffer for it—they will
extinguish my "brief candle." I tremble for my ballad & *me*. You will
however be kind to us as usual—much too kind—there is the only
danger!–

> Your attached
> E B Barrett

•   •   •

1. Bryan Waller Procter (1787–1874), poet, dramatist, and biographer, published
   under the pseudonym Barry Cornwall *The Works of Ben Jonson, with a Memoir of his
   Life and Writings* (1838).
2. Thomas Noon Talfourd (1795–1854), M.P. from Reading and a friend of MRM's,
   wrote *Ion*, the play that brought MRM to London in May 1836.

TORQUAY–
[SATURDAY] AUGUST 3.^d 1839

•   •   •

Day after day I have waited for this poor parcel—and besides, for
Mr Horne's reply to the enquiry I directed his way, via Mrs Orme, as
to whether he w.^d write a scene or poem of some sort, quickly & instantly for Miss Mitford's annual. I wrote to her by the post *next* to
the one by which your letter reached me. It appears that Mr Horne
has been out of town—as far as I could understand what she wrote to
me two days ago,—& this very day, I have received a most obliging
letter directly from himself, from which here are extracts.– "I beg of
you not to imagine that I am affecting to be, or really being, impertinent, when I say I never yet wrote a word in an annual,—and as I
never could afford to buy one, nor ever lived in a house with one, so

I never read one. It would give me great pleasure if I thought I c^d do anything that would be agreeable to Miss Mitford and yourself, in the work in question—but I really dont know what is wished. Anything I can do, pray command me, & to save time, allow me to tell you what I cannot. I know very well that the *majority* of the annuals entertain certain views of Art, to the bettering of Nature beyond all measure. The hands & feet of all the females excite pity,—their figures frighten one,—& perplex no less with scepticism as to how they are to *continue*. Nor are these hourglasses redeemed from the disbelief they excite as to all organic humanity, by the features & expressions of the faces— for 'each seems either'! I c^d not write of such without being guilty of offence to their arbitrary perfection."————"If you please, let me have some landscape with the least possible refinement or elegance in it, & the most old ruins. Amidst these, something might be built in descriptive or dramatic poetry,—but I can do nothing at all with the ladies & gentlemen—— You will preceive, no doubt, from all this, that I have derived my impressions from probably the worst annuals—to w^h Finden's Tableaux may be quite an exception. If this be the case and I can look at several of the subjects, I may be induced or compelled to alter my opinion—".

There are the extracts! I am personally quite unacquainted with Mr Horne—but you will see through all this playfulness & oddity of satire upon the annuals, that he is at your disposal, & a willing victim besides!—— It will be right for me to send my own expression of thanks to him for his letter to me—& this I shall do on Monday, & I hope I shall not be wrong in telling him that you will write *directly* your instructions to himself. His address is 75 *Gloucester Place, Portman Square.* Of course he w^d like to select a subject, sh^d you have more than one drawing unappropriated—but otherwise a few words from you w^d win him into contentment, even without the old ruins. Have you not *heard* of his Cosmo de' Medici? He is a man of indubitable genius. I feel THAT quite distinctly, although I have read only a little of his poetry—and then his heart turns to the old poets as well as to the old ruins—& *that* I like, very much!——

• • •

But if your table is not filled, I do think you will like Mr Horne– And you will in any case, write to him—wont you?——

Ever dearest Miss Mitford, I feared that you might interpret my silence into a distaste to y^r criticism! You were wrong—very wrong—

if you did!——— And altho' you recall your first impression, yet I am afraid more weight is due to it than to your merciful re-consideration. I had imagined that the penitence was implied, even were it not directly expressed by the words "Take pity on me—Let the sin be removëd" —and to tell you the real truth, I have been taught to "walk softly" upon all subjects connected with theologisms by the repeated intimations of my obstinate proclivity towards them. Let it *be* an obstinate proclivity!— I do hold, & do not slacken in holding, that all high thoughts look towards God, & that the deepest mysteries, not of fanaticism but of Christianity, yes, *doctrinal* mysteries, are,—as approachable by lofty human thoughts & melted human affections,— poetical in their nature. It w^d be a great mistake if I were to defend my own poetry from any imputation of intruding religious subjects, & of calling "vasty spirits" whether they will come or not. I do not defend it. I only maintain that all such appearances of intrusion, arise from my own incompatibility, from some want of skill in *me*, & NOT from any unfitness of the subject—the subject meaning religion generally, & not such questionable selections as the subject of the *Seraphim.*–

Do you remember anything of my stanzas upon L E L. Well! I heard of Mr Kenyon's speaking very kindly of them—& saying besides that it was a pity the *last* stanza was not cut away—that I w^d bring in religion upon all possible opportunities. And such things have made me, not afraid of my own opinions, but nervous sometimes about introducing wrongly or dwelling too much—and, in the ballad in question, I was satisfied with making as I thought one meaning clear & tried not to be too *verbally* theological —doing this very particularly in writing for an annual—not for *you* my beloved friend who never sent me any "advices" of the sort, but for your readers of whom you say such unflattering truths. Your "slightest of all readers" make an admirable pendant to Mr Horne's ideal of the engraved "ladies & gentlemen"!– In regard to yourself—[(]y^r own opinions)—I am sure they will agree with mine, against every experience of non-success or mal-success on the part of so many "religious poets", that the fault is more likely to lie in their not being poets than in their being religious—& that one truth is self evident—*wherever there is room for* HUMAN FEELING *to act, there is room for* POETICAL FEELING *to act*. We cant separate our humanity from our poetry—nor, when they are together, can we say or at least prove, that humanity looking downward has a fairer aspect than humanity looking towards God. I am afraid that the matter with some of us, may be resolved into our not considering religion a subject of *feeling*, of real warm emotion & feeling—but of creed & form & necessity. If we feel, it is wrong to show that we feel!—& this, only in religion!– Because you are kind to me, I must love you—& nobody will call me wrong for doing that. It is only grateful & natural that I sh^d love you—& there is no want of decorum & picturesqueness in loving you. Because Christ died for me, I must love HIM—but it is very wrong of me to say it,—& very improper—& above all things very unpoetical! Oh! the pitiful inconsistencies of this mortal world! And the inconsistency would be nothing, if it were not for the cold—if it were not for the cold & the baseness!––

Well! but it is easy to make the penitence more evident, dearest Miss Mitford—& respecting the short lines, which of them are the worst? I will try, & do what I can–

The address is,

R. H. Horne Esqr
75 Gloucester Place
Portman Square
London.

I have heard that he piques himself upon being very like the pictures & busts of Shakespeare!– People feel differently on every sort of subject. If I were like Shakespeare I sh^d be quite distressed, & take to wearing a wig, & green spectacles immediately. I sh^d be ashamed of being like Shakespeare, & afraid of profaning the shrine—I really should!——

Love to dear Dr Mitford. I must send more cream, as he liked the last.

Your ever attached
EBB.

I am going on very comfortable—my brother George is with me—& my dear Arabel is coming—& Papa is coming—& all this makes me very glad & happy—— But I am likely to remain here until next year– I am afraid there is no escape from it!—— Do you ever talk or dream of coming this way? I wish I had the loadstone which lies under y^r threshold——

I had a very kind note from dear Mr Kenyon just before he went to Three Mile Cross. "Miss Mitford's lovely village" by the way, is praised in last month's Blackwood, in the *"Picture Gallery"*–

FRIDAY– [LATE JANUARY 1840]

.   .   .

D.ʳ Scully has condemned me to a dynasty of blisters—each to be applied to the chest every three days for two or three hours at a time—which just answers the purpose of a minor kind of flaying– Not that I am worse. But the spitting of blood which never has quite ceased, always increases with the fall of the thermometer—& it is found absolutely necessary to divert as far as possible (which is not very far) the morbid course of the circulation.

Have you seen M.ʳˢ Gore & M.ʳˢ Trollope in their late avatars? "Preferment", with an undeniable cleverness, is dull & heavy—besides the *hardness,* as inseparable from that world-illustrating species of composition as from an old walnut shell. As to "One fault", with neither dulness nor heaviness, the book seems to *me* far less clever than M.ʳˢ Trollope's books generally or always are—and I am at a loss about the title, the applicability of the title, seeing that it is suitable neither to the work which is far from having *only* one fault, nor to the hero who really does in my eyes concentrate in his magnificent person most of the faults & the worst ones, I can remember without "farther notice"—while the poor persecuted & perfect heroine has no fault at all . . , if it be not that she might "have DONE IT" more gracefully, in making her proposals to that second husband with whom the third volume *leaves her*– But then again she was wet & in a hurry—there are excuses for her. It w.ᵈ have been different if she had waited to change her stockings—& by the way, Eureka,!—in that one omission lies the *one* FAULT! ——

Talking of Geraldine & converts, —did you ever meet with an account partly translated partly composed by Miss Schimmelpenninck, of the Port Royal?[1] It is long since I read, & will be longer before I forget that most interesting account of the most interesting establishment which ever owed its conventual name & form to the Church of Rome, & its purity & nobility to God's blessing & informing Spirit–

They have come to warn me about the post. My beloved friend, do write whenever you can without crowding your employments unpleasantly, & *never* at another time.

My sisters say they w.ᵈ intrude their kindest regards—& mine *are*

with dear D.! Mitford by permission—–& intrusion too—fancying &
wishing all sorts of seasonable good to both of you!–

Your most affectionate
E B Barrett–

1. *Geraldine: A Tale of Conscience* (1837) by Emily C. Agnew reminded EBB of Mary
Anne Schimmelpenninck (1778–1856), who wrote a history of the Society of Port
Royal, a Cistercian nunnery near Versailles, since both books were concerned with
Catholic doctrines.

TORQUAY.
[FRIDAY] 6.th MARCH 1840–

My beloved friend,
    I was hesitating whether or not to write when your letter came
telling me to do so. I *wanted* to write very much—to assure you of my
gladness about 'the PLAN': and then again what you said in regard to
the pressure upon your time seemed to say 'Tais toi Jean Jaques' to
me. All your affectionateness c.d not prevent my letters taking up time
in reading as well as answering. Pray my ever dearest Miss Mitford,
dont let them teaze you. Now dont write to me again for . . how
many weeks? No– The time shant be measured or it will look too
sadly long—but dont write until you have time to throw away by
handfuls– It will be kind to *me* if you dont.
    And I am the more remorseful for my in-the-way-ingness (I re-
commend that word to your authorship) because I do feel about to be
useless in your new undertaking. People have different manners of
reading, & I know that very many from the Laureate downwards, are
in the habit of filling voluminous commonplace books. I put ashes
upon my head in the confession that I am not one of them. 'Every
woman to her humour!' That commonplacing always seemed to me
wearying work, & scarcely calculated, in my own particular experience, to make amends for the expenditure of time which it exacts. I
have a legal sort of memory, & when my associations imply the existence of a passage, I know tolerably well where to find it out. Poor
Sir Uvedale Price[1] used to call me "a good ferret." Books of mere reasoning & philosophy, I have often fixed in my memory by an analy-

sis—and pages of such analyzing are somewhere nailed up in old boxes of papers, in Wimpole Street—but such, even if I c^d reach them, w^d be of no manner of use to you or anybody in the world– Extracts from books I have scarcely any even there. I never did care to make them—except in the case of books which I was not likely to have access to again. Yes!—and a little MS book beside me now, has extracts from the Greek Fathers &c arranged so as to show their views of certain doctrinal points. And here is a long arch-angelical passage from Swedenborg[2] whom I intended to part from eternally at the time I clipped that lock of hair!– Oh how can I be of use to you?–– You know Fuller, old Fuller,[3] I dare say– Otherwise, two pages of dislocated oddities from him, sh^d go to you, in my handwriting, & might prove usable as quotations applicable or unapplicable. Shall I send *them*?

How can I be of use to you? I am a ferret in a cage here—lying in bed as weak as a baby, & out of reach of books such as might profit you most–

The plan is delightful—I mean for *us*, the readers, the world,—your letters being always very attractive parts of you, & your *early* letters essentially & relatively interesting, of necessity. Do they refer to any particular subject—I mean, are they what are called 'literary letters' or *scenic* letters—or do they gossip "at their own sweet will" (think of Miss Roberts[4] attributing those words to Miss Landon!) on all sorts of subjects? There!—I meant to ask no questions. But it will do as well,—if you dont answer any!–

Surely it is a book for selling—& living besides—whatever name you put to it. And it seems to me that nothing can be better than Mr S^it Talfourd's suggestion, which I w^d modify by your own in some such manner as this

Letters before Authorship
by an Author.

Surely that arrangement cannot be objectionable on the ground of length,—while it is perfectly applicable & expressive, & catches the ear. I shall be so very glad to hear of triumphant success & profit & praise together. And I shall be sure to hear of it,— if I live out a few months longer. May your undertaking prosper my beloved friend— *may* it!–

In the meantime I am very sorry that you sh^d be so hummed

about by the great swarms of your admirers . . altho' I really could'nt
help laughing at the diffident request of the lady unknown, praying
for the transcription of her three volumes. Such shadow falls from
such laurels!—but people are pardonable for fancying that the Miss
Mitford of our village sits in a perpetual sunshine of her own which
all their Alexandering cant disturb,—& that moreover she has an om-
nipresent smile, to smile the whole world round at once!— Oh I can
well believe that *you* are more pestered than others even of equal notoriety—& the reason of it is a crown above the crown!—& not because you are taken for "a good-natured fool". What a reason to
suggest!——— *That* made me laugh too!—

As for me, you *have* spoilt me to be sure—but the new pinnacle
you forsee for me "above the notoriety," made me laugh again.
[']'Thrice the brindled cat hath mewed". No—no—dearest Miss Mitford! I shall always be safe, *below* the danger of notoriety,—were I to
live more years than I am likely to do months.

And yet I do believe that I can match your modest lady with another—an absolute stranger to me & mine, who wrote to me several
years ago to beg me to lend her a thousand pounds! She wanted the
money, she said, to enable two young men to go to the university:
and understanding that I was an only child & an heiress & very eager
about literature besides, she thought me just the person to apply to!—
After my first astonishment, I really did rather admire her for making
such an effort, in despite of all conventionalities, in behalf of literature & two aspiring lovers of it. I really admired her benevolence &
her boldness. Something of the sort too, I said in my reply—explaining the truth that I had ten brothers & sisters, was no heiress; & observing—which at that time was literally true—that if she had asked
me for a thousand half-pence I c^d not have given them to her. Can
you believe in the fact of her writing again, to desire me to collect
forty pounds *among my friends*—I a stranger to her, among them
strangers to her, for others strangers to both parties?—and in the worst
fact of all (discovered by me long afterwards) that the two aspiring
geniuses were related to her benevolence very closely—the one being
her son & the other about to be her son in law?—!— And she a lady—
in family—education—& position in society! This does beat the three
volumes!—— Yield the palm to me! ——

People who are not "ladies" say sometimes . . "I am afraid you
are not agreeable". Well!—in that sense of the word (& also, perhaps
in worse senses) I cant be agreeable to *you* today—no, not at all,

dearest dearest Miss Mitford!– Dear Dᵣ Mitford is a magistrate & a country gentleman, & my own dear Papa was both all his life until the last very few years—but still a country gentleman & a magistrate *per se* I cannot say much eloquent praise of– I have known a good many—& . . . I leave the species to *you*. You shall be laureate to them—and I will hide myself somewhere behind Ma^dme de Staels' petticoats at the other side of the room—

> Blessings be on them & eternal praise
> The poets!–

· · ·

And, what is the cockney school? I never cᵈ make out. Hazzlitt Leigh Hunt Keats Charles Lamb, Barry Cornwall—. What is *common* to these gifted writers, that we shᵈ make a school with it? Is it not their locality which gave the name—& still less reasonably than the Lakes gave another? And are any of us the worse for living in London, if we dont roll in the dust of the streets? And altho' there have been & are among these writers, sins of coarseness & affectation & latitudinarianism, did any one of them all ever perpetrate such an enormity as Mᵣ Ainsworth's Jack Shepherd,[5] he, who for aught I know, may keep sheep in the wilderness—with a crook on one side & Burns's Justice on the other?

· · ·

And will you ever forgive all my disagreeableness—my impertinen[c]es, my contrariousness?– Here are contradictions enough for a lifetime—even a woman's!– But I am always *sincere* in writing to you—& none the less in assuring you, dearest dearest Miss Mitford of my true & grateful & *uplooking* affection.

Your E B Barrett–

· · ·

1. Sir Uvedale Price (1747–1829), gardener and scholar who admired EBB's *An Essay on Mind, with Other Poems* (1826) and for whom she made notations on the proof sheets of his *Essay on the Modern Pronunciation of the Greek and Latin Languages* (1827).
2. Emanuel Swedenborg (1688–1772), Swedish mystic in whom EBB had a lifelong interest.

3. Thomas Fuller (1608–61), English divine whose meditations were whimsical expressions of wisdom.

4. Emma Roberts (1794–1840) in *"The Zenana" and Minor Poems of L.E.L. With a Memoir by Emma Roberts* (1839) said that LEL never dreamed her verses, "gushing, as she has beautifully expressed it, of their own sweet will," could provoke harsh criticism.

5. William Harrison Ainsworth (1805–82), whose *Jack Sheppard: A Romance* (1839) was regarded as an "enormity" of vulgarity, here linked with Robert Burns's "The Jolly Beggars."

TORQUAY

Tragedy and Adjustment
1840–41

In July 1840 tragedy struck the Barretts when EBB's eldest brother, Bro, drowned in Tor Bay. EBB, who was closest to him of all her family and who felt responsible for his presence in Torquay, was prostrated for months and never completely recovered from the shock. The following January, despite her worries about her father, MRM had the happy thought of giving EBB Flush, offspring of a Mitford spaniel, whose antics helped divert EBB and provided a subject of enduring interest to the two friends. For the marooned and unhappy EBB news from Three Mile Cross was a lifeline, as MRM presided over pets, flowers, and wayward servants amid a wide circle of correspondents, including one at court, the queen's dresser, Marianne Skerrett (1793?–1887), whom EBB calls "Miss Skennet." In July MRM brought to EBB's attention *Pippa Passes*, a new work by a virtually unknown poet, Robert Browning. Although MRM, who had met Browning socially, was not favorably impressed (partly because at almost thirty he was still being supported by his parents), EBB instinctively identified him as a "true poet." Her sympathy with artists shows in her defense (25 July 1841) of two other writers: the poet-journalist Leigh Hunt, accused of bad taste, and her correspondent R. H. Horne, whose reputation suffered from an early eccentric work ("the black book"), *Exposition of the False Medium and Barriers Excluding Men of Genius from the Public* (1833). During the spring and summer

44

of 1841, as MRM pondered a subject for a new drama (never written), EBB was well enough to begin a collaborative effort with Horne on a drama, *Psyche Apocalypté* (never completed) and to sit for a portrait ("the poor picture") by Mrs. Matilda Carter, a popular miniaturist, while she waited impatiently to be allowed to rejoin her family in London.

MONDAY– [OCTOBER OR NOVEMBER 1840]

My beloved friend,

You have not thought me ill or—worse still—unkind, for not writing?– I feel bound more than I ever remember having felt, in chains, heavy & cold enough to be iron—& which have indeed entered into the soul. But I do love you still—& am rather better than worse—likely, I do suppose to live on. In the meantime, thank you thank you for your letter, & *both* of you dear Dr Mitford, & my beloved friend, for your affectionate sympathy. Months roll over months. I know it is for good—but *very hard to bear.* And now—at least a week ago—my kind physician, after having held out hope from time to time, for the sake I do suspect now of drawing me onward, brought me his ultimatum—that he cannot sanction my attempting to leave this dreadful place before the spring– He told me he had wished & prayed it might be otherwise, but he was convinced now that in the case of my removing even to another house *here* much less to London, the consequences w^d be fatal.

After all, I suffer so in staying that I w^d dare it & go– But my saying this is quite vain, with Papa & my sisters looking on– They wont hear of it. So I stay– They are well I thank God.

You wont miss me dearest Miss Mitford in the Tableaux – I know & knew you w^{dnt}—except in your illogical affectionateness. Then Mr Horne does not contribute? Mind you dont think of sending *me* a copy– I shall try to see it—& such a largesse w^d be quite out of place considering the circumstances.

May God bless you always– My sisters['] love to you—& mine to Dr Mitford. *Can* you read?

Your unchangingly affectionate
EBB–

Notwithstanding this trembling hand, I am better & stronger—& more tranquil as to my thoughts. I suffered from what was called *congestion of the heart*—& was in so singular & frightful a state of weakness as not to be able to sleep for five minutes together without *fainting*. For weeks they watched me in their kindness night after night—only ascertaining the transition by a sigh, or the sudden coldness of cheek & forehead. And now I can sleep for an hour or more at a time—& the faintings are almost quite gone. Dearest Miss Mitford—I do truly love you. Love me a little. You understand so well—& will—besides—that I want them all to go & leave me here with my maid for the winter. I sh.d be far easier & happier if they w.d—*far easier*. But I fear they wont go—dear things!–

So far I had written—& now I hear thr'o M.r Kenyon that dear D.r Mitford has not been well & that you are in distress. Oh do do, write—if you can—when you can– I must not lay a straw's further weight on you my beloved friend. May God bless you *both*–

> Your ever attached
> EBB.

·   ·   ·

> Three-mile Cross
> Jan. 14, 1841.

I write, my beloved friend, by my dear father's bedside; for he is again very ill. Last Tuesday was the Quarter Sessions, and he *would* go, and he seemed so well that Mr. May thought it best to indulge him. Accordingly he went at nine A.M. to open the Court, sat all day next the chairman in Court, and afterward at dinner, returning at two o'clock, A.M., in the highest spirits—not tired at all, and setting forth the next day for a similar eighteen hours of business and pleasure. Again he came home delighted and unwearied. He had seen many old and dear friends, and had received (to use his own words) the attentions which do an old man's heart good; and *these*, joined to his original vigor of constitution and his high animal spirits, had enabled him to do that which to those who saw him at home infirm and feeble, requiring three persons to help him from his chair, and many minutes before he could even move—would seem as impossible as a fall of snow between the tropics, or the ripening pine-apples in Nova Zembla.

All this he had done, but not with impunity. He has caught a severe cold; and having on Saturday taken nearly the same liberties at Reading, and not suffering me to send for Mr. May, until rendered bold by fear I did send last night—he is now seriously ill. I am watching by his bedside in deep anxiety; but as silence is my part to-night, and I have prayed (for when those we love—*so love*—are in danger, thought is prayer), I write to you, my beloved friend, as my best solace. Mr. May is hopeful; but the season, his age, my great and still increasing love, and the habit of anxiety which has grown from long tending, fill me with a fear that I can hardly describe. He is so restless too—so very, very restless—and every thing depends upon quiet, upon sleep, and upon perspiration; and yet, for the last twelve hours I am sure that he has not been two minutes in the same posture, and not twelve minutes without his getting out of bed, or up in bed, or something as bad. God grant that he may drop asleep! I read to him until I found that reading only increased the irritability. Well, I do hope and trust that he is rather quieter now; and I am quite sure that I shall myself be quieter in mind, if I can but fix my thoughts upon you. Heaven be with you all! Ever yours,

M.R.M.

THURSDAY– [21? JANUARY 1841]

My dearest dearest Miss Mitford I am so grieved in this new grief of yours —and although I did "read the last page first" & carried from it all hopeful inferences, yet the hope is scarcely like enough to certainty to make me easy, or less earnest in my petition to hear how dear D! Mitford is now. Send me some broken words, my beloved friend—will you? And oh may God be near your prayers, & blessing you beyond them.

I sent a little cream as soon as the lazy farm-people here would let me have it— Indeed I delayed longer than my wishes in applying for it—because I did want to send with it, besides Chaucer, M! Horne's Cosmo which M! Bezzi seems to hold fast with both hands & much resolution. I never saw him (M! Bezzi) you know—& he is said to be an *arch*-amiable person. But I am in the confidence of one fault . . his tendency to the 'retinence' of books. Several books he has of mine, besides Cosmo—and really my prospect of seeing them again becomes more cloudy to my own perception every day.

Tell me just what you think of Chaucer—will you, dearest Miss Mitford?

Oh and I do trust that by this time you may have a freer heart for the thought of such things. The *cause* of the attack was sufficiently salient & evident to exonerate the constitution from unprovoked failure: and a little more prudence (such as the evil itself will naturally induce) will give room (may God grant it!) for the health which returns, to remain.

Do give my love to dear D.ʳ Mitford—my thanks (again & again) for the kindness of his thought of me at such a time, & my hope . . . my humble hope, limping after all the rest . . of his being able & inclined perhaps to take a little of my cream!—& so, confer on it, a dignity above any pertaining to M.ʳˢ Trollope's dear "crême" of transcendent lords & ladies at Vienna.

How I thank you for Flush!—dear little Flush—growing dearer every day. He has fallen upon evil days at Torquay,—for a report of 'mad dogs' has alarmed the magistrates & loaded the guns, & we dare not trust him out of the house. But he runs & leaps within it enough for exercise & keeps up his spirits & his appetite—only the latter is becoming scrupulous—demurring to any *un*buttered bread. In fact, Flush prefers muffins. However we go on delightfully together—that is, Flush & I & Crow (my maid) do. To the rest of the household he is decidedly hostile—will scarcely bestow a mark of courtesy upon either of my sisters, runs away from my brothers, & is coldly disdainful to one little page who has done everything possible to please him & is in despair at the result. But Crow he is very fond of—& he prances up to the side of my bed in an ecstasy to hug the hand he can reach, between his two pretty paws. We are great friends. And when my sisters & brothers are with me, there he lies . . quite down-hearted– – responding to no notice . . waiting patiently, as it seems, until he can celebrate their departure by a round of leaps!– Is'nt it strange?– We cant make it out at all. Perhaps he may associate Crow & myself with his deliverance from the basket, & love us out of gratitude—but why he sh.ᵈ be such a hater of the toga (which really is the case) & so little to be won upon by my *sisters* even, is a riddle to us all.

I have not seen the 'Hour & Man' yet.[1] This is such a place for books! But I shall soon, nevertheless.

Oh of course . . judging by extracts . . Toussaint's eloquence is Miss *Martineau's*.

Do send me good news—if God give the power!–

Ever yours in truest affection
EBB.

•   •   •

1. *The Hour and the Man: A Historical Romance* (1840) by Harriet Martineau about Toussaint l'Ouverture (1743–1803), the Haitian liberator.

[SUNDAY] MAY 30th [1841]

•   •   •

What Mr Horne and I are engaging ourselves in, is a mere *Lyrical Drama*; & the title of it, is to be "*Psyche Apocalyptic*"! —the subject, as is obvious, balancing itself between the high fantastical & the high philosophical—the hero neither a Manfred nor a Faust (we shall keep clear of either) but pretty nearly as mad to vulgar eyes, and suffering persecution from the hauntings of his own soul,—the Psyche—seen in vision, and heard in solitude or crowds. Ah—you shake your head!– I feel it,—as the Olympians did a Jove-shaking —I feel it all this distance off. But we are to have real situations, I mean tangible—men and women talking loud out to one another—& only Psyche is purely psychical. There will be joy and grief—a child and a bridal—we are not quite in the clouds—we keep one foot on the ground.

The mystery is, how *I* shd have the vanity to consent to a combination with Mr Horne,—whose genius I take high measure of. And besides—there does seem to me an objection to such combinations in general, even with more balanced powers—and to this moment I am not sure how I shall succeed in working by allotment, after the necessary fashion.

The truth is, that Mr Horne long & long ago, more than a year ago said in one of his kind letters that 'he shd like to write a Lyrical Drama with me.' I answered more laughingly than I cd now . . joke to joke, as it seemed to me—it was very ingenious in him to want to set up a show, with a dwarf and giant together—some nonsense of that sort—not all nonsense either. Then he was serious and pressed his wish upon it. And I was made serious—and we talked or rather wrote it over—& it was agreed to be done some time—sometime when he and I became acquainted face to face.

A pause came—when this spring Mr Horne (half out of kindness, and the wish to amuse my mind, and perhaps *whole*) proposed that we shd begin at once—desiring me to consider for a subject. My thoughts grew fantastical, and hummed down upon Psyche—and I was surprised at his accepting the suggestion eagerly,—as a difficult subject but still feasible, and a very fine one. We were agreed in a minute. And now he is arranging the sketch I sent him, into *acts* (oh we call them 'acts' I assure you) and dividing the labour between us. You see the weak sides of Mr Horne and myself bend the same way—to the *mystic*. That is why we agreed,—and the only excuse for such a partnership.

• • •

How is dear Dr Mitford? How are *you*? You were not well, when you wrote. You sit up too late—you do everything too much, even to loving . . no, not loving, . . thinking well of . . *me*!–

God bless and keep you.

The picture—ah the poor picture!– I will tell you of *that* another day. Papa said it was'nt like!!– I and the grand Sultan are not people to have our likeness taken.

Your faithful & affectionate
EBB.

Not a line of the dramatic poem is written. Nothing but the plan. We daudle and dream. Mr Horne declared I was asleep & dreaming—and now he has gone down to Wolverhampton on government business about pots & pans & pits, NOT poetry but pottery–

Flush sends his love–

Do you know Mrs Sigourney[1] —The American poetess? I had a very flattering letter from her just before she sailed, saying that she had tried long & vainly for my direction–

Is the Mr Edward Quillinan[2] who married Mr Wordsworth's daughter, the 'Love & War' Quillinan.

Do write when you have time to throw away– Nobody picks it up so gladly as I—because—-no room for reasons.

1. Lydia Howard Huntley Sigourney (1791–1865), Connecticut author of *Pleasant Memories of Pleasant Lands* (1842).
2. Edward Quillinan (1791–1851), poet and novelist, married to Wordsworth's daughter Dora, published the novel *Love and War* (1841).

[MONDAY] JUNE 14, 1841

Thank you my beloved friend for your kindness in writing & wishing to have me within teazing distance– Ah!—I hope you would'nt have reason to repent it if I were to go!– I should be on my guard, and never say "Do come," and *look* it as seldom as possible.

I have told Papa about the house, but have urged nothing,—because under the circumstances & in the state of feeling natural to me at this time, my only full contentment can be in his doing his own full pleasure. I want to be with him & in a situation which w^d least threaten a future separation—a want which involved the objection to Clifton, I c^d not keep concealed. But if his wish remain fixed upon Clifton, even to Clifton I must go. And in any other case, the reason is strengthened for my suspending every form of interference.

I came here, you see, not indeed against his desire, but against the bias of his desire. I was persuaded—he was entreated. On his side, it was at last a mere yielding to a majority.

Well!—& what has been the end?– The place . . no! I will not say that it was accursed to me—but the bitterness suffered in it has been bitter, (in regard to present endurance) as any curse. All the sorrow of my life besides, & that life not free from sorrow, showed without sting or agony in comparison with the deep deep woe of last year.[1] It was the sharpest laceration of the tenderest affection—an affection never agitated till then except with its own delight. Oh my beloved friend—There was no harsh word, no unkind look—never from my babyhood till I stood alone– A leaf never shook till the tree fell. The shade was over me softly till it fell. And although what I cannot help feeling as an unnatural tenacity to life, prevented my following my beloved, quickly quickly as I thought I sh^d,—and although I have learnt even to be calm & to talk lightly sometimes, yet the heavy sense of loss weighs at my heart day & night, and *will*, till my last night or day.

There is much much to love, left to me, close to me always– But there is no one close to me always, to whom I can say 'Is this which I have written, good? Is it worth anything?' and, be sure of the just answer. The nearest sympathy, the natural love which was friendship too, is not close to me now.

I have thrown down my paper & taken it up again. It was wrong, very wrong, to write so– It has pained your kindness, & done no good to me—except indeed for the pleasure's sake of speaking out a pain. Take no notice of it dearest friend!—ever kindest & dearest you are!—— I know that the stroke fell in blessing & not in cursing, & that when we see each other's smiles again in the light of God's throne, not one will be fainter for the tears shed here. Blessed be God in Christ Jesus, who consummates grief in glory.

But you will understand from all, that my poor most beloved Papa's *biases* are sacred to me, & that I w^d not stir them with a breath. Yet he says to me "Decide". He is so kind, . . so tender. No love of mine can echo back his, as far as the demonstration goes– I love him inwardly, I was going to say better than my life . . but that is worthless, was so always, & is now so most of all.

I shall like you to know Papa—ah, you smile at my saying *Papa*—I am too old for such a baby-word I know—but he likes to be called so, & therefore I dont like to call him otherwise even in thought– I heard him say once "If they leave off calling me 'Papa', I shall think they have left off loving me". I shall like you to know him. You will certainly like & estimate him. Mr Kenyon does thoroughly– Mr Horne, who has seen him once, has begun to do it already. He is not poetical, or literary even in the strict sense—but he has strong & clear natural faculties & is full of all sorts of general information. I have consoled myself sometimes when you were abusing the professional literati with the thought that you w^d be sure to like 'Papa'. You like, you know, sensible men who dont make a trade of their sense,—reading country-gentlemen who dont write books. I have hopes of you.

Well—and thus then it remains, I have put him in possession of your report about the pretty house—but have received no notice of his decision, or of any sort of decision about any place. Thank you, thank you, for thinking of me in reference to the Chiswick show.^{2} How kind! how *welcomely* kind! and how probable it is, as far as any pleasure can be probable, that I may see you somewhere this summer!–

•   •   •

No– The picture, they said in Wimpole Street, was not like. The head was too large, & the features too large, & the expression a void. So said the critics there. Those here, consisting of my sisters & two brothers & one or two persons who had looked at me (some time ago) for an hour or two, vowed deeply on the other hand that no picture ever was will or could be a more complete facsimile of the thing pictured.– Well—but it was for Papa, & Papa was dissatisfied. So I begged him to return it & let the artist muse upon the means of amendment. She mused,—drew out her brushes, perhaps in some little fluttering of annoyance,—& straightway made all the critics of one mind—straightway everybody said "Oh, it is'nt like at all now!" Was'nt it provoking?–

And then my sisters went to her & prayed her to come again & do something—& she came & did it, took away something of the wooden look, & left the whole under improvement. So "the critics here" say now "It is very like—*only not quite so like as it was at first*",—and what they will say "there", remains yet unknown. A satisfactory business altogether!

Is your picture like?– I mean the one you yourself had painted—happier in its destination than mine. I liked to hear of my thought being your thought once on a time. Love *will* do the same things.

•   •   •

My dearest friend, in what you say of me you speak wisely & truly as far as your kindness lets you. A cold mystical poetry strikes & falls from us like the hail—it does not penetrate or abide. And in this work, if M! Horne & I ever compass it, as well as in others, I will try to clasp & keep in mind what you tell me, & make my access to human feelings *through* human feelings– The plan of the work in question admits of the natural workings of humanity: there are real persons & events—there is not a naked allegory, or a mere embodiment of abstractions. Even the Psyche herself, with her persecutions & her terrors, is intended to present an absolute & universal truth, not barely incident to our humanity but common to every thinking human being. However I sometimes fancy that the work, whether for good or evil, will never pass much beyond the threshold of its conception.

M.͎ Horne lingers– He seems quite earnest about it—but he has been oppressed with business (England never cares you know, to give leisure to her poets) & is just now suffering from the *hooping cough.* I had a letter from him to say so two days since, from Broadstairs where he fled for change of air. He says "There's a re-juvenility for you."!— but I really fear that he has been & is still exceedingly unwell.

But although I admit your verities, I will not deny my mysticism. The known & *the unknown* both enter into our nature & our world. Our guesses at the invisible belong as much, & more nobly, to the part played here by the spirit within us, as do our familiar thoughts upon the flowers of June– Our terror before 'Psyche', (as in my view of her revelation) is not surely more alien to our humanity, than a child's or a poet's pleasure in a daisy.

At the same time I quite submit to the truth of your remarks— only entreating that your view (& it need not) may not *exclude* mine. I confess to a love & reverence for Goëthe above any to which Schiller c.ᵈ move me. Goëthe was surely the greater genius—and he did not, as you admit, neglect the humanities, in their strict human sense. It was Shelley that high, & yet too low, elemental poet, who froze in cold glory between Heaven & earth, neither dealing with man's heart, beneath, nor aspiring to communion with supernal Humanity, the heart of the God-Man. Therefore his poetry glitters & is cold—and it is only by momentary stirrings that we can discern the power of sweet human love & deep pathos which was in *him* & sh.ᵈ have been in *it.*

Do you call me ungrateful, or stupid? Have I not the sense of kindness or its memory, never to thank you until now for the geraniums? Ah Papa did better. He told me that the gift, together with the recollection of all your goodnesses to me, touched him so, that he could'nt help intruding a note upon you. It was well done of him— and *you* did not call it an intrusion, I know as well as if you told me.

They will take great care of the geraniums—they must: and if Wimpole St is left to itself this summer, the pots must transmigrate to *me* with the gardeners.

I have been up day after day, & an hour at a time, & bore it gallantly. *I am going away.* Pray for us, my beloved friend, that we may meet really, & not in hope alone.

> Your ever attched
> E B Barrett–

·   ·   ·

1. Bro's death by drowning.
2. The annual flower show at the Duke of Devonshire's gardens in Chiswick, outside London. MRM and EBB visited them at the time of their first meeting in May 1836.

[Saturday] July 17 1841.

. . .

Thank you, thank you for Browning's poem.[1] My thought of it crossed your question about my thought, Mr Kenyon having kindly sent me *his* copy ten days since. But I must tell you besides that I read it three times—in correspondence with Mr Chorley's four—& in testimony both to the genius & the obscurity. Nobody sh.^d complain of being forced to read it three or four or ten times. Only they w.^d do it more gratefully if they were not forced. I who am used to mysteries, caught the light at my second reading—but the full glory, not until the third. The conception of the whole is fine, very fine—& there are noble, beautiful things everywhere to be broken up & looked at. That great tragic scene, which you call "exquisite"—& which pants again with its own power! Did it strike you that there was an occasional *manner*, in the portions most strictly dramatic, like Landor's, in Landor's dramas, when Landor writes best. Now read—

> —"How these tall
> Naked geraniums straggle! Push the lattice—
> Behind that frame.—Nay, do I bid you?—Sebald,
> It shakes the dust down on me! Why of course
> The slide-bolt catches– Well—are you content
> Or must I find you something else to spoil?–
> Kiss & be friends, my Sebald!"

Is'nt that Landor? Is'nt it his very trick of phrase? Yet Mr Browning is no imitator. He asserts *himself* in his writings, with a strong & deep individuality: and if he does it in Chaldee, why he makes it worth our while to get out our dictionaries! Oh most excellent critic 'in the glass house['] !–

After all, what I miss most in Mr Browning, is *music*. There is a want of harmony, particularly when he is lyrical—& *that* struck me with a hard hand, while I was in my admiration over his Paracelsus.

This is for *you*—I *do not know him.*

Ten oclock—& not a word of the last subject—the last dread subject!– I will write tomorrow. But I must say before my eyes shut tonight, that I thank you most gratefully & fondly, beloved kindest friend, for the frankness of your words. Oh advise me always—tell me always what I ought to do—or ought'nt– It is so, that I feel sure of your loving me.

I will write tomorrow—but do not wait until then to be in true grateful attachment.

Your EBB–

Can you read? My hand shakes, . . goes east & west . . today— & it is *tonight* now.

I have sent for the *Literary Gazette.*

1. Robert Browning (1812–89) had published *Pippa Passes* in April as the first of a series later collected under the title of *Bells and Pomegranates.*

[SUNDAY] JULY 25. 1841

My kindest, ever beloved friend,

I understand, I acknowledge, I love all your love. It was only *you.* And yet I thank you as if it were more than you! The frankness & truthfulness of it are so dear to me, that I say once more, . . Ever be so with me, my beloved friend, and do not suffer a reserve to deprive me of an advantage.

I have sent for the book [1]—that is, I have asked Papa to send it to me directly—*without* telling him the 'because'. Of all particularly particular people he is chief; and I sh^d not like for obvious reasons, to startle him in his particularity by what may prove, as I hope & believe it will, the shadow of a silence, the negative of a negative & to be treated negatively. If it sh^{dnt} . . why what shall I do? How difficult, yet how necessary, to retreat from this poetic alliance—which has been so long pending—& the papers preparatory to which, are actually prepared!–How shall I get up a 'caprice' dramatically, & not ungratefully?–Well—it is my own fault as my vexation!

I see too that you think the John Bull-Fraser-people may say all sorts of disagreeable things, even if the black book turn out a Biblical commentary. But then, sh^d we mind it? Mr Horne means to say in the preface (so he wrote to me once) that the work is the joint production of two persons *who had never seen each other*. Now if he said so, nobody w^d have the power to dissert upon our degree of forgone intimacy—w^d they?–

After all, as I told you before, the whole thing if left to itself, may & probably will, break like a bubble, I said to him some time ago, that if his delays were so abundant, it w^d take several generations of people like me, to work with him to the end of Psyche. He is overwhelmed with business of various kinds– That work of Tyas's, the history of Napoleon, is his you know—besides the preliminary Essay to Schlegel[2]—besides some Mexican directorship—besides, oh I cant tell you what!–

Yes—the disadvantage is to *me*. I shall say afterwards—'Tout est perdu hormis l'honneur.' There is honor to my own *consciousness* in working with him, but when we have both done, everybody will ascribe the weak parts of the performance to *my* responsibility, & all the good to my coadjutor's. When a man & a woman write together, it's almost always so—to say nothing of poetic degrees– But this I sh^d not I sh^d not mind. The critics could never mortify me out of heart— because I love poetry for its own sake,—and, tho' with no stoicism & some ambition, care more for my poems than for my poetic reputation.

•   •   •

And this, bringing me to Leigh Hunt, reminds me that I do not wholly agree with you in regard to him. I think he has been wronged by many,—& that even you, your own just truthful & appreciating self, do not choose soft words enough to suit his case. For instance— it never was proved either to my reason or my feelings that *Rimini* had an immoral tendency. Indeed my belief is exactly the reverse. The final impression of that poem, most beautiful surely as poem, appears to me morally unexceptionable. The 'poetical justice' is worked out too from the *sin itself*,—& not from a cause independent of it,—after the fashion of those pseudo moralists who place the serpent's sting anywhere but in the serpent. We are made to feel & see that apart from the discovery, apart from the husband's vengeance on the lover, both sinners are miserable & one must die. She was dying, without that blow– The sin involved the death-agony!– Who can read these things tearless, & without a deep enforced sense of [']'the sinfulness of sin"?

•   •   •

The Examiner under the Hunts, came a step before me—but I have here, in the house, a volume of his collected poems—the effect of which, to judge from my own pulses, is for beauty & for good. Now I sh^d like to lecture you out of that book! My text book sh^d make amends for my impudence!– I w^d begin with the verses to his sick child

> "Sleep breathes at last from out thee
> My little patient boy—"

I w^d dare you to read *that* without a tear! & then again as a prose gossiping essayist—his delightful Indicator! – Oh I plead for Leigh Hunt. He has been very unfortunate, & very imprudent as to money affairs —but it is the way of poets, as a race,—and we c^{dnt} be very hard upon him for wasting too much money (one story went so!) upon a stair-carpet,—could we—should we, dearest Miss Mitford?– Now how I *am* teazing you.

Thank God for the escape, my beloved friend—the *second* escape within so short a time!– The thought of that flame mounting & burning, made me tremble almost like your Flush! Do tell me that you are really none the worse for the fright. Such frights do not do good—although *your* mind is comparatively safe, in the sevenfold wrapping of care for others.

•   •   •

Thank you for your delightful letters! Thank you for the "royal gossip"– *They* do not need a royal gossip or a gossip royal of any sort to be delightful—to be three times welcome—to be my fairy gifts of sunshine for the hour on which they fall! A word about the garden—about Flush,—how it beams & makes me glad! Still the long Windsor letter had its charm. I sate down with you & Miss Skennet in the Monkey heat, & saw the queen & the queen's baby, & the prime minister musing in a scene to himself!– I enjoyed it all—& wont deny my entertainment,—for all your "fishing" questions with large hooks!–

Seriously—gravely, gratefully, I feel deeply my dearest kindest friend how many golden guineas of time I cost your dear kindness. I give them back to you in more golden affection—but my hand strikes against your gift in *that* kind also, & I find myself still your debtor.

And so let it be!– There is a tender pleasure, you shall not grudge me, in remaining

> Your indebted as attached
> E B Barrett!–

•   •   •

There has been the dreadful regatta today—& through shut windows & close-drawn curtains I could'nt help hearing the cannons firing & the people shouting! It has been so painful—so hard to bear! And I hoping all was over, took up this letter to turn aside my thoughts from the morning's sadness. This house is the lowest down on the beach, of all! W^d we were gone!——

God bless you! I knew your sympathy before you uttered it. Ever yours.

1. Horne's *Exposition of the False Medium and Barriers Excluding Men of Genius from the Public* (1833), advocating a Literary Institute for writers. MRM has suggested that EBB's reputation could suffer from an association with the eccentric Horne.

2. Horne had done the text for *Tyas's Illustrated History of Napoleon*, parts 1 and 2 (1839) and had sent an introductory essay on Schlegel's *Lectures on Dramatic Art* to Carlyle in 1839 for his comments.

[Thursday] August 5. 1841

Now for Flush's turn . . after the poets!– And he may "side the gods" as well as another.

I think I told you, I am sure I meant to do so, that pretty as he was when he came here first, he is prettier now and does indeed grow prettier & prettier every day. He is not merely fatter comparatively, but fat positively—& *how* we cant quite make out, for his appetite matches in delicacy a May Fair lady's at the close of the season. It is the milk, I suppose, that does it. He is fond of milk—& when any is brought to me in a cup he wont let me drink a whole half without a hint that the rest belongs to him. He waits till his turn comes, till he thinks it *is* come—and then if I loiter, as I do sometimes pretend to do, M! Flush tries to take possession of the cup by main force. His ears which you were inclined to criticise are improved—grown thicker

& longer, and fall beautifully in golden light over the darker brown of his head & body. He is much admired for beauty—particularly for that white breastplate which marks him even among dogs of his colour— Flush the silvershielded!–

But the beauty sh^d come last! I assure you that he does not in intellect & sensibility disgrace his high lineage!– I c^d tell you two or three volumes of wonderful stories upon either count. If I were another Scheherazade I c^d save my head by talking of Flush.

What really astounds me sometimes is his intelligence of words— not of gesture, not of countenance but articulate words . . Whisper them in his ear & its the same. Crow says (*she* taught him, which accounts for the ceremony) "Go to Miss Barrett"—and up he rushes to my side in a moment. Nay—if she says so in another room or down stairs or even out of doors, straightway he is galloping to my door, & I hear him turning the handle after his fashion, not scratching dog-wise, but turning & shaking the handle, in a way which suggested itself to his observation as the ordinary means of opening a door. Nobody taught him *that*—but he always does it—& the effect is curious. Then if you say to him "Kiss me Flush", he does it directly. "Lie down"—"Be quiet"—the action follows the phrase.

His greatest pleasure of all is to be taken out to walk—and when some of the walkers pass through my bedroom into one adjoining to put on their bonnets, you sh^d see Flush's eyes brighten as he leaps off my bed to investigate the subject & discover if really they are going. The sight of a head in a bonnet stirs him into an ecstasy. He dances and dances, & throws back his ears almost to his tail in Bacchic rapture. More than once he has lost his balance & fallen over. And then if after all, the cruel person in the bonnet sh^d say . . "No Flush! I cant take you today". Ah then is the change! Now dont think me romancing,—but at the utterance of those words, he stands still, suddenly still, looking up to the cruel eyes in visible consternation! He stands so, just a moment,—and then leaps up to me, & kisses my hands & face after his fashion, that I may intercede for him. Now I do assure you it is'nt romancing! He always does this. It is not once or twice—but always. I am his friend & take his part and spoil him— and in every disappointment & fright he always comes to me, that I may do my best for him. And if in the going out business, I can do nothing,—and the sentence is repeated "No Flush—you cant go out today" . . why then, Flush is a philosopher & lies down again by me

& never tries even to follow the bonnet out of the room. Now is'nt it clever of Flush?

•   •   •

But when everybody cries out "I never saw such a coward as that dog is," my apology for him is just this. It is the predominant sweetness & softness of his disposition which keeps him aloof from the "shadow before" of 'wars alarms'. He says to himself—"Now this may be the first step to a fight—and it being quite contrary to my principles & temper to fight, I shall beware of taking it". Flush has never, since he has been here, hurt any living thing or tried to hurt it—& he wont do so. Even the other day when that naughty boy Edwin tied a live mouse by the tail to a chair's leg, & Flush's friend the kitten, yet too young to slay, was trying to beat it down with its paw, Flush stood by superior, close by, with eyes as large as four, looking Crow says "very much amused" but "never attempting to touch" the poor little victim himself. She cut the string & let it escape.

The friendship with the kitten continues fast as ever. It runs after him like a puppy—and he thinks nothing of carrying it up stairs in his mouth. Then he lies down, & suffers the little snowy thing to roll over him & play with his ears & thrust its paw into his mouth. There is love on both sides. But Flush has a passion besides, for young children & babies. So have I—and if ever one is carried in for me to look at, as happens now & then, he is in ecstasies—dancing round & round the room after the person carrying it,—& carressing it after his fashion most tenderly. When Arabel goes into a cottage & Flush is with her, he is by the cradleside in a moment, with his nose pushed under the bedcloaths—till the poor mother comes to the rescue, in the natural belief that her baby is about to be eaten. It's just the same in the street. If he meets a nurse & baby, he forgets all strangership & dances round it, & pulls peradventure at its frock. A child sixteen months old came here the other day. He was delighted—w^{dnt} lie down—could'nt keep still a moment,—& made the poor child scream more than once with his fearful familiarities,— & won its heart at last by suffering it to feed him with breadbutter which he w^{dnt} take from any hand but just that little infantine hand. So there they settled down at last, his two paws upon her knee & his eyes on her face! No notice from Flush to anybody else as long as she stayed!– Even the kitten was neglected,—& took comfort by playing with his tail while he wagged it unconsciously–

. . .

A letter sacred to Flush! Well—you asked me for his history, so must pardon the length of it. It's a post[s]cript to the letter yesterday.

Do let me hear how you are beloved friend! If many of my thoughts end in you, this of Flush *must*. How he makes me think of you! How every pleasure he gives me, is one drawn from you! How I love him for *your sake*!—which is the sure way of loving him dearly.

God bless you my beloved friend. There are faults of construction in Cosmo—but in Gregory the constructive faculty seems to me strong. At the same time it might not do upon what we call the stage.

Ever your attached
EBB

. . .

LONDON

Wimpole Street
and Publication
1841–42

EBB was finally reunited with her family at Wimpole Street in London in September 1841. In October MRM, accompanied by her maid "K," journeyed from Reading for the first meeting of the friends in three years. MRM supplied to EBB's artistically inclined sister Arabella an introduction to her old friend, the painter Benjamin Robert Haydon (1776–1846)—also a friend and correspondent of Keats—who began a correspondence with EBB. During the winter and spring of 1842, EBB abandoned the *Psyche* collaboration with Horne, who was preoccupied with George Stephens's efforts to stage *Martinuzzi* in defiance of the "theatrical monopolists," and at the request of the *Athenæum* editor Charles Dilke turned her attention to writing a series of essays on the Greek Christian poets and the English poets. In her [27–28] March letter she takes issue with MRM's condemnation of all evangelicals as narrow-minded, pointing to her own maintenance of catholic literary tastes in the face of strong evangelical convictions. Her reference in this letter to Mary Wollstonecraft Godwin (1759–97), author of *A Vindication of the Rights of Woman* (1792), and her interest in the *Memoirs* (1798) published by William Godwin indicate how early EBB's feminist views had taken shape. Her reading at this time included an *Autobiography* and the *Theory of Pneumatology*, both by the German physician and mystic Heinrich Jung-Stilling (1741–1817)— evidence of her growing interest in parapsychology—and the letters of

Samuel Richardson (1689–1761) along with his novels *Clarissa Harlowe* (1747–48) and *The History of Sir Charles Grandison* (1753–54). She also read Emerson and Carlyle, characterizing the latter as a "great prose poet," an idea developed in an essay on Carlyle she supplied to Horne for incorporation into his *New Spirit of the Age* (1844). In her letter of 1 April, responding to MRM's expression of pride and affection—she had been particularly impressed by EBB's poem "The House of Clouds," published the preceding August in the *Athenæum*—EBB vividly recreates the circumstances of their first meeting six years before.

50 WIMPOLE STREET
MONDAY SEPT 13th [1841]

My ever beloved friend,
    The first line written by my hand in this dear home is, as it sh^d be, written to you. I arrived on saturday just after post time—& yesterday being sunday there were no means, you know, of passing a letter upon it. I c^d only read over & over *your* letters, & thank & bless you for them!
    I write only a line. I am tired of course, with a sense of being thoroughly *beaten*,—but bad symptoms have not occurred—at least the spitting of blood increased *very* little in proportion to what might have been expected—and the whole amount of God's mercy to me is told in the fact of my being *here*. "How great is the sum of it"! Here—with Papa—in the midst of all left! No more partings—nor meetings which were worse!—almost *much* worse, sometimes! I thank God for the undeserved mercy!–
    For the rest, there was of course much to remember & suffer both in leaving Torquay & coming *here*. But my weakness helped to spare me—and now, I try to be alive only, or most, to the sense of blessing.
    Thank you thank you for your too much kindness!– The precious ringlet! It might serve, as far as the preciousness goes, to hold a city by—only being cut off, it is precious still. The fable ends there—and the truth begins. And is'nt it truth that I love the least part of you?–
    You say too much—far too much! It's all too much kindness. Give my love to dear Dr Mitford. How close we are now!—and how I w^d say a hundred other things which I cant!–

Goodbye– God bless you!
Dont you know that Martinuzzi has perished. I fear so–

Ever your
EBB–

50 WIMPOLE STREET
WEDNESDAY [13] OCT. 1841.

•   •   •

However it may be, I am angry with myself for talking of 'a full house.' It was wrong of me—& a mistake besides. The house is large for London—and although our family is large too, there is a room for you, a large room,—large enough for K. besides yourself, if you liked her to be there with you & if she could be accommodated on a sofa— & this without *any degree of inconvenience to any of us*–Think of it—keep it in your mind—dearest Miss Mitford. There is the room ready for you at any time. I only wish we could offer one to Dʳ Mitford—I only wish we could. But we are so many—and the long coats I find, take up more room than the jackets I left behind me! Many as we are, we have one heart between us in relation to the affection & admiration due to you. No! I cant put it quite as you tell me! I cant keep it all as affectionate thankfulness for your goodness to *me!* I cant keep away the admiration from working besides—and I would'nt if I could. You remember, I dont share your opinion upon the "good for nothing-ness" *par excellence* (a construction scarcely odder than the opinion) of authors & authoresses. And oh—dearest Miss Mitford—if I did not fear to shock you, I *could* say something dreadful of *you*—! nothing less than that you never cease, waking or sleeping, grave or playful, in letters or conversation, to appear & be that very terrible thing what-ever it is, that you are in your published works. Therefore how can I say to Papa what you tell me—that you are nothing like an author-ess?– How can I? Where is my conscience? Indeed I can say no such word. Never was there a more perfect unity than that between the individual & the writer in your case. Do forgive me for thinking so— because *that* was one of the *whys* that *I* loved you at first sight—& *that* too *was* one of the *whys* that the whole world of us loved your writings long before any first or second sight of mine. They are earnest writ-ings,—sealed to universal truth by an individual humanity.

But I must tell you of Arabel's visit to M! Haydon & M! Lucas, by the grace of your goodness to her. M! Haydon was not at home— "out of town" the servant reported him to be, admitting her however without hesitation into the fresco room– Set (Septimus) went with her, & they both turned their eyes round & round in search of the angel Uriel & could scarcely believe they had found him in the form of what they both talked of as "a sketch in the corner". This however was of course the *fresco*. Do you call to mind the artist's enthusiasm about his new creature standing in the gap of the wall? Now—although Arabel is unlearned upon frescos & did not probably expect rightly, yet we may gather from her report & Set's behind it, that nothing generally striking & obviously great has been effected in the new fresco apocalypse. I should like much to know how others of your friends under the same circumstances, have been impressed or unimpressed. Do tell me. Arabel was utterly disappointed—"*That* all!!" *That* was her feeling.

•　　•　　•

M! Lucas was very kind & pleased them in everyway—talked of Prince Albert & his talents—"If he had studied five years under Raffael, his remarks could not have been acuter" —thought him very handsome, & the Queen charmless if you except the pleasant countenance & youthful freshness. There were too earnest enquiries about you & D! Mitford & the probability of your coming to town–

Arabel said "Did you ever paint a portrait of Miss Mitford, M! Lucas!" "Oh yes!—but it was a failure—he had destroyed it—" (prophane man!) "he had made a great mistake,—& instead of preserving her characteristic of simplicity, dressed her up in a hat & feathers. All was wrong together."[1]

•　　•　　•

I had a note from M! Horne today, to express his remorse at having wandered to "things less worthy" than Psyche,—& "to return". I did not "whistle him back" I assure you—nor even "sign him back"—but as he sends me the modeling of the third & last, department of our drama, little remains I suppose but to set to work. I had been 'revolving in my altered soul' all your gracious & good advice about a subject, & having been haunted for a long while before it came—oh long long ago,—by one of the interdicted ("*A day from Eden*" —half dramatic) was beginning to clear my mind by writing it off previously to doing something better. But this Psyche has the first claim of all you see—has'nt she? There is no room or excuse for a departure on my side—is there?– I think not!– And indeed Psyche, if we only write up to her feet, will make a noble subject—will *show* as a noble subject. Oh I think so– I do indeed!–

I said to M! Horne that you as well as another less worthy person, had admired the energy under a certain tarpaulin hat – Was I wrong to say "*you*"? I hope I was not. It would give pleasure I knew. And thus he replies, confessing the identity. "The tarpaulin hat, having weathered every storm & vicissitude, is preserved as a trophy of a traveller who visited every place he intended, and after six or seven thousand miles, arrived at his mother's house with one halfpenny. I had a great mind to send it off straight to you (the hat—not the halfpenny, for that alas!—was obliged to go long since) but when I routed it out, the thing was too real & w^d have much soiled the idea"– I have made them laugh here by saying that if he *had* sent it to me, I w^d have hung it up by my bust of Plato! ——

You are spared my "House of Clouds" today. Crow cant find the Athenæum. I will send it to you—but for today it's too late.

Give my love to dear D! Mitford!– God bless you both.

Your ever attached
Elizabeth B Barrett–

1. A picture of MRM by Lucas in "hat & feathers" does exist, however.

50 WIMPOLE STREET
[TUESDAY] NOV. 2^d 1841

Thank you my dearest dearest friend for doing what it was at once so kind & so wrong to do—writing that long note to me when you were tired & when it was too late to write at all. The two words "Quite safe" were the only ones I asked for—and if I had known (as I might,—knowing *you*) the excess that asking for them w^d induce, I w^d have tried to be reasonable instead & to suppress my fear of the railway. Well—but you are no longer tired I hope—and here is the dear letter surviving its own evil. I will think of that, and love you my beloved friend for everything.

Ah—you are too kind to me!—both of you—dear D! Mitford & you!– And how at the end you deceive yourselves in a way which makes even my grave gratitude smile—pretending yourselves to be obliged,—& thanking others for your own goodness! What a curious delusion it is, dearest friend! You for instance, coming this long way by that noisy railway, just to see *me*—as in your naïveté you admit— and immediately turning round to thank me for my infinite kindness in being not actually a flint, & pleased to see you!– You for instance, with your touching kindness & varied powers of charming, falling down in the midst of us all like a goddess—& then thanking every- body who by imperfect gesture of hand or knee acknowledged the av- atar!– As to Papa he is quite overwhelmed. He stopped me in the midst of the delivery of your message to him. "What had HE done"— he said—"What had been in his power."? What have *I* done, is to be said still more emphatically. What have I ever done,—ever since I first looked at you—but honored you as all the world does, and loved you as I could'nt help?

I am only just awaking from the dream which began last thurs- day. Since saturday, I have been rubbing my eyes. It was so strange, so supernatural to me—so happy besides! How hard to thank you. We *talk Miss Mitford* now, constantly. I am still nearer to you my beloved friend!– and altho' the more you know of me, something must ever more be taken from the superfluity of your estimation of me, yet as you never can find out that I *do not love you*, I am not afraid of falling down the worst depth—while your improved knowledge of what is *mine*, of those who are the dearest to me, and their own experience of the charm which is in you, must draw us more closely together. May God bless you always!– I am not worse as to health, indeed.

·   ·   ·

Half an hour ago I received a letter a *psychical* letter, from Mʳ Horne, which made me smile almost to laughing, it struck with such an unconscious rebound against your *love-opinion* upon my dramatic faculty. Now hear what he says: & "My enemy does not say so" — but my friend—one who is most generous in his general praises, & most, not merely inclined but resolute,—to think well of my poetry. Now hear—& hear besides that I in my inmost conscience recognize his judgment on this point, as being very nearly if not altogether just & righteous as Daniel's!— "—Inasmuch as I have perceived . . or fan- cied I saw . . that all the different characters in your various writings, are not very different, nor very much of characters in themselves, but rather the medium or vehicle of certain abstract thoughts & images &

principles; and forasmuch as they are not of any age, nor of any period of time, nor of any sex character nor physiognomy—but *pure abstractions*, & as such perfect, though not dramatic——"

That is, perfectly undramatic. I need'nt quote any more—need I? And oh how convicted I feel!–

My beloved indulgent friend's
own EBB—

What am I to say from everybody? 'All the love they dare['']. Mine to dear D.ᵣ Mitford. Thank God he is so well. Do say to K. how sorry both Crow & I are that she w.ᵈⁿᵗ come in. Of course I had not repeated your excess of kindness to M.ᵣ Horne. It was a coincident contradiction.

50 WIMPOLE STREET
[TUESDAY] Nov.ᵣ 9. 1841

•   •   •

I turn away to brood upon all the kindest words you say upon all of us. I thank God day by day, for His unspeakable mercy in bringing me home again—whether to live or die, be it according to His will. You can understand what the deep gladness must be . . although YOU never experienced the bitter anguish[1] of bestowing evil, unmitigated evil, where you w.ᵈ only cause good. The scars of that anguish I shall take down with me to the grave. Things past remain present—*some things*. And however I look around me & love them all, dear things,— for *my best beloved*—I may as well say it for it always was so—for *my best beloved* I look up to that Heaven whence only comes any measure of true comfort & adequate endurance. The crown fallen from our heads as a family, can be restored only there.

But it is wrong to write so to you. Do not notice it. It is wrong. May God bless you ever & ever.

Your attached
EBB–

---

1. A reference to the deep trauma and sense of guilt caused by her brother Bro's drowning a year earlier in Torquay.

[Saturday] March 3ᵈ [*sic* for 5ᵗʰ] 1842

My beloved friend too kind always to me, there goes to you today another Athenæum with its burden of Greek poets. I may end by tiring you of them after all . . & yet I almost fancy to myself that you will care something for Gregory's [']'Soul & body" which strikes a sprightly note in the midst of his more solemn minims. In the meantime I embrace as if I were a Brahmin martyr, though in quite a different spirit, your column of prophecy. You the dearest prophetess in the world, & dear Mʳ Kenyon & I myself shall be nearly sure to walk round it since you say so! I hail the omen "a good bird" as the old Romans wᵈ call it, & singing like a nightingale!

· · ·

I have seen Mʳ Kenyon. I saw him either the day on which my last letter went to you or the day next to it,—& the first word which he, in his evil conscience uttered as he passed the threshold of my door, was . . . *"Don't ask me if I have written to Miss Mitford"*. Well!— then he went on to tell me of his Bath expedition—how immediately upon his arrival there in the midst of his Landors & Crosses & Eagles[1], a dumb devil took him, in the shape of a cold, & he cᵈⁿᵗ speak a word. That was disappointing & vexatious of course to every one of them—& he appears to have scarcely been able to speak again until he went out of hearing, back again on the London road. And thus perhaps he had not much pleasure in being away—at any rate he did not talk of the journey as one talks of pleasures—& between ourselves, dear Mʳ Kenyon did not seem to be altogether in the satisfied sunny spirits one is used to associate with the name. Not that he did not smile, & laugh even, & talk with gaiety & brilliancy—but the sparks did appear struck accidentally—the buoyancy & abandon were not in their old places. I said to myself "He is out of spirits plainly['']'. My fancy very likely! Dont take much note of it lest it be my fancy. He congratulates himself on his return to own quiet back room which you may remember, & from which he has shut out the world with his folding doors. That is his illusion! For you know & I know, that the world can slide in at a back door as well as a front, & that our dear friend's solitude is confined to . . perhaps . . half an hour before breakfast. I asked him when he was going away again– "Never!" "So you said the day before you went to Bath". "No, no. I always meant to go in the spring to Bath, if not then—but now I am quite settled".

You see we may be sure of him for a fortnight—or even three weeks!—there's no knowing! Dear M! Kenyon!

Thank you my dearest friend for wishing to lend me Richardson's letters in the five lost volumes—& promising me the one within reach. But since I spoke, I have found them all six at Saunders's library, & they are at this moment waiting to be read at my right hand. I rejoice in my sympathy with you,—(it is more honor!—& a pleasure, oh surely a pleasure, besides!) regarding the love of details, & of all memoirs & letters in which the great Humanity is revealed to us by a thousand little strokes. "Sands make the mountains" —& still lesser grains, this large Human Nature. I quite quite agree with you. It has always been my impression that if Sir Charles Grandison had appeared in three volumes like the novels of our day, he w^d have been *unreadable*. But we come to love the personnages of that work as we do many people in the world, by force of knowing them long, by force of being tired of them, by force of recognizing the neutral tint of our common life in the very tedium of their dulness. I do think just that of Sir Charles Grandison. As to the divine Clarissa she is a book apart, a poem apart—a beatitude in a fiend's mouth! There is no praise fit for her beyond our tears.

Will you give me a handful of sympathy for Flush's misfortunes—not that Clarissa's suggested them,—however "by your smiling you may think to say so." You may have heard of Miss Trepsack, a very dear old family friend of ours, who lived *simply as a friend* in Papa's family, has held him an infant in her arms besides each of *his* infants, & now having lodgings in a street near to us runs in & out (she can still run I assure you) of this house & calls us "her children". Now you understand who our dear *Trippy* is—for we call her impertinently just *that*—& now you have only to learn that dear Trippy who cant bear dogs in general, has dropped down into love before Flushie, & gives him cakes so often that Flushie's first ceremony upon meeting her is to examine both her hands & then push his nose into her bag. Well. Flush went out walking with Trippy & Arabel yesterday, & was taken into a confectioner's shop & presented with a sponge cake for himself. Flush is too great a coward to eat even a cake in a shop, with a strange man staring at him, & far too gentlemanly to eat it out in the street—therefore the gift was wrapt up in paper & given to him to carry home "to Miss Barrett"—all of which he perfectly understood & acted upon. He had carried it with the gravest satisfaction quite up to this door—when on a sudden—behold, there was a vision of the two great dogs, Resolute & Catiline, who also, on their part, were coming in from walking, & met him on the threshold. Now Flush's delight in the society of these great dogs is something quite wonderful—& more especially as they in their tender affection very often almost swallow him up. Even his love of cakes is nought before his love of the dogs! Therefore on he sprang,—into their very mouths—& down in his emotion, fell the precious cake—& up in the same minute was it snatched by his beloved friend Catiline & swallowed with a mouthful. Poor, poor Flush! He did not see the catastrophe—but on the subsiding of his passionate delight he looked about for his cake round & round in vain—smelt into everybody's hands,—went on his hind legs, feeling with his pretty front paws all round my tables, & at last had recourse to most vehement coaxing that somebody might give him his cake. Of course, the end of my story is that I sent out for another one, & that he ate it with many signs of satisfaction. But think—in the meantime—of poor Flushie's anxieties! And that treacherous friend Catiline!

God bless you my ever beloved & kindest friend! My love & most affectionate wishes to your invalid. How are the servants.

Your own EBB–

1. Friends of John Kenyon: Andrew Crosse (1784–1855), scientist noted for his claims to have produced insect life with voltaic currents in a water battery; Rev. John Eagles (1784–1855), a painter who contributed to *Blackwood's* under the pseudonym of "The Sketcher."

[SUNDAY–MONDAY] MARCH 28 & 9th
[*SIC* FOR 27-28] MARCH 1842 –

It is Sunday & there is no way of sending a letter to you my beloved friend—but it is a day to speak what is in my heart, & the heart moves your way without thought of the day. And this is what is in my heart!

Are we so far apart my dearest friend? Do we think so differently on a point scarcely unimportant? Ought I to deny my convictions for the love of you? Surely not! you will say so as I say so! That I love & admire & revere you . . *that* you KNOW! But I sh^{d} be more unworthy of the least of your love than I feel myself to be now, If I c^{d} sacrifice or *appear* to sacrifice in the cowardice of silence any one opinion or principle which I hold honestly.

In the first place, we do quite differ in regard to our mutual estimation of the mass of persons called "religious", that is,—making high religious professions,—whether in the church or out of it. All these persons—of whom I know more privately & domestically than my beloved friend appears to know—all this mass of persons, except such as are hypocrites, hold strongly by my affection & respect. I believe them to be right & safe—justified before God. I believe that it is right to think earnestly & not to be ashamed of speaking earnestly, our belief in the gospel of Christ & our hope by His death! I believe that Christ's *will* is, that we sh.ᵈ speak aloud our love for Him—that it is the natural result of our natural affections that we sh.ᵈ speak them all—why not our love which goes upwards? But you will agree with me in your admirable candour my beloved friend, that by the great mass of the world this upward love alone is unspoken! Is it unfelt? Is it a subject of shame? Those inferences remain.

I do believe then that the persons in question, are both in doctrine & in word *right*—& if I do not say 'I am *proud* to be numbered among them' it is because I w.ᵈ rather be humble in the same place.

The individual case you mention is exactly twice as revolting (I eagerly agree with you) as connected with a person of the class in question—but I appeal to your justice not to condemn a class for the corruption of an individual! it is as you observe a very large class (I thank God it is) in the church of England & out of it . . almost all the dissenters—*all*, as far as profession goes—with the exception of the ice-bound unitarians; & if in all classes —whether political, philosophical, artistical or philanthropical,—there are hypocrites, why sh.ᵈ you expect the religious class to be free from the taint! Even the apostles had their Judas—did you ever mistrust John for Judas? Surely not! Nor shall this infamous man who did you so much harm . . nor SHOULD he . . . . forgive me my dearest friend . . wrench your opinions & affections into a universal wrong. I could tell you instance upon instance of the actions of noble Christian hearts & hands which might well neutralize the poison of that man's wickedness. There is M.ʳ Groves of Exeter, in the receipt of five thousand a year from his profession, who gave up everything, nay, gave *away* everything, & went into the east without purse or scrip, a missionary on foot, with a noble heroism. The taunt of "Methodism" has drawn tears from many meek eyes I know . . while the heart sate firmly on its throne of a strong purpose. The lives of many have been cast away . . the blood of their life pouring from their dying lips,—through a life-devotion to preaching Christ's truth! And all this to be remembered in Heaven! Should we forget it here? If God loves it, should we not love it? Let us think twice before we say we do not.

Yes! they are narrow in taste for the most part. They hold strange opinions, strange contractive opinions on the subject of literature & the arts—which I call a contracted spirituality as well as a contracted taste. Because the whole atmosphere of God's creation (man's works being a part of it, even as the bee's geometry is) is a medium of beholding God—& we are not called upon to look away from the creation up to God, but to look *through* the creation up to Him. It thus appears to me that their notions on the subject of literature & the arts are defective *spiritually*—I do think so!

People of very different opinions generally, fall into a similar mistake! Mr Dilke for instance, wrote to beg me to avoid as far as possible in my papers the mention of the name of Christ (& I writing upon the Christian poets!!!) because it was painful to people's feelings to see that name mixed up indifferently with the ordinary subjects of the journal. Of course I did not enter upon an argument with Mr Dilke— but I thought within myself—"Here is just the mistake of a large religious class. *They* say, Christ's name must not be named in conjunction with ordinary literature—& therefore we who hold by the name of Christ, must shun the ordinary literature.["] The mistake is identical you see—the inference only being different—religious persons forsaking literature,—& worldly ones avoiding Christ's name! I mean no disrespect to Mr Dilke—but I am emphatic upon a mistake which is in my eyes dangerous to the world & melancholy for the religious. I agree with the latter from my heart . . that the place unfit for the naming of the redeemer's name, is unfit for the thoughts of the redeemed. The inference is as right as the premises are wrong!

Still it is not everybody in the class in question who holds the opinion . . & you must not consider it so. The Evangelical part of the establishment, & the methodists are the most narrow—the independents the most liberal. I have heard Shakespeare quoted from the pulpit in dissenting chapels—and Mr Hunter a congregational minister, a dear & valued friend of mine, has all sorts of reading even to a partial knowledge of the old dramatists.

For my own part, I holding by the convictions of my soul to these Christian societies in all their chief doctrines & yet so far from being "unco guid"[1] that I am guid in no possible sense, . . you know very well how little I have stayed my thirst in any matter of literature. There are not perhaps many women in England even beyond my age who have tasted of such hundreds of muddy waters as I have—muddy & pestilential as well as the clear & pure—all sorts of abominations in & out of philosophy—as Hume & Hobbes & Voltaire & Bolingbroke, coming down from Lucian in the antique—manifold attacks, atheistical & otherwise on what I reverence as the truth. Reading *everything,* it has been said, does nobody any harm—& yet I sh^d scarcely like my sisters to touch all that has strengthened the truth to *me* through an antagonistical iniquity. Still, without referring any more to these philosophies so called, . . my conviction is that general literature sh^d be as open to the devoutest soul as the meadows are! I sh^d as soon say do not look at the sun—do not listen to the nightingale—as do not read the poets! The opinion is as monstrous in my ears & to my understanding as to yours.

·   ·   ·

In regard to poetry—whether exclusively religious subjects be or be not the best adapted to poetry—I am sure that we shall agree my dearest friend in the opinion that the tendency of poetry must be upward—that religion should virtually enter into it—that Humanity cannot be considered philosophically without a reference to its relations God-ward & Heaven-ward. One might as well (& better) leave a man's mortality out of his humanity, as his immortality. We shall agree in this—shall we not? *Let* us, my dearest friend!

"We were placed on this earth to love each other"—yes! but we know from the supreme book if we do not from our own experience that the love is warmest, truest, purest, which is the overflow of the love to God—even as we hear your own Coleridge say

'He prayeth best who loveth best' —

love & prayer being reciprocal helps. Therefore it w^d not be true in philosophy to insulate in poetry the bare human love! *It has been done* I know! And that it is done too often is exactly what I mean to lament in wishing for "Christ's hand upon our poetry". I wish it for poetry['\]s sake & philosophy's as much as I wish it for religion's. I beseech you to consider what I mean before you decide that you will have no sympathy with me in the opinion!–

• • •

As to the drama, I believe there is a prejudice as well as an opinion—& that your conjecture respecting the revolting influence of the amphitheatre may be connected with it. The theatre I am persuaded *might be* a means of great moral good. That it is not so now however—that it was not so even under James the first, that it was so fearfully the contrary under the second Charles, may justify utterly the absence upon principle of any person. Do not mistake me my beloved friend! I do not blame you or others for attending the theatres—in all liberty of conscience. I sh.^d not blame my own brothers & sisters for doing it—if Papa had a less particular objection. But I quite see the sufficiency of the objection as it is seen by him & others. Do you know how Mr Macready[2] has been attacked for even trying, even beginning to try to suppress *the saloons*—(the miserable application of which is very well known)—& how it has been declared that no theatre can exist at the present day without a saloon—& how, if it could, the effect w.^d be to force vicious persons & their indecencies into full view in the boxes—!! Now this appears to me enough to constitute a repulsive objection! & I who have read hard at the old dramatists since I last spoke to you about them,—Beaumont & Fletcher Massinger Ben Jonson all Dodsley's collection, —can yet see that objection in all its repulsiveness! . . & read on!

Dear Mr Kenyon came here again yesterday (Sunday) I am writing now on monday—& overwhelmed me with the unexpected supernumerary visit of kindness! Mr Browning, the poet, passed saturday & a part of sunday with him, & pleased & interested him very much! He has bad health—swimmings in the head—& a desire (if any loosening of family ties sh.^d give him to himself) to go to a Greek island & live & die in the sunshine. Mr Kenyon says he is "a little discouraged" by his reception with the public, which I am very sorry to hear . . but "a strong sense of power" which is equally obvious may obviate the effect of the depression.

• • •

Do you know Carlyle's writings? I am an adorer of Carlyle. He has done more to raise poetry to the throne of its rightful inheritance than any writer of the day,—& is a noble-high-thinking man in all ways. He is one of the men to whom it w.^d be a satisfaction to me to cry 'vivat' somewhere in his hearing. Do you recognize the estate of mind when it waxes impatient of admiration & longs to throw it off at the feet of the admired? I have felt it often!

You have not been well, my dearest dearest friend! Those newspapers—those newspapers! Do say particularly how you are! Be sure that I c^d not *mistake you*. Try not to mistake *me*—or rather try to love me through what appear to you *my* mistakes—& through what *are*!——

Happy! "you are happy!" You startled me with the sound of the word! I am *content* my beloved friend at least!

George said smiling one day by my bedside a great truth which I smiled at too though sadly. He said "When I hear people say they are content, I always know that they are miserable". It is a great truth with some modification—for certainly I, for one, never felt satisfied, content, I call it—until the illusion of life was utterly gone. When I think of the future *now* . . I think of something to be done, something to be suffered,—not of what is to be enjoyed. It is not when we talk or write lightly that we do not feel heavily—it is not at least so for me. My only individual hopes now are prospective actions & duties. My castle-building is at an end! A great change has passed both upon my inward & outward life within these two years. I scarcely recognize myself sometimes. One stroke ended my youth.

And so be it! even so! It must have ended some time—& it is as well ended suddenly as more gradually. Bearing this vacancy at my side, I may bear the rest patiently.

And I am you see contented—quite calm—fearless even of the future. I am at leisure too & able by God's grace to count the MUCH which remains—to think of the beloved faces near me still—& of such a dear & precious friend as yourself in the same world with me—& permitting me to love her, heart to heart, as at this day!

May God bless & keep you my beloved friend! I never can thank you enough for all the comfort & sympathy I have received from you. I beseech you to bear with, a little longer,

your ever attached
EBB

Yes—I know Mary Wolstonecraft. I was a great admirer at thirteen of the Rights of woman. I know too certain letters published under her name: but Godwin's Life of her I never saw & sh^d like much to do so.

The exquisite letters of Meta Klopstock![3] *Exquisite* is the only word of them. They have been extracted in different works—& I was familiar with nearly all of those in Richardson's Correspondence before my acquaintance with it.

I have read the 'Cavalier'—but years ago. I must see it again. Nothing in Defoe fastened upon me much, except Robinson Crusoe & The Plague—which last you know of course, & which is still more a romance than the other –

Have you received Miss Seward's letters—with *mine?* I sent them by the railroad on friday I think. I do hope too that you received the last Athenæum —the one containing my last paper? Papa directed it himself to you.

•   •   •

1. Cf. Robert Burns, "Address to the Unco Guid, or the Rigidly Righteous" (1787).
2. William Charles Macready (1793–1873), the actor-manager of the Drury Lane Theatre.
3. Meta Klopstock (1728–58), wife of Frederick Klopstock, author of "The Messiah" and known as the German Milton. Richardson's *Correspondence* contains four of her letters, one telling of her courtship by Frederick.

Three-mile Cross
March 24 [*sic*] 1842.[1]

Thanks upon thanks, my beloved friend, for the kindness which humors even my fancies. I am delighted to have the reading of Anna Seward's letters. Perhaps we both of us like those works which show us men and women as they are—faults, frailties, and all. I confess that I do love all that identifies and individualizes character—the warts upon Cromwell's face, which, like a great man as he was, he would not allow the artist to omit when painting his portrait. Therefore I like Hayley, and therefore was I a goose of the first magnitude, when, for a passing moment, just by way of gaining for the poor bard a portion of *your* good graces (for I did not want to gain for him the applause of the public—he had it, and lost it), I wished his editor to have un-Hayley'd him by wiping away some of the affectations—the warts—no—the rouge, upon his face.

My love and my ambition for you often seems to be more like that of a mother for a son, or a father for a daughter (the two fondest of natural emotions), than the common bonds of even a close friend-

ship between two women of different ages and similar pursuits. I sit
and think of you, and of the poems that you will write, and of that
strange, brief rainbow crown called Fame, until the vision is before
me as vividly as ever a mother's heart hailed the eloquence of a patriot son. Do you understand this? and do you pardon it? You must,
my precious, for there is no chance that I should unbuild *that* house
of clouds; and the position that I long to see you fill is higher, firmer,
prouder than ever has been filled by woman. It is a strange feeling,
but one of indescribable pleasure. My pride and my hopes seem altogether merged in you. Well, I will not talk more of this; but at my
time of life, and with so few to love, and with a tendency to body
forth images of gladness and of glory, you can not think what joy it is
to anticipate the time. How kind you are to pardon my gossiping, and
to like it.

God bless you, my sweetest, for the dear love which finds something to like in these jottings! It is the instinct of the bee, that sucks
honey from the hedge-flower.

[M.R.M.]

1. This letter should bear a date after EBB's of [27–28] March 1842.

[FRIDAY] APRIL 1st 1842.
IS'NT IT *spring*?

Your dearest & too touching letter O my beloved friend, is among the
things for which I cannot thank you adequately when my heart & eyes
are fullest!– May God bless you—*love you*!

•   •   •

Often & often do I look back, leap back in spirit over the great
gulph of darkness between my *now* & my *then*, & think of the moment
when the door was first opened to me of the permission to love you.
Did I ever tell you just how it was? Mr Kenyon had been asking me,
asking me,—like a king beseeching a beggar to take a dukedom—
pressing me on all sides with kindness to pass an evening at his house
& see Wordsworth. Now I w.^{d} have gone on a pilgrimage to see

Wordsworth ever since I was eight years old—& if the indispensable condition had been pebbles within side of the pilgrim shoon, I w^d have gone even so. But at the end of a pilgrimage, I sh^d have seen Wordsworth alone in his niche,—kissed his feet & come away . . & he peradventure w^dnt have seen *me*! It was altogether different going into Mr Kenyon's den of lions & lionesses—& I was frightened into absolute shame at the sort of roaring implied by my imaginativeness. I know Mr Kenyon was half angry, thro' all his kindness, at my long drawn perversity—& I was near crying in the conflict between what I wished & feared, & what dear Mr Kenyon tried to press beyond the fear. Who can judge aright for another who has lived a peculiar life, in no sort of society except of books, & shy at the best, as to manners—? "I loathed that I did love"! – Well—at last the temptation took the form of a softer devil. He, not the devil but our dear friend, asked me to think no more of the great party but to consent to come to a very small one, where Wordsworth w^d be again—& *Miss Mitford* . . & then he told me of your gentleness & dearness. So then I said "yes"—half ashamed & half afraid still!—and then again in the morning came a note from him to propose my going with himself & *you* . . & *you*! to the Zoological gardens. Oh how I remember the words—I am sure he measured them so as to encourage me into some estate of common sense—"you will become acquainted" (thus they ran) "with an amiable person whom you will be certain to like, & who is prepared to like you". Prepared to like *me*! I resolved at once to go, & set my teeth as for the the [*sic*] desperate purpose of it—couldn't do anything during all the interval at books or writing . . dawdled about . . walked up & down stairs, looked out at the window—said to myself so as to keep myself firmly buckled up in resolve, "I shall be glad *after it is over*! I shall be glad I have seen her, all my life afterwards (O unconscious prophetess!) & in the meanwhile it will only be a few hours pain". Think of me as you please, but I do assure you that when the carriage was heard to be at the door, my knees trembled so that it was a hard thing for me to get down stairs to it. And then, . . the first sound from your lips which reached my ears . . embleming all the rest . . was said in reply to something Mr Kenyon said & I c^d scarcely hear in my confusion, something to the effect that I "sh^d have a protectress now"—"*I hope, a friend*". Those were the first words I ever heard from your lips—& there was a tone, a significance of kindness in them which went beyond the words & made me love you in [a] moment. I loved you before as all the world does & for much the same reasons—but the heart-to-heart love began just then! You were Cæsar to me in a moment!– Dearest friend . . bear with me as you have done. It is for *you* to bear with *me*!

Your eyes are growing older you say & you cant see the violets so well this year as on others. Now do not anticipate the growing older. When your eyes grow older,—I mean when age begins to affect them,—you will see more clearly than you do now. You are short-sighted—are you not?—like me & M.r Kenyon & Papa. Well—that species of defective sight *improves* with age—because it arises from the too great convexity of the pupil, which it is the effect of age to flatten. So YOU SEE you have made a mistake & are growing younger instead of older. I am so glad!–

Poor M.r Browning! Was that extreme irritability of nerve supposed to be occasioned by the disappointment, or the exercise of an overwrought faculty? After all I cannot wish with you that he be turned to occupations of less excitement. In the first place, C.D he so turn? In the second, dare we ask silence from such a poet? It w.d be like asking a prophet to forbear his prophecy—he has a word to speak from Nature & God, & he must speak it!–

Certainly M.r Browning does speak in parables —& more darkly than . . even . . . . some other of your friends. But he is a true poet. I estimate him very highly—& so do you—& so must all who know what poetry is & turn their faces towards its presence willingly.

The "Rhymed Plea"[1] is admirable "after its kind" —but with all my true & admiring regard for its author & his writings I could not be content to receive it as sole comforter for the absence of higher inspirations.

My prose style like Carlyle!– To remind anyone in the world of Carlyle were praise enough & too much! Miss James's praise made me feel glad for a moment . . as if it c.d be true.

And yet you are quite right. He does not write pure English . . no, nor quite pure German—nor pure Greek, by any means. But he *writes thoughts*. He reminds me of Leibnitz's plan for an algebraic language, —altho' *his* plan is not algebraic—but he *writes thoughts*. There is something wonderful in this struggling forth into sound of a contemplation bred high above dictionaries & talkers—in some silent Heavenly place for the mystic & true. The sounds do come—strangely indeed & in unwrought masses, but still with a certain confused music & violent eloquence, which prove the power of *thought* over *sound*. Carlyle seems to me a great prose poet. At any rate he is a man for the love & reverence of all poets, seeing that he, almost sole among the present world's critics, recognizes the greatness & the hopefulness of their art.

I, presume to offer my admiration to M! Carlyle, my dearest friend! No—you have not spoiled me quite up to that point or pinnacle yet.

Thanks upon thanks for the lovely violets. They deserve to lie enfolded in your letters– I wish I deserved to receive them, as well!

May God bless you ever. They always drive me away from you with this post hour. Say how the face-ache is! & go on to love.

your own grateful
EBB–

• • •

1. Kenyon's *Rhymed Plea for Tolerance: In Two Dialogues with a Prefatory Dialogue* (1833) argues in heroic couplets against a strict interpretation of creed.

Three-mile Cross
April 9, 1842.

It will help you to understand how impossible it is for me to earn money as I ought to do, when I tell you that this very day I received your dear letter, and sixteen others; that then my dear father brought into my room the newspaper to hear the ten or twelve columns of news from India; then I dined and breakfasted in one, then I got up. By that time there were three parties of people in the garden; eight others arrived soon after—some friends, some acquaintances, and some strangers; the two first classes went away, and I was forced to leave two sets of the last, being engaged to call upon Lady Madalina Palmer, who has an old friend of both on a visit at her house. She took me some six miles (on foot) in Mr. Palmer's beautiful plantations in search of that exquisite wild flower the buck-bean (do you know it—most beautiful of flowers? wild, or as K[1]——puts it, "tame?"). After long search we found the *plant* not yet in bloom. Then I hurried home, threw my own cocoa down my throat, and read to my father Mrs. Cowley's comedy, "Which is the Man?"[2] and here I am (after answering, as briefly as I can, many very kind letters), talking to you.

My father sees me greatly fatigued—much worn—losing my voice even in common conversation; and he lays it all to the last drive or walk—the only thing that keeps me alive—and tells every body he sees that am I killing myself by walking or driving; and he hopes that I shall at last take some little care of myself and not stir beyond the garden. Is not this the perfection of self-deception?. And yet I would not awaken him from this dream—no, not for all the world—so strong a hold sometimes does a light word take of his memory and his heart—he broods over it—cries over it! No, my beloved friend, we must for the present submit. There may be some happy change. He may himself wish me to go to town, and then— In the mean while my heart is with you. Ever yours,

M.R.M.

1. "K," or Kerenhappuch, MRM's new maid.
2. One of several light comedies by Hannah Parkhouse Cowley (1749–1803).

Three-mile Cross
April 27, 1842.

No! my dear love, I am not now about to write on the subject of the South Seas.[1] The first volume of any size that I printed was on the story—which came to me from a friend of the American captain who visited them—of Christian's Colony on Pitcairn's Island. A large edition was sold. Then I published a second edition of a volume of miscellaneous poems; then another volume of narrative poems called "Blanche and the Rival Sisters." All sold well, and might have been reprinted; but I had (of this proof of tolerable taste I am rather proud) the sense to see that they were good for nothing, so that I left off writing for twelve or fifteen years, and should never have committed any more pen-and-ink sins, had not our circumstances become such as to render the very humblest exertions right. My dear mother's health was then almost what my father's is now; only then we were three, so that, except by staying at home, I was not so absolutely chained as I am now.

Well, perhaps if I could be all the time I covet, among the sweet flowers and the fresh grass, I should not enjoy as I do the brief intervals into which I do contrive to concentrate so much childish felicity. Who it is that talks of "the cowslip vales of England?" is it you, my beloved? The words are most true and most dear. Oh! how I love those meadows, yellow with cowslips and primroses; those winding brooks, or rather *that* winding brook, golden with the water ranunculus; those Silchester coppices, clothed with wood-sorrel, wood-anemone, wild hyacinth, and primroses in clusters as large as the table at which I write! I do not love musk—almost the only odor called sweet that I do not love; yet coming this evening on the night-scented odora with its beautiful green cups, I almost loved the scent for the form on which it grew. But the cowslips, the wild hyacinths, the primroses, the violet—oh, what scent may match with theirs? I try to like the garden, but my heart is in the fields and woods. I have been in the meadows to-night—I ran away, leaving my father asleep— I could not help it. And oh! what a three hours of enjoyment we had, Flush, and the puppies, and I! I myself, I verily believe, the youngest–hearted of all. Then I have been to Silchester too. My father went there; and I got out and ran round the walls and coppices one way, as he drove the other. How grateful I am to that great gracious Providence who makes the most intense enjoyment the cheapest and the commonest! I do love the woods and fields! Oh! surely all the stars under the sun, even if they were brighter than those earthly stars ever seem to me, could not compare with the green grass and the sweet flowers of this delicious season!

I mistrust the feeling of poetry of all those who consent to pass the spring amongst brick walls, when they might come and saunter amongst lanes and coppices. To live in the country is, in my mind, to bring the poetry of Nature home to the eyes and heart. And how can those who do love the country talk of autumn as rivalling the beauty of spring? Only look at the texture of the young leaves; see the sap mounting into the transparent twigs as you stand under an oak; feel the delicious buds; inhale the fragrance of bough and herb, of leaf and flower; listen to the birds and the happy insects; feel the fresh balmy air. This is a rhapsody; but I have no one to whom to talk, for if I mention it to my father, he talks of "my killing myself," as if that which is balm and renovation were poison and suicide.

Heaven bless you, my most precious! My father's love. Ever most faithfully your own,

M. R. MITFORD.

1. EBB had recommended to MRM the history of John Williams (1796–1839), a missionary to the South Seas whom EBB had heard and admired at Sidmouth. He was clubbed to death by natives of the New Hebrides in November 1839.

Three-mile Cross
May 4, 1842.

Charlotte Smith's[1] works, with all their faults, have yet a love of external nature, and a power of describing it, which I never take a spring walk without feeling. Only yesterday I strolled round the parklike paddock of an old place in our neighborhood—an old neglected ride, overgrown with moss, and grass, and primroses, and wild strawberries—overshadowed by horse-chestnuts, and lilacs, and huge firs, and roses, and sweet-brier, shot up to the height of forest-trees. Exquisitely beautiful was that wild, rude walk, terminating in a decayed carthouse, covered with ivy; and, oh! so like some of her descriptions of scenery! My mother knew her when her husband was sheriff of Hampshire; and she lived in a place (about four miles from the little town of Alresford, where I was born) where the scenery and the story of the "Old Manor House" may still be traced. There was a true feeling of nature about Charlotte Smith.

Of the three—Wordsworth, Southey, Coleridge—how very much the greater poet Coleridge seems to me! Poor Cowper! I never doubted his insanity, knowing as I did his kinswoman, whose melancholy tale I must have told you (Mrs. Frances Hill, sister to the Eve Hill of the letters, and his first cousin) whose madness was always said to be hereditary.

There could be no question of the taint in the blood. That the hands into which he fell were not likely to administer the best remedies, even with the best and purest motives, there can be as little doubt. So you have actually seen and known one who believed in that melancholy tenet! I always held the imputation to be untrue: it seemed to be so impossible that any one mind could at once believe *that* and the mediation. Yours ever,

M.R.M.

1. Charlotte Smith (1749–1806), poet, novelist, translator of French poetry, and author of *Rural Works* (1795).

[SATURDAY] May 14. 1842

Dearest dearest Miss Mitford,

You are welcome as more than daylight at all hours of the day . . & I c^d not restrain my exclamation—acclamation it was rather . . of 'Oh how delightful!' when I felt by the thickness of the substance between my fingers & thumb what a long letter I had before me for coffee time at six oclock, instead of at nine in the morning. Two sheetfulls in your own handwriting!! Flushie jumped up in a sympathy of rapture, & wanted very much to hold it all in his mouth—but no! Flushie!—you may eat my muffin if you please but nothing at all, . . not the least bit in the world, . . out of my letter!– There, you & I have our divided interests!–

Which reminds me that I c^dnt help reading to Crow your beautiful story of your Flush,—& that mine immediately took up the gesture of listening intently gathering his ears over his great eyes as if he saw a hare, or rather a crow in a field (his more familiar wonder & a very favorite subject of observation out of the carriage window in the days of his traveling—) & patting about his little paws everytime the word 'Flush' 'Flush' occurred. Be sure he thought I was reading about *him*! I know he thought so!– It was very natural that he sh^d, you know!

•   •   •

Is his sister found at Reading? Yes! I take courage from Ben's argument—I had thought of it before. If anybody stoops to hazard a salutation upon Flushie's head—a most awful growl together with a shrinking gesture are the consequences. Supposing that his cowardice may preserve him from any possible danger, I certainly need not be uneasy. Still, there are peculiar risks here, in London. Dogstealing is carried on as a profession—& only the other day, while Henry & Major Nugent . . a blind neighbour of ours were walking together, a little spaniel belonging to the latter was snatched up, thrown headlong into a sack, & run off with. The poor little thing was recovered . . but after several days anxiety—& what w^d my Flush do & what sh^d I do under such circumstances? Flushie w^d cry piteously—& I sh^dnt be very much wiser I dare say. He always cries, directly anything goes wrong—if you go on reading for instance without paying him proper attention! nay, just now . . just as I was writing of this morbid sensibility,—up came a little plaintive note of complaint as much as to say

'Oh how dull it is!'!—but I have patted him well & he has kissed me in turn & now he has re-disposed himself into a ball close beside me with very sufficient resignation.

.   .   .

While I write, Mr Kenyon's ready kindness has sent me Tennyson's new volumes, which I see include the old—or at least some of the old—with a little note to explain his more kindness of having wished to get to me & of having been 'circumvented'! I had not sent him your message because I expected to see him day after day—but now I shall use no delay & write to him what your wishes are about his going to you. I *cant* doubt that he will go if he can—and I *dont* doubt that he can!

.   .   .

In much of this, you will perhaps, upon thinking it all over, agree with me. The point on which we rather differ is connected with the question whether a pen & ink person must necessarily become selfish in becoming sensitive. I say 'No' to it, in the very loudest voice I have the power of attesting with. Those who yearn most for sympathy are according to my impression, the very people who sh.^d be readiest with sympathy—and if they are backward instead of ready, why my doxy is, not that it arises from their being of the Pariah race pen-&[-] ink people, but radically & independently of all 'inkhornisms' as Hall the satirist says, ... *selfish* people. Agree with me my beloved friend as far as you can—and for the rest forgive me the differing–

.   .   .

And tell *me* how you are. I am anxious about you through all this nonsense. For my own part, I am better—yet have been "bad at heart" since I wrote last. Oh yes! I have two prophets for good—you & Dr Mitford—& I believe you both as in duty & hopefulness bound–

Your own EBB.

.   .   .

[SATURDAY] [4? JUNE 1842]

•   •   •

And now I am liking to think of you as established in your garden room, in sight of the beautiful furniture of Nature's placing & hanging & coloring, whether of flower or bough. How I long to see you— though in a dream! I w^d give a waking day of most other pleasures for such a dream as *that*. The coming here, the seeing you here, is not however one of them. I c^d not willingly forgo seeing you here—& perhaps shall have to do so against my will—for you do not open a crevice of hope—nor a keyhole! Well! it is not to teaze that I talk of it, but only to show to you that I think of it—in part—and in part, that I cant help it. The fulness of heart you know, makes people talkative. What makes them hopeful?– That is less obvious—but perhaps the fulness of the heart too! At any rate I do hope on about seeing you here this summer.

Mr Kenyon has not been here for a fortnight—although I invited him to come & hear my Æolian harp. My Æolian harp. Because I admired it, Papa gave it to me,—so that the winds have to pay me now in music for all the harm they have done me hitherto. Winds! I am a pretty person to talk about winds—I who have been gasping the whole morning through for lack of a breath, the thermometer witnessing to 76. Why I sh^d be glad now for the verriest east wind, only to breathe by its sweet grace. There never was much hotter weather in England!–Even Papa whose ideal of a temperature is taken from an oven, & who envies in his inmost soul every penny roll on the breakfast table . . . . even Papa admitted last night that . . . . 'the tea was too hot.' Those were the precise terms of his complaint! Not a sigh against the sun, for the world tho' it were baking—only against the tea because it was boiling! I said simply "That is a triumph".

In the pause between these paragraphs I have been helping Flushie to his bread & butter & cream cheese, . . & now he is gone to his task of local discovery (I have moved yesterday & today for the afternoon into Papa's bedroom to which there is a communicating door with mine) walking backwards & forwards & round & round & smelling with philosophic subtlety at every chair & table. He clearly does not like it as well as my room. He wishes himself & me well out of it. He echews *[sic]* his place upon the sofa, & does not consider it safe to settle any where. Poor Flushie! If you c^d but have seen him as I was moving! how when I stopped to rest, he threw himself upon

me in a passion of condolements & kisses . . & how he followed
closely & anxiously every step, ending all by another layer of kisses!
He clearly disapproves the whole arrangement, from the first to the
last—& now to declare his opinion openly & be conscience-free of the
least responsibility, he has stretched himself on the floor. It is an expressive gesture!–

Yes, my dearest friend—yes & no! No, I have'nt read Gosip-
pers[1]—& yes, I will. I have sent for it these three times to Saunders
& Ottley, & must buy it, I rather think if I wish ever to behold it.
And that shall be done.

Yes! besides, to Emerson's letters. Or rather, yes, to the letters,
& 'no' to Carlyle's preface—because I read the American edition. M!
Kenyon lent the book to me, the book belonging to M! Crabbe
Robinson[2] whose hair stood on end when he heard of its being lent
to me! "Why" he said "that book is too stiff even for myself—and I
am not very orthodox."– In fact the book, for all its cold calm air of
philosophy—most inhumanly serene—is very extravagant in some of
its views. It sets about destroying (& this is a sufficient symptom
of extravagance) the personality of every person, & speaks of the Deity as of a great Background to which every created individual forms
a little porch!!! For the rest, there are beautiful & noble thoughts in
the book, beautifully & nobly said. The chapter upon *Love* is very
fine. Do tell me, if this Emerson crosses your path, what you think
of him. Miss James asked of my thought instead of yours, just, I suppose, because she knew of my Carlyleship & because Carlyle has
taken him up. But as it happened Carlyle's introduction is precisely
& only what I have not read of the volume in question.

Think of Flushie's being dreadfully jealous of the Æolian harp!
He heard me say "Beautiful beautiful" (a word sacred to his ears) &
squeezed quite close to me & tried every possible means of reawaken-
ing me to a sense of his surpassing merits. Is not that amusing?

Ever & ever your EBB.

1. *The Gossippers, or The Neighbours: A Story of Every-day Life* by Frederika Bremer, the
   Swedish novelist, translated by Mary Howitt in 1842.
2. Henry Crabb Robinson (1775–1867), solicitor, foreign correspondent, and editor of
   the *Times*, whose famous diary records his friendship with a wide circle of authors,
   including Wordsworth, Goethe, and Coleridge.

LONDON

Support and Strengthening of Bonds
1842

In a quiet summer of 1842 EBB began planning a new volume of poetry (eventually to appear as *Poems* (1844). She and MRM pursued the perennially fascinating topic of John Kenyon's marriage intentions, particularly toward his frequent companion at this time, Sarah Bayley. A new topic of interest was mesmerism, popularized by the experiments of Dr. John Elliotson. A highlight of the summer for both friends was MRM's laying of the cornerstone of the new Reading Library on 31 August 1842, with elaborate ceremonies. As Dr. Mitford's health declined throughout the fall, however, MRM increasingly enlisted EBB's aid, especially for the composition of some light verses for a miniature annual, *Schloss's Bijou Almanack*, she was editing. EBB agreed, against her better judgment, since producing verses on order for such an oddity (the *Bijou* was approximately the size of a thumbnail!) seemed a trivialization of poetry. She struggled to satisfy the harried MRM who, after requiring several revisions, published the verses as her own. Along with gifts of food and medicine, EBB kept up a steady stream of practical advice and religious consolation to Three Mile Cross. A half-in-jest earlier defense (26 July 1842) of the "Miss Ps" of their acquaintance, unmarried women writers with pretensions to youthfulness—("it is better to be eighteen than forty, for marriageable women," EBB wrote sympathetically)—takes on added interest in light of her defense (31 October 1842) of Robert Browning's domesticity. John Kenyon, probably the source of such details, was at this time trying to introduce her and Browning, but she resisted the idea of his calling on her. A letter of praise from Wordsworth, however, gave her intense pleasure at this time, when she was beginning to experiment with the sonnet form.

[MONDAY] JULY 4. 1842

My ever dearest friend, the Fates are certainly rejoicing in cross stitches, these are ever so many post days. For the second or third time—nay, I am sure it is the third,—I have received your letter while you were receiving mine, with a most adroit mal-appropriation of subject-matter & sentiment. Nevertheless cross or not, I never can be otherwise than in delighted goodhumour at hearing from you—particularly when you say, as in this last dear MS, that in the case of your troubles thickening beyond all bearing, you will drop *me* last!– It is on the strength of such a kindness that I write so soon.

Another attempt—or assumed attempt on the queen's life! A boy—having the appearance of an errand boy,—& the pistol loaded with tobacco pipes—and a standerby snatching it out of his hands while he was preparing the gunpowder in the park! What is this strange popular mania of queen-shooting?[1] What is the motive? & what the end? In the meanwhile the despots of the earth sit safe— the Austrian emperors remain according to Mrs Trollope, "our angels" —& nobody thinks of even smoking a tobacco pipe at them, much less of shooting it. It is only citizen Kings, & liberal queens that their people address themselves to shooting. I am very angry—angry & sorry & ashamed. Who shot George the fourth? Not even I—says the sparrow. Poor Victoria! Let the coolness be what it may, there is an undercurrent—she is a human being & a woman! and is more over conscious that of those who reproach her most, nobody has said that she has not wished to benefit her people according to her light. And the end of it all is,—she is set up for a mark to such little boys in her dominions as are pleased to play with pistols! It is worse than bad–

I hear that people go now to see the poor queen leave the palace for her drive, with a disposition to be excited, with an idea of seeing her *shot at*: there is a crowd at the gates every day!– Mr Hood proposes in an epigram in the last New Monthly, to change the name of

Constitution Hill for Shooter's Hill—but the subject is too grave for jesting on.

By the way, were you not amused by Hood's letter[2] on the copy-right, in the Athenæum? *I* was; & far more so, than by those elaborate merriments which however adroit & clever,—and he is the master of his art,—do sometimes rather weary me than make me gay. Do you not confess to the same feeling? Laughter as by literature professed, seems to me like religion as by law established, rather legal than cor-dial. And however this may be in general, the effect of Hood's gai-eties are very particularly in my experience gravities, from one end of the Comic annual series, to another.

Oh yes, yes! my beloved friend, you are very right I am sure. We do agree really & effectually when, as in so many cases, we agree to differ,—because we, so, agree to *be true*. If truth were not above all, my place w^d be under your feet: but truth *is* above all,—& therefore you allow me to sit at your side with an equal opinion. That is your homage to truth even more than your indulgence to me; & I believe with you that it is better & happier for both of us as well as more right & 'reverent' in the German sense that it sh^d be so.

In regard to the drama, I have been at the theatre—I have seen Shakespeare in London—but it was when I was a young child: and I admit to you willingly that in reading & taking pleasure from the writ-ten Drama, my ideas of it never enter the theatre from first to last. I have a notion,—that the theatre interprets between the dramatic poet and the unpoetic multitude,—& *always* where the poetry is high, des-ecrates it in translation. I believe in a high spiritual Drama clear of the theatre—& the higher & more spiritual, the more clear. This is my creed—my doxy—my superstition—put the most good for nothing word you please into connection with it. I am ignorant quite, dramati-cally—according to your view of the dramatic: & it is impossible for me to escape that 'gentle contempt' with which the better instructed look down upon the blanker mind. Let yours be as gentle as you can, my dearest dearest friend—& leave room by its side, for as much love as possible–

   • • •

Yes! now I am turning my face to doing something in poetry— well aware that if ever I do anything, it must be *there*. To succeed in pleasing you makes my heart beat at this distance from the goal—

even at the thought of the possibility of reaching it. But I must think for a subject. M! Kenyon said some time ago, [']'You ought to write a poem on a classical subject." I told him your suggestion upon Napoleon—& he shook his head– And I shook my head on the classical subject—because I object to the want of truth: not having been "suckled in that creed outworn."

Your paragraph from M! Robins is delightful—& to me in an especial manner from the interest with which I must read everything about your old home. Ah!—how your fate reminds me of our own! We were thrust out of our paradise in Herefordshire,—Hope End, where poor Papa had built & planted & adorned—not for himself or his! It is a painful subject, amongst us, & never mentioned . . And yet now that another stroke —(to the heart this time) has fallen,—I rejoice at our removal from a place so cruelly full of memories. I w^d not stand there once again, not for the whole world besides.

It is thus that our adversities recoil into blessings!– How many tears the adversity in question cost us! & I do not wish one of them back again in their source.

May God bless you my beloved friend! I trust your Marianne did not relapse into illness thro' the grief you speak of. The post goes–

Your own EBB–

1. This shooting in which a pistol was loaded with tobacco occurred only two days after clemency was granted to the perpetrator of an earlier attempt on the queen's life.

2. Thomas Hood (1799–1845), author of "Song of the Shirt," and editor of the *New Monthly* and the *Comic Annual*. In two June 1842 issues of the *Athenæum* he argued for an international copyright law, particularly in view of American abuses.

Three-mile Cross
July 25, 1842.

I have had two or three interesting visits lately, dearest. One, the last (to-day), from a Dr. Carter, a friend of Dr. Elliotson,[1] and a believer in, if not a practicer of, animal magnetism. He has traveled all through America, North and South, visiting Chili and Mexico, doubling Cape Horn, rambling over Juan Fernandez, etc., etc. He says that allowing for a little coloring, Stephens's "Central America"[2] comes very near the truth; prefers South America to North; but declares that, after rambling over all that is fairest in Europe, Greece, Italy, the Peninsula, the lovely islands of the Pacific, all that is called finest in point of scenery, he knows nothing so beautiful, for mere beauty, as our own dear England. The Americas are on too large a scale, he says; neither the eye nor the mind can take in a whole. I can understand this. And the result of their too bright skies is a want of atmospheric illusion—of shifting shadow—of that transition which is as expression to a lovely face.

I wish you had seen Dr. Carter, you would have been pleased with him. He told me what I did not before know, that Mrs. Trollope is a thorough-going mesmerite, constantly at Dr. Elliotson's, and believing through thick and thin. Another thing which he told me gratified me greatly: being ill in Spain, home-sick and longing for some English or Englishlike book, he sent to see if such a treat could be procured, and received a Spanish translation of "Our Village!" So few English works are published in a Spanish dress that it is a real compliment, and I tell you of it just as I told my father, because I know that it will please your dear heart.

Another visitor is Lord Brougham's[3] thrice-charming and thrice-excellent sister. She is full of life, and spirit, and brilliancy—as clever, Marianne[4] says, as her brother, and kind cordial, generous, frank, and full of all that is admirable and all that is charming. We have only spent one afternoon together, and I feel that we are friends for life. She says that her brother's health and spirits are better than she once feared they would be. He finds in constant employment a medicine for great grief—the loss of his mother weighing even more heavily than the loss of his daughter. Both were to be expected, but Miss Brougham said that she believed her brother had reconciled himself to the one as inevitable—had even assigned to it (through the foresight of the medical men) something very near the actual date; whilst the green old age of his mother, the absence of change or decay either of health, spirits, or faculty, had blinded him to the danger, so that the shock, the surprise, was greater in the death of the very old than of the very young.

He has lost one eye, and the other fails him, so that he dictates instead of writing. His newspaper is the "Sun." He has never had the courage to revisit Brougham since his mother's death, and Miss B. says she doubts if he ever will. His place in the south of France is his great amusement; and the giving judgments in the House of Peers.

How I wished for you during Miss Brougham's visit! God bless them both! Ever your own,

M.R.M.

1. Dr. John Elliotson (1791–1868), the mesmerist who resigned his professorship at London University when action was taken against him for his "magnetic" experiments in 1838.
2. John Lloyd Stephens (1805–52), American travel writer, author of *Incidents of Travel in Central America, Chiapas, and Yucatan* (1841).
3. Henry Peter Brougham, first Baron Brougham and Vaux (1788–1868), Lord Chancellor 1830–34, was an amateur scientist with a reputation for eccentricity.
4. Apparently Marianne Skerrett (1793?–1887), MRM's friend who was dresser to the queen.

[TUESDAY] JULY 26. 1842–

•   •   •

And now, you are to reward me for my docility & obedience (I deserve most of your praises full as well as this of my own) by sitting down directly if you please, & telling me the whole story about Miss Pickering. Oh! you *are* a knitter of a mystery!– I am curious to the very extent of my capacity. "Bridecake—bridecake"! Why do you mean, can you possibly mean, that Miss P. the second,[1] *signified* to you that M.ʳ Kenyon proposed to her or meant to propose to her, or considered her directly or indirectly "par amour" —? Is that your meaning? Now I do beseech you,—if any compassion for or sympathy with an unfortunate victim of curiosity remain with you, tell me your story. I wont tell it over again to M.ʳ Kenyon—be sure of *that:* but if I see him before he goes abroad, I *will* assuredly ask him if he is acquainted with Miss P the second, & how she stands in what Howell calls "the horizon of his love".[2] I may say *that*—all except the last word, for which of course I sh.ᵈ give small change. I may look in his face & talk of Miss P the second & think . . . . metaphysics. I w.ᵈⁿᵗ betray you dearest Miss Mitford—not for a wilderness of bridecake! so do, do, open your chronicles in my sight!—& consider the weakness of our common womanhood by eschewing further delays!

It seems to me that (talking of womanhood) your pen & ink odiosities do beguile you (for *you*) into wonderful injustices sometimes.

For instance, is'nt it hard for women in the majority,—hard for them not as "great writers" but as petticoated creatures, to go down hill in the dreadful metaphorical sense of growing old? Dont they slip down, creep down backwards, & send all spectators over the stiles? Do the devotees to German stichery get down any better in general than the Miss *Ps*? I trow not. And even if you are right in straightening your remark within such limits . . why you sh.^d be tenderhearted my dearest friend & consider. Miss P. the first, wishes to propose; Miss P. the second, to be proposed to. Now how effective can the most active exertions towards those meritorious ends, hope to be, without a little youth for a groundwork? One might faint nine times at forty, & dead away, and in vain, when the mere asking for hartshorn at eighteen w.^d *do* it. The inference is clear—it is better to be eighteen than forty, for marriageable women—that is, for women resolved on being married—and it is clear to me besides that your Miss P the second, is far from being such a 'fool' as your Master Ben[3] took her for.

And now, tell me all about it & about it. Oh no—be sure if our dear Mr Kenyon sh.^d turn out to be bewitched, it was not achieved by the novels. He keeps Wordsworth & Tennyson in his house until weeks count up into months without reading a page of them: he is not likely to read a Miss P. But I who read more of good & bad than I dare confess, & who of late years have stretched out my hand for literature, more sometimes to be languid & half asleep over than for thoughtful purpose, know her novels very well, & have found the degree of amusement or beguilement I sought, from several of them. Nobody can praise them for good writing to be sure,—nor for any other sort of elevation above the commonplace: & the degree of talent shown in them, lies in a slovenly form,—& is not strong enough by nature to stand alone without pains. But there is a degree of amusement to be confessed in the books—at least by me when I am sleepy—& there is an amiableness & good feeling which I was always pleased to confess. Did you ever read a line, a page of them? or try to do it? I dare say not. I heard once that she professes to hate writing, & writes to live. She writes rapidly, because without *an ideal:* which is a very common reason for uncommon facility.

Well! and dear Mr Kenyon came to see me on sunday. It was cold & rainy by the Lakes, & he & his companions (oh! who were they?) were forced to have a fire every day as it came. He saw Mr Wordsworth by two half hours, & thought him out of spirits—"depressed" was the word!—suffering much from his eyes, & wearing a green shade. He did not go near poor M.ʳ Southey whose case is worse & worse—not recognizing even his wife! – He didn't see M.ʳ Hartley Coleridge! I asked him if he had enjoyed it all,—& he laughed & told me not to ask questions. And yet, & yet . . if M.ʳ Crabbe Robinson was one of his companions, . . Miss Baillie⁴ was another! Yes—it is true! And the circumstance was not so much told to me as betrayed to me,—which makes it significantly true. Oh bridecake, bridecake! was this the Miss Baillie who travelled into Devonshire?—to Ross? the very same. Whether the Miss *B* shall clash finally with the Miss *P.* you know better than I do—but verily I am beginning to think that this dear M.ʳ Kenyon of ours will come to belong particularly to somebody distinct from us, *in bridecaka bridecakorum.*

•   •   •

I am delighted with your chronicle of your visitors, & most delighted about the Spanish translation of Our Village! Thank you my dearest kindest friend for telling me! Was it a *good* translation? But the *fact* proves the *fame.* There is a pleasure,—which you will acknowledge,—in the consciousness of having lived & thought not in vain,—& of being a means of extending intellectual influences & innocent enjoyments to the ends of the world. Such a pleasure may well correct the sharpness of many pains—& it is yours proudly & happily my dearest dearest friend,—& your friend's to *see!*–

The Black Mountains Papa went near, are Welsh & not Irish. Arabel & Occy have gone not quite so far today . . to spend the day at Hampton Court with some friends of theirs.

M.ʳ Kenyon & I talked of you of course. Today M.ʳ Bezzi is to arrive as his visitor; & on next monday, they set out on their continental tour—resolute to return in the second or third week of October.

I had heard of M.ʳˢ Trollope at D.ʳ Elliotson's. indeed one of my brother's met her there—but that was more than a year ago, & she was then less a believer than an investigator. Anybody could talk *me* into it in half an hour.

Will you give my love to D.ʳ Mitford? Will you try to go on to love me?

Your EBB–

•   •   •

1. Ellen Pickering (?–1843), a prolific minor novelist who wrote for a livelihood, here called "Miss P. the second." "The first Miss P" is Julia Pardoe (1806–62), a travel writer and friend of MRM.

2. In a letter of 30 May 1619 to Richard Altham, James Howell (1594–1666), historiographer to Charles II, wrote: "Though you be now a good way out of my reach, yet you are not out of my remembrance; you are still within the horizon of my love."

3. Ben Kirby, the Mitfords' handyman.

4. Sarah Bayley (?–1868), a close friend of Kenyon who, at his death, left her £5000 and his house at Wimbledon.

[Monday] August 1. 1842.

My beloved friend, I am close to you again, not to teaze you long today, but to set myself right in your judgment, which I am quite sure is turned my way with a black condemnation cap. How c^d you think me in earnest in taking the part of the fair majority of fair ladies, as to the question of their sunsetting? When I said that women, determined to be married, sh^d have an eternal youth passed to them by acclamation, you surely, surely c^{dnt} think me quite grave in my reasoning?

And for the rest,—why, although I am, to be sure, a hero & heroine-worshipper by religion, I am *not* a worshipper of Ps . . (I appreciate a certain letter just before it too well for *that*!) and if I take the part of Pen & Ink in masses, even inclusive of the P. department, it is only when you seem to me hard upon Pen & Ink & *P* women, for such frailties as they share in common with needle & thread women, according to the proverb & reproach of all generations. It is as far from me as the Georgium sidus,[1] to defend such frailities—to do anything in fact but laugh them to scorn. Only it seems to me too cruel logic, my beloved friend, to blame Pen & Ink *as* Pen & Ink, for sins to which Needle & Thread are equally subject. When young ladies of forty wish to pass for eighteen they are very silly—and I willingly moreover w^d grant to you that silly women with an assumption of teaching the world through "my publisher," do emblazon their silliness wonderfully. I scarcely dare to ask you to grant to me in turn, that "my publisher" is not the source of the silliness, & pen & ink not an *originating* but simply a collateral weakness.

Oh—we shall never agree!– It certainly does appear to my perverseness, that you, having the literary side of the world turned to you, upbraid it for *worldliness* . . the quality of all corners of the octagon—& that all these dreadful pen & ink people, (convert them in a miraculous moment to needle & thread & guns), as surely as the last, w^d be none the less selfish & affected for it. Are not personal vanities, I mean dress & face vanities, & social vanities, dinner & visiting vanities, as bad, of as rank a smell to Heaven, as literary vanities? Indeed, I fancy so—although, as I granted before, people who profess the *metier du genie* have the less excuse for acting & talking like noodledums.

After all, I am sure I sh^d join you in hating the P's, & many other *a b c*'s besides. Nay, after all I am very sure, that if I were teazed & haunted by them as your own dearest self, I never c^d be half as kind & goodtempered & gracious as *you* are. I c^d have thrown a bunch of nettles after *P. II*, after *she* threw off your nosegay!

But this is the particular point upon which we diverge particularly. The canaille of literature may be as bad as the rest of the world, as other *canailles*, & as you say. But I am a hero-worshipper, & it is difficult, nay, impossible for me to believe that the hero, the true genius, is not morally greater, more generous, more faithful, more tender-hearted than the troop of vulgar men. Will you believe harm of your Fletcher? of the whole world's Shakespeare? Will your own heart let you think either poet a selfish, insensible man? Do not their books testify against such thoughts? W^d you turn back such books as no good witness? For my own part I receive the witness reverently, as if it were the voice of an angel. And however I may be, & am actually, ignorant of the personal manners & moods of the gifted men of our day, my *instinct* is to love & reverence them as men, & in a trust unshaken by a suspicion. And if *that* is very perverse,—why, *you* my dearest kindest friend, sh^d be the last to be very angry,—if you love me the least bit in the world. W^d it have been right of *me* not to love & reverence *you* a long time ago, nor keep a heart wide open for you? Had I been of your sect, I sh^d have fancied all manner of evil of you—now, sh^{dnt} I? Therefore I was right to be ready to love you,— & that I am justified, doubly trebly justified, nay, glorified to the very hem of my perverse doctrine, by the event,—is too well proved to gainsay. Ah my dearest dearest friend! what a luckless person you are, to undo in your own person the most available of your arguments!– But we wont quarrel about who are the naughtiest "in this naughty world", all the days of our life—shall we? And here is Crow come to ask for my letter for the post, & put an end to the quarrelling for today.

• • •

M! Kenyon went away yesterday. I did not see him—had a little note for farewell, & he said in it that I was to speak to you of him when I wrote to you next. His opinion of Miss Baillie as a "reasoning woman" is very high.

Ever your most attached EBB.

• • •

1. The planet Uranus, discovered in 1781 and named for George III.

[TUESDAY] AUGUST 30. 1842

My dearest friend's letter must take from me a few words of answer today—altho' so much of it is unanswerable—& the very ink seems to turn into water as I try to write– Thank you briefly for your dear affectionateness! I was almost uneasy after the impertinence of my petition to you—but your *'nos'* are soft as *'yeses'*.

I wish you had told me the day upon which you were to act chief Architect in Reading, so that I might be present in spirit. In the meanwhile it is very pleasant to be sure of D! Mitford's being better enough to admit of this little absence; and even his desire for you to accept the honor intended by it, seems to me a satisfactory proof of his own consciousness of improvement– Do you not think so? Oh yes! he must be better. And now, I do hope & trust & pray, you are going to bed regularly again, & reposing yourself *for his sake* from this dreadful succession of fatigues whether of watching or emotion. 'Three weeks without going to bed!' Indeed I cannot bear to think of it,—& I cant choose but suspect, even from your own story of how it was, that you might have slept often & often when unnecessarily anxious thoughts kept you awake. And yet there shall be, ought to be no scolding. Unnecessarily anxious thoughts are too often necessary thoughts—and ministering angels will be true to their natures!–

But I must suggest one thing. Do have if you have not had, whenever these watchings become necessary again, a sofa by the bed-side of the invalid, & *lie on it* when you do not sleep. During my worst of illness—at the time when sleep was the bare signal for fainting fits, & when it was dangerous to leave me lest death & sleep sh! come together—there was a sofa by my bed—& my dear sister lay on it half

the night & my kind Crow the other half—& in this way they exchanged & bore up against exhaustion for weeks & weeks. It was not
my fault—I did what I could, when I was conscious,—& wanted a
nurse to be hired; but that was not permitted—through too much
kindness it was'nt: and the sofa provided a degree of repose which w^d
have been unattainable in the easiest chair in the world. If you were
to undress to a dressing gown & lie on the sofa my beloved friend, I
am sure it w^d be better–

Flushie hates to see me write & has just settled himself half under my arm & half on my knee. How calligraphic I am likely to be!
Oh Flushie! settling yourself to sleep too!

No, no, no!—my dearest friend!—I am perverse, I am adverse,
& most perversely adverse to the out-of-town proposition. No, you w^d
not press it if you knew exactly how we all are, & how *I* am, above
all. Dr Chambers did not think it desirable for me to leave London
in the summer, before,—told me in fact "that I was as well here in
the summer as anywhere"—& Dr Scully who writes to me occasionally, does not recommend beyond the wheeled chair. I always think
that the opinion about what is called "London unhealthiness" is
rather a *sentiment* than an opinion– If we were bricked up in the city,
we might talk of thick airs or no airs—but here, on the very verge of
the country, some two hundred yards from Regent's Park which
opens out to "Hampstead's breezy heath" it is all imagination to cry
out for 'air'. Then I have the whole breadth of the house & five windows through which to *inhale*—Papa's door being always open now to
admit a free current of . . . a whirlwind if it pleased to come . . &
carry me away to the Surrey hills. Now how sh^d I be better in a little
close lodging house—between a draught & a coup de soleil . . being
stifled—or, by a happy alternative, catching cold? And even if I
avoided fatigue & went only a walk's distance away—say, only to
Hampstead! Still, I must give up a good deal—my evenings with
Papa, for instance!—to say nothing of my *vow*. Oh no, no! Thank you
a hundred times for your great & earnest kindness—but you must not
try to send me away from my new found consolations. And I, so well
too!—so wonderfully well!– Not strong, you will say– And indeed,
feeble enough. But still, stronger, & likely to be stronger still, if the
wheeled chair answers as I mean it to do, as soon as ever we can *catch*
a day at once cool enough & warm enough for an experimental day–
Observe,—you, my beloved friend who are *not* 'perverse',—that a
chair likely to move smoothly upon a level pavement such as it is be-

fore our door, w.^d not move *so* smoothly upon gravel walks, such as may be commendable gravel walks in lodging house gardens. No, no! If you come to London, *when* you come to London—for the hypothesis is too dear to be put hypothetically—you shant come to make mischief between Papa & me, nor to scold *me*, but just to give the pleasure you cant help giving wherever you go,––*that*—& more than *that*!–

      •   •   •

Is M.^r De Vere[1] given to literature at all—I mean as a reading man, not a pen & ink man? I can quite understand the effect of the re-action of a generous impulse,—& to such, that bitter hard-cored & hard-rinded orange Protestantism must indeed give very sufficient incitement. Still, where a man thinks as well as feels, & where his first religious impressions are not associated with Roman Catholicism, it is wonderful to me where he finds the energetic credulity necessary to the act of becoming a Roman Catholic. There is a great distinction . . do you not admit?—between a R Catholic by birth & education—and one by choice & *conversion—inversion* I w.^d rather say! Not that a man, or woman either, sh.^d remain in any sect or persuasion, because he was born in it—(we are all bound to consider & examine, & find, if possible, better reasons for our belief, than the habit of it . .)—but that habit & association will have & use a certain weight & bias, which if not good, yet excuses partially the evil. I hope that your M.^r De Vere may resist his impulse.

As to Charlotte Elizabeth[2]—yes, I have read that little book you speak of, & several of her little books besides. Her bitterness & narrowness towards the R Catholics,—her bitterness both in religion & politics,—I admit & lament to the roots of my heart. She is a very devoted woman, & lives to God nearly as if she lived with Him—and I believe that in exciting to religious feeling her books have done much good & especially among the young. She is not deceived, my dearest friend, I *think*. Her high & worthy object has been to incite to religious feeling—& her little books which are otherwise graceful enough & of a prettiness very pleasing to a youthful taste, have been taken to the hearts of many for teaching & blessing. The plague, the curse on them is their *sectarianism*!—a word, by the way, which w.^d drive the poor woman mad if she c.^d see me apply it to her—to her who rejoiceth in the Church of England "the whole & nothing *but*"! —, & opines that 'sectarianism' means simply the other side of the

Church door. Poor unconscious Charlotte Elizabeth!—she is intensely sectarian after all!–

I do not know her personally, & although I have heard her name, I have forgotten it. But my traditions tell me that she is very excellent & amiable—unmarried, elderly,—& so deaf as scarcely to hear through a trumpet. Her friends talk to her with their fingers. You learn by her books how fond she is of flowers.

For the rest, be sure that I do not count her prevailing fault a slight one—& that, on the contrary, often & often when I wished to choose a giftbook for a little friend of mine, & held Charlotte Elizabeth's graceful stories with their heavenly aspiration, in my hands longingly as "the very thing", . . I have put them down again with a sigh for 'the fault'. When the 'milk of the gospel' grows sour, pestilent is the sourness!–

As to Wilberforce[3] & his memoirs, I agree with you very much, both as to him & them. He was a good man but made of narrow stuff. And then,—if the keeping of *spiritual journals* be advisable—which I very much doubt!—the publication of them cannot certainly be so. Even D.r Johnson c.d not bear that exposure—far less c.d Wilberforce, who was a man so little in all things that his very wings were scant.–

Romilly's[4] memoirs have interest—but "Let my soul be with" Wilberforce, altho' Romilly was the greater & more intellectual man. Not that I am an enthusiast about *him*—& not that "great" appears in any sense a word for *him*: & it is wonderful & chilling to me, his unconsciousness,—apparent at least & unbroken to the observation, by voice or sign, throughout these memoirs,—of the Spiritual Realities beyond his humanity. Is it not so? I think it was my impression.

I quite pity you in your chief masonship! Oh my dearest friend, how nervous it is sure to make you!– And yet I, a little enter into the pride of the honor & glory of it, just as D.r Mitford & K. do—& I am glad of the judicious discernment of the Reading people. Tell me more!–

And now I must gather together & count up my little sheets. Surely I have written half a quire to you—*Miserere*! –

Ever your attached EBB–

• • •

1. Aubrey Thomas De Vere (1814–1902), Irish-born poet who converted to Roman Catholicism in 1851.

2. Charlotte Elizabeth Tonna (1790–1846), editor of the *Christian Lady's Magazine* (1834), and a prolific writer.
3. William Wilberforce (1759–1833), M.P., and Evangelical philanthropist whose *Life* was published posthumously in 1838.
4. Samuel Romilly (1757–1818), an advocate of penal reform whose *Memoirs of Samuel Romilly Written by Himself* appeared posthumously in 1840.

Three-mile Cross
Sept. 2 [*sic* for 1], 1842.

You may imagine, my beloved friend, how very much my dear father is restored when I tell you that carrying with us, and sending on before, the four persons absolutely necessary to help him in and out of his very low open carriage, he was well enough to attend at the stone-laying ceremony yesterday (Wednesday), and that the exertion, as Mr. May foretold, rather did him good than harm. It was really a pretty ceremony. I suppose there'll be an account of it in the Reading paper next week; if so, I'll send it. Perhaps, after reading, you will be so good as to return it, since I should like to keep the detail. If ever I am ungrateful enough to bemoan my isolated position, I ought to think over the assemblage in the morning, and at the evening tea-party and concert (where my father insisted on my appearing for an hour), in order to feel the thankfulness that thrilled through my very heart at the true and honest kindness with which I was received. It was an enthusiasm of man, woman, and child—hundreds—thousands—such as I can hardly venture to describe, and it lasted all the time I staid. Indeed, the pleasure amounted to pain, so confusing was it to hear the overpraise of which I felt myself unworthy. But it was not the praise that was so touching, it was the kindliness, the affection. My father cried, K—— cried, Dora Smith cried, I think more than all, at the true, honest, generous heartiness of the people. There is in Reading a very eloquent man,[1] really eloquent, and it is a high and rare gift. He is a physician, young and deeply religious, very clever, very scientific, and one who interests himself greatly in the instruction of the people, giving courses of lectures every winter. He spoke the oration, a very fine one; and if the reporter have done him justice, you will see that he is a speaker of no common stamp. If the account be badly done, I sha'n't send it; but will then write again to supply the omissions of this letter; taking for granted frankly, my most dearest, that to you it will be as full of interest as such a thing happening to you would be to me. Think how full of thanksgiving were my prayers last night that my dear father had enjoyed such gratification.

I must see the "North American Review," and the condemned tragedies,[2] chiefly the "North American." I know very well Mrs. Stirling, the mother of the poet.[3] His father is the most trenchant and violent writer of the "Times." Mrs. Stirling is very charming—a Cornelia-like woman[4]—stately and noble, whose pride in her son is charming. It is long since I have seen her. No, Mr. Milnes is not cold! I love his poetry.

Heaven bless you, my love! I am tired to death. Ever your own,

M.R. MITFORD

1. Identified as Dr. Charles Cowan.
2. The "condemned tragedies" were George Stephens's *Martinuzzi* and Charles Darley's *Plighted Troth*, the subject of a satirical article in the July 1842 *Fraser's*. EBB thought Horne the author of the article, a copy of which she sent to MRM.
3. John Sterling (1806–44), contributor to various periodicals under the pseudonym "Archaeus." He and EBB were reviewed in the July 1842 *North American Review*.
4. A reference to Cornelia, "Mother of the Gracchi" (second century B.C.), Roman tribunes. She is famous for saying to a woman who wanted to see her jewels, "These are my jewels"—pointing to her sons.

[WEDNESDAY] SEPT 14. 1842

My dearest friend, here is the newspaper back & thanks upon thanks for the pleasure of the sight of it. I admire your chief orator—and I admire & love the chief 'personnage', & applaud with all the applause & exult in all the exultation, & do not wonder that Ben cried! Ah!— & how it must have affected with a deep joy which was also tenderness, D? Mitford. What it must have been to *him*, those shouts & upturned faces! I almost wonder that he c^d bear it at all in his weak state, altho' I perfectly understand that if he c^d exult instead of being overcome, . . rise upon the swell of the emotion, . . the effect w^d be beneficial physically. May God bless both of you through each other—each by each! still longer on earth; & afterwards, so, make His Heaven sweeter to you!

Are you personally acquainted & do you see much of the physician who spoke? I liked very much indeed what he said of not looking to science or to any means purely intellectual for national regeneration. It is just as I could have chosen it to be said; & just also, as scientific persons generally w^d be loth to say it. He is bold to speak the truth. "Knowledge puffeth up,—but Love buildeth up" —and the Love of God is the glorification of Love, even as God is Love Itself. I know of nothing that can build us up, except LOVE in the high intense divine meaning: & the strutting vanity assumed by Science & Philosophy is as offensive to the contemplative man whose eye is upon his *nature,* as to the contemplative angel whose eye is toward Deity.

. . .

Since you are interested about Mr Stirling besides somebody else, I mean to send you the North American Review,—& Fraser for July, for another reason. Mr Townsend (are you aware?) is an enthusiast about Mr Stirling's Archæus's, poetry, which I never c^d be & confessed it. Mr Simmons[1] writes excellent thoughtful verses,—but (for confession the second) I must demur to receiving them as inspired poetry. Reading them for instance, after Tennyson's, do we not "fall from Heaven" as the French say? Milnes is a poet—Browning is a poet—Tennyson is a poet. When we come to Sterling & Simmons, we cannot assert it of them unhesitatingly. *My* voice, at least, I do confess . . *stutters.*

Are you aware (and if you sh^d not be, do not tell it again) that the violent paper against poor Mr Reade in Blackwood,[2] was *by Mr Landor?* It was indeed. Yet nobody, I think, c^d have guessed it "by the style".

Dearest dearest Miss Mitford, I am going out in the chair today for the first time & directly, & can write no more. But you must hear first how well I am, & that for several days the *spitting of blood* which more or less beset me nightly, has quite stopped. Oh for another summer to grow strong in! Only, winters & weaknesses are good for us. May God bless you always!–

Ever your attached
EBB–

. . .

1. Bartholomew Simmons (1804–50), Irish poet and contributor to *Blackwood's*, especially known for his poem, "Napoleon's Last Look."

2. John Edmund Reade (1800–70), minor poet, whose *Record of the Pyramids* was harshly reviewed in *Blackwood's* for July 1842.

FRIDAY [*SIC* FOR WEDNESDAY]. OCT. 19. 1842—

My dearest friend, I have fancied that you w^d prefer having the verses a day sooner, & therefore I send them directly. They ran away from me with their double rhymes, before I considered properly; but as you did not object to the last I sent you, & as the double rhyme does certainly always seem to *me* to give an appropriate lightness to the short lyric, I venture to leave the verses as they are,—in their natural state. Your relation of Mr Schloss's judgment made me smile. 'Beautiful & sublime'. Why the book must be too small to hold us! That *you* sh^d be 'beautiful' is no wonder at all; and I suppose I am 'sublime' because nobody can understand me. At any rate it is a great satisfaction to me, that *so far*, I have not spoilt your success; and I thank you my dearest friend, for making me aware of it.

Indeed after reading your welcome, welcome letter yesterday (twice as welcome to me as the queen to Scotland!) I was very thankful for the great mercy of joy & tears vouchsafed to you after that *terror* which I c^d well comprehend. At eighty two my beloved friend, we do not recover into youth—and yet I do begin to think that you may be spared some time longer from the final stroke. "An excellent pulse"! and for the improvement to *continue*, as your note of this morning gives evidence, suggests still more hope. May God comfort you,—however He may direct the issue of present circumstances. I often think that in praying for even such a temporal blessing as the life of our dearest friends, which we feel surest & clearest of *being* a blessing to us, we pray yet in the dark,—not knowing evil from good. In Heaven, we may presently call good, evil,—& evil, good; & the chiefest afflictions under which our hearts break here below, may there appear our chiefest benedictions.

Thank you for your kind tolerance of my sonnet on the picture. Do you know Mr Haydon is so pleased with it that he talks of sending it to Mr Wordsworth, and requested me to publish it in the Athenæum, on account of some impossible good which he attaches to its publication. Of course, I c^d not say 'no'; but whether Mr Dilke may not, remains to be proved: for Mr Haydon says rightly that the Athenæum people dislike him, . . are cold to him, . . as they are indeed to the whole world of art, with the exception of musicians. Before I sent the sonnet away yesterday, I tried to alter that line with 'releast' to the end of it, —but could not, for the better. The sonnet structure is a very fine one, however imperious, and I never *would* believe that our language is unqualified for the very strictest Italian form. I have been exercising myself in it not unfrequently of late.

Ah—you speak more severely of Mr Browning, than I can say 'Amen' to . Amen w.^d stick in my throat —even suppose it to rise so high. There is a unity & nobleness of conception in 'Pippa passes' which seems to me to outweigh all the riddles in riddledom—and verily a great many 'lie hid' in the same 'Pippa'. Give me my choice,— only give me my choice, between Mr Milnes's genius & Mr Browning's, & you will see if I don't take the last & say 'thank you'. I am sure I ought to say it for what your goodness leads you to say of *me*— but indeed, indeed, Pippa, dark as she is, is worth all those rhymes you speak of—in my eyes, not blinded by friendship. Do you know that Mr Browning is a great favorite (I mean as a man) of Mr Kenyon's? Mr Kenyon spoke to me warmly of his high cultivation & attainments, & singular humility of bearing– And he is weak in health too! I sh.^d like to hear you praise him a little more, indeed.

I have had one or two kind & interesting notes from Mr Haydon, who speaks of you as admiringly as I like almost. "She is a noble creature" he says—"never flinched in all my misfortunes". I like *him* too, & am grateful to him. But as to seeing him yet & here, . . oh no, my dearest friend, I c.^{dnt}! Why, do you know, that, last summer, Mr Wordsworth had himself the infinite kindness of proposing twice to Mr Kenyon, to come to see me—& Mr Kenyon said 'no'. Not that *I* said 'no'. I c.^d not have articulated it to Wordsworth! I c.^d rather do so to the queen. But 'no' was said; & now, how c.^d I say 'yes' to anybody in the world?

Next summer, perhaps, it may be different——but who am I, who talk of next summers?

It is very cold—which is probably not likely to be injurious to your dear patient. Of the Kenyons, I hear nothing at all.

I smile in triumph over your feeling about Anna Seward's Letters.

Ever your most affectionate
EBB–

• • •

[Friday] Oct. 21. 1842–

•   •   •

I will make you acquit M.ͬ Kenyon next,—altho' you can have little thought to spend away in acquittals or condemnations. But indeed *he* did nothing wrong, nothing in the world otherwise than kind, in that 'no' he said to *the* KING. He had heard me talk, & my sisters talk still more, of the harm it did me to be excited by seeing people or by any other exciting cause—and once, not long before, he asked me whether he might not bring M.ͬ Browning who kindly wished to see me,—and I answered "oh no, no! I cannot indeed". And my sisters explained to him how it was that directly I saw anybody, my heart stopped short, & I left off sleeping. So you see when M.ͬ Wordsworth had the goodness to propose what he did, M.ͬ Kenyon acted considerately as he always does in answering what he answered. Only if I had known at the moment, *I* could not, as I told M.ͬ Kenyon afterwards, have articulated the 'no'. I w.ͩ have seen M.ͬ Wordsworth—if I never were to go to sleep any more!–

Ah! spine complaints,—and mine are very different. The horse-racing which has gone on in my blood w.ͩ astonish people used to mortal pulses. And altho' I am far quieter, tranquillized wonderfully in every way, of late, yet I sh.ͩ not be so well, even now, if people came often to see me. I am excitable by nature, excitable by illness—& not as strong in spirits as in days gone for ever. This winter I must be quiet—and when we are together again I will listen to all your wise counsel & take every shred of it I can—provided you dont advise me to go away from Papa again.

And that reminds me, how astonished *he* w.ͩ be if I had M.ͬ Horne & M.ͬ Browning up stairs in my bedroom!! He w.ͩ certainly open his eyes & set me down among the *inclined*-to-be- "good-for-nothing poetesses." I for my own part, might be very well ['[']inclined' to do it, . . if I were equal to it otherwise—for I absolutely agree with you that it w.ͩ be not only innocent, but what is quite another thing, *proper*. You do not speak of the 'Damned tragedies' of Fraser, by the way.

And by the way again, I do not mean to praise '*Strafford*'. I praise 'Paracelsus'—I praise 'Pippa passes'—I cannot indeed wish the poet of either, in another *metier*: & I shall be renowned at last for my supreme obstinacy—shall I not!–

Do I vex & trouble you instead of distracting you, my beloved friend? Perhaps so. But then, you will put the letter away when you are not equal to reading it, & it will be sure to be silent in a drawer. I wish I c^d look at your face one moment, to know whether you are killing yourself or not. I am uneasy about you my beloved friend.

• • •

Your own attached EBB—

[THURSDAY–FRIDAY] OCT. 27th [–28] 1842.

• • •

Papa is my chaplain, . . prays with me every night, . . not out of a book, but simply & warmly at once,—with one of my hands held in his & nobody besides him & me in the room. That is dear in him,— is it not? And he with his elastic spirit & merry laugh!– One might as little expect such an act from the youngest of my brothers (at first sight!) as from him. When I was so ill he used to do it constantly I think, and altho' I c^d not understand what he said, through the wanderings of my mind at that time, yet I had a sort of vague satisfaction in seeing him kneel down there & in feeling that he was praying for all of us. It was strange, my state *then*, & looks to me from hence like a dreamed of dream! I am sure I never prayed myself for a long while. I seemed to lie too near to God to pray—as if the sword were close to my neck, & I, lying without hope or fear, c^d not *speak* to the striker. It was power & weakness meeting together—my sense of power in *Him*—my sense of weakness in myself. It was no doubting of His mercy, none of his love—but the Hand had struck me & I c^d not speak.

And here I am writing all sorts of mournfulnesses to you when I ought to write gaieties. I shall be sent to that drawer which I hired, you know, for the particular use of such letters of mine, as make themselves disagreeable. I shall certainly be sent to my drawer. In selfdefence I will tell you that our dear Mr Kenyon comes home today at three oclock; and that tomorrow he is to have a dinner-party. So you think me old enough to have twenty gentlemen in my bedroom if I please, according to the order of the garter! Agreed! but then, but then . . this Papa of mine would, even if I were fifty, most certainly demur to it. He is twice as 'proper', do you know, as I am who have the misfortune to be a "good for nothing poetess"?– He is indeed. And besides, I am scarcely inclined & fit yet in anything but age, for any of the twenty except dear M.ʳ Kenyon—not in strength, not in spirits—and besides, next summer when I am, you say, & I hope sometimes, to see all my gods and ONE GODDESS, I shall take my place for a part of the day in the back drawing room. I was down stairs four or five times this year,—and if I can but keep up . . . . . . oh yes, yes! you shall do whatever you please with me next year my beloved friend, . . provided . . . . always provided . . . . . !

M.ʳ Haydon sent my sonnet to Wordsworth—did I tell you? And to my astonishment, to my great great pleasure this morning, a note very gentle & gracious, from Wordsworth himself was in my hands! I shall throw myself at M.ʳ Haydon's feet for procuring me such a pleasure! he was *the means* of it obviously!– The great poet speaks of the obscurity of the line you remarked upon, & suggests an alteration which unhappily is just too late for the Athenæum, but which is available for a republication. A letter from Wordsworth! Dont tell anybody, but I *kissed it*. And he speaks so kindly of his intention of calling upon me when he was last in London!–

. . .

Your own
EBB–

M.ʳ Wordsworth says most kindly "The conception of your sonnet is in full accordance with the painter's intended work, and the expression vigorous; yet the word "ebb" though I do not myself object to it nor wish it altered, will I fear prove obscure to nine readers out of ten.

A vision free
And noble, Haydon, hath thine art release.

Owing to the want of inflexions in our language, the construction here is obscure. Would it not be better thus?– I was going to make a small change in the order of the words but I find it w.ᵈ not remove the objection. The sense as I take it, w.ᵈ be somewhat clearer thus, if you c.ᵈ tolerate the redundant syllable.

By a vision free
And noble, Haydon, is thine art release."

I quite agree with you my dearest friend, as to the honor done by the *candor*. That he sh^d stoop to criticise a verse of mine is felt by me as if he praised it. He says besides that he has received "much pleasure" from other of my writings, & speaks of his wish to have come to see me last year, very kindly indeed. I am touched & charmed by all of it—and in making up 'my *bills*', *calculate* that I owe it indirectly to you. Now, do you not see? Through *you* came my knowledge of Mr Haydon—through Mr Haydon the sonnet-making & sending & rewarding! To *you* clearly!

Ever & gratefully your attached
EBB –

[Three Mile Cross] [October ? 1842]

. . . At last it occurred to me that the best for him would be to move the large articles of furniture with which our entrance-hall is filled, and restore the little parlor to its office of a sitting-room for him, put up my dear father's bed in the hall, condemning both the front-door and the one from the staircase, leaving none but that from the parlor and that from the kitchen, and going in and out myself from our back-door. This has been accomplished, thank God, without disturbing him. A bed is put up in the kitchen for his nurse. I shall sit up when needful in the parlor, and the large fires of the parlor and kitchen, and the double doors and double carpets with which we have lined the hall, make that a most warm and comfortable bedroom. Heaven be praised! Now he can have his two favorite arm-chairs in the little parlor, and be moved from one to the other as he gets cramped, and Flush[1] and I can sit at his feet. Poor Flush! how he has been watching the operations, and how thoroughly he approves them! I wish you could see him. Mr. May will be delighted to find that, besides a comfortable bedroom, we have got a nice little parlor for him—change is so essential. Now he can get up as early as he likes, and stay up as long; and, instead of the stove which Mr. May suggested for the hall,

he will have the nice open grate which he likes so well, and his favorite round table, and his own two chairs.

I cannot tell you the relief that this is to us all. I have been so
worried, besides the anxiety and the grief and the fatigue, that this
one relief is an unspeakable blessing. It seemed so hard that the dis-
comfort of moving up and down our cottage stairs should be added to
such feebleness. Now he will at least have no outward want of room
or appliances; and as to visitors being forced to come in at the back-
door, and pass through the kitchen—why, friends will not mind it,
and acquaintances I should not dream of letting in.

I do not apologize for sending you this detail, my beloved friend:
you will sympathize with me, I know, and this lodging my father has
been a most serious matter to me. Ever since his dear master has been
so ill, poor little Flush has either slept at his door—across the door—
or in my room, which he never used to do. It seems as if he could
not bear to leave us, and there is a look of pity in his sweet countenance, a fellow-feeling which I cannot describe. The gentleness with
which he kisses his master's hand now is quite charming.

Poor K. is very good to me—indeed, I must say that everybody
feels strongly and rightly towards my dear father. They are kind to
me in a great measure for his sake. Poor as he has lately been, he has
done so much good—good that mere money could not do—by un-
compromising, unflinching justice. Whoever was oppressed had a
friend; whoever sought aid in any proper object had a zealous, hearty
advocate. Be sure, my beloved friend, that when I say a country gentleman's life is one of widespreading usefulness, I speak of what I
know. There is not a poor person within ten miles who does not bless
my dear father—ay, and many not poor, who sought advice, and a
helping hand, and a voice never silent, when it could promote the
welfare, or the prosperity, or the harmless pleasure of others. Forgive
me when I say this: but why should I not? All the authorship in the
world would never win the love and respect that awaits upon a character so firm in the right and so full of active good-will towards his kind.
God bless him! Even in his own extreme feebleness he neither forgets those whom he could help (his last relapse was brought on by an
attempt to go to the bench last Saturday to serve a neighbor, and, although forced to return without alighting, he accomplished his object
by sending for his brother magistrates to the door), nor his gratitude
towards those who are so good to me. Even to-night he spoke to me

of "dear Miss Barrett." Once again, beloved friend, I do not ask you to forgive this—I should not love you as I do if I could doubt your sympathy.

[M.R.M.]

1. MRM's spaniel, sire of EBB's Flush.

[MONDAY] OCT. 31. 1842.

• • •

And now let me stand in the sun for a moment before I say 'goodbye'. I shall come to the rescue of poor M. Browning,—'out of the spirit of contradiction', you will be of opinion. But consider! He is very fond of his mother & his sisters! And instead of accounting it effeminacy that he sh^d fear their "taking his horse away from him", I call it affectionateness that he sh^d not bear to do what w^d occasion them anxiety. If he had been afraid himself, he w^d himself have abjured the horse—and that *we* might have called effeminacy—but love, love, . . who dares say a word against the influence of love? It is strongest, be sure, with the strongest.

• • •

[EBB]

LONDON

Changing Roles and Widening Horizons
1842–43

By the time of Dr. Mitford's death on 11 December 1842, EBB was writing the beleaguered MRM almost daily. Over the next months she anxiously followed the progress of a subscription begun by MRM's friends to pay debts accumulated during her father's illness (a fund that ultimately reached £2000 and allowed MRM her first taste in years of freedom from financial pressures). In April MRM journeyed to Bath, ostensibly to rest, but undoubtedly also to remove her maid Kerenhappuch ("K"), who had recently borne an illegitimate child, away from gossip. This delicate situation, and MRM's recovering of her Bath letters for later publication (never realized, although some of the material appeared in her *Recollections of a Literary Life* in 1852), help account for the dearth of MRM letters from this period when she remained in close touch with EBB. EBB's emotional 19 June 1843 letter shows the persisting trauma of Bro's loss, but the more characteristic zest with which she describes (in 24 May) her love of reading letters and chides MRM for her impractical travel plans (to Yucatan!) shows her markedly improved health and spirits. The two women had by now virtually reversed roles, with EBB busy not only with her poetry—some of which was appearing in *Graham's Magazine* and thus enhancing her reputation in America—but with critical essays for Horne's *New Spirit of the Age* (1844). Having yet to meet Horne in person, EBB was alternately mortified and amused at MRM's inviting back "Araminta" (as they called him) after complaining of his taking three baths a day and hunting hares and heiresses in the Reading neighborhood. In September, Flush was snatched (not for the first time) by dog thieves and an excited EBB rises to dramatic heights in recounting the story of his rescue.

[MONDAY] DEC. 11. [*SIC* FOR 12] 1842–

It is over . . the suffering of your beloved one—and now it is for *him*—(IF the sense of human tribulation *be* permitted to reach the delivered spirits)—it is for *him* to lean over *you* pityingly & tenderly . . you have changed your relative positions. My dearest dearest friend, in all your natural affliction, you will not at least be afflicted that he now sh.ᵈ be happier than you are: & every tear you shed & every bitter thought which turns into a sigh, simply prove that he is. Think so, my dearest, dear friend! I expect that the tender generous love which has done so much in working for & watching & softening the life you lament, sh.ᵈ become the most active human cause of your consolation.

For the rest—thank you, thank you, for caring to see me *now*. I receive the expression of that wish as the strongest, dearest & most touching proof of your affection. I am very grateful for it. And if I am not with you my beloved friend, it is not because I do not wish it— and if I am with you constantly in my heart & hope, it is the necessity of my earnest love for you which leads me to you.

I am sorry & penitent for having neglected to ask you to send *me* a list of persons to be written to, & to offer myself as your secretary. Can I do anything now in that way or another? Shall I supply you with paper, for instance, . . the mourning paper which is dear in country towns? Suffer me to send you a supply. For your future, I will not write of it today—but I *think* of it & of YOU always, always.

I wish I c.ᵈ look with you on that serene beauty of death,—where the last footstep of the happy spirit has touched the earthly remains into a celestial peace. I never saw the dead. You are happier in your sorrows my dearest friend, than I have been in many ways. And, so, justest!

You go to bed early, & sleep late . . do you not? you take nourishment & wine—do you not? will you not? will you not for my sake, my dearest Miss Mitford? This shivering, I cannot like to hear of,

whatever M! May may argue of it. You are exhausted, overagitated—
how can I like to hear of it?– I beseech you to repose—to cast your
spirit into the arms of God,—& your body on the bed—& draw the
curtains & lie quietly. You may trust K———— surely with a good part
of the painful business which is necessary—and it is necessary for *you*
to be tranquil & quiet, & rescue, so, your heart & brain from certain
evils of your position. I am very glad that M! Geo. Dawson will be
with you. But quiet, quiet! that is necessary. I beseech you my
dearest dearest friend, to spare yourself—& your health. You have
done beyond the work of *the love of women—that* was for others—the
memory belonging to you as a crown for your heart for ever & ever!
Now you must repose. Now you must be quiet! And if that too must
be *for others*, let it be for *me*—let it be (if my vanity does not exceed
in imagining such a thing) for *me*—& I will be very proud & thankful,
I promise you.

If you do not tell me *not* to send the paper, I mean to send it.

May God bless you in Jesus Christ! in Him who was 'made perfect', as a Savior, 'through suffering', —& of whom it is said 'He
wept', when men spoke to Him of the grave of a friend.

Does little Flush keep close to you? My Flush never sees me
shed tears without running to kiss me & rub his little brown ears
against my face. He learnt love from *you*. There is no wonder that he
sh.d be complete in his lesson.

Believe, my beloved friend, how near I am to you in thought, in
prayer, in sympathy of tender affection.

> And in all these things I
> am your EBB–

> Three-mile Cross
> Dec. 15 [*sic* for 13] 1842.

My Beloved Friend,—I thank you from the bottom of my heart for
your dear, precious letter. You would be astonished at my composure—*I* am. I have scarcely shed a tear since Saturday. And I woo
cheerful thoughts, and take all care of myself, as *he* would have
wished. If ever spirit were in heaven, *there*, through the mercy of
God, and the atonement of the Savior, is he—whose faith and trust
were in that mercy and that atonement—whose last moments were

peace—whose every thought was of kindness to man and trust in heavenly mercy through the mediation of the Redeemer. And so, feeling and knowing that to have kept him here, even if that had been possible, would have been to detain him amongst care and sorrow, in feebleness, helplessness, and suffering—it would indeed be a wicked selfishness, not to strive, with all my strength, for resignation and for cheerfulness.

It would be a base ingratitude to you, too, my beloved friend, and to the many, many kind and affectionate people who are around me. I can not tell you how good and kind every body is. It seems as if they were inspired with your spirit. Those whom he best loved will follow him. I have just strewn flowers over him (the lovely chrysanthemums that he loved so well, that he helped me to strew over my dear mother), and he looks with a heavenly composure, and almost with his own beautiful color, the exquisite vermilion for which he was so famous, on his sweet, serene countenance. I could not touch him. Mr. May desired me not. He said there was danger in renewing the chill, which has now passed away. I mean the shiverings. So that I am greatly better, my beloved friend, and when I get into the air again shall do well. Still, I am alone; that is the thought that clings to me, though when I think of you, sister of my heart, it presses less heavily.

I read Tennyson. "Locksley Hall" is very fine; but should it not have finished at

> "I myself must mix with action,
> Lest I wither by despair?"

It seems to me that all after that weakens the impression of the story, which has its appropriate finish with that line. What do we not owe to such a poet? One, who can be thought of at such a time!

I must limit my correspondence. I have written above a hundred letters; and now feel that some, who had real claims, have been forgotten. Heaven bless you, my beloved friend!

Ever faithfully yours,

M. R. M.

[WEDNESDAY] DEC. 14. 1842.

·   ·   ·

It is very very good of you to think of me at this time so as to take the trouble of directing Mr Schloss to send me a *Bijou*. When it comes it shall be a real jewel to me—because I shall value whatever is mine in it, for the sake of what is yours. And now for the reviews! I have an ague to think of them—never, I may truly say, was half so frightened of them as now . . never. Suppose it turns out that scissors of mine have clipped off your shadow & left you related to the Schemils!! –

You are probably quite right about the superfluity of the latter stanzas of Lockesly Hall, altho' I did not observe it at the moment. I always *mean* to buy those poems —and had it been done, I might have, as commentators say, 'examined the text'. Now I simply trust to you & am the further, probably, from error on that account. That Lockesly Hall *burns* with life & passion. What is your reason for refusing to the poet, the *constructive faculty*? I have been thinking & do not come to a result. It appears to me that there is more evidence in these volumes *for* the probable possession than against,—& that such a strong tragic soul works in the last poem we have spoken of, as would soon, if it willed, supply itself with a body. The "Two Voices"! What an astonishing power of subtle thought in a silver-vibrating language! He takes a high place, by that composition, among those metaphysical poets, who have (not Cowley as Johnson dreamed) but that high prince of riddledom, the thoughtful Ld Brooke[1] at their head.

I have heard that Mr Tennyson prefers to all his other works the 'Vision of Sin', at the end I think of the second volume or near the end. Do look at it. The opening is full of power,—the versification wonderful, giving proof of a master's hand . . & *wrist* too. Still, & notwithstanding Hazzlitt's dogma about authors always being right in the appreciation of their works —in which by the way I am tolerably sure that Mr Hazzlitt was wrong, . . I cannot rank this poem even with the poet's highest—much less *above* his highest. Can *you*?

Mr Browning's last 'Bells & Pomegranates,[2] I sigh over. There are fine things—yes, and *clearly* fine things. But there is much in the little (for the publication consists of only a few pages) which I, who admire him, wish away—impotent attempts at humour,—a vain jangling with rhymes . . I mean of *mere* rhymes . . and a fragmentary roughedgedness about the *mounting* of some high thoughts. It is astonishing to me that it occurs to nobody else . . but when he rises into the Drama . . his manner of being graphic & passionate reminds me so of M.r Landor that I am absolutely startled. There are no particular imitations, but the manner strikes me as identical. It *did*, in that magnificent, passionate scene in Pippa Passes, which M.r Horne so justly praises. Is my imagination in fault? I sh.d not be sorry if it were. I admire M.r Browning; & recognize him always as a true original poet whenever I consider,—& that is not seldom,—how great a thing it is to be one.

•   •   •

[EBB]

1. Fulke Greville, Lord Brooke (1554–1628), Renaissance poet, courtier, and biographer of his friend Sir Philip Sidney.
2. *Dramatic Lyrics*, the third in his series *Bells and Pomegranates*, had appeared in November 1842 and contained "My Last Duchess" and "Soliloquy of the Spanish Cloister" among others.

[MONDAY] JANY. 2. 1842 [SIC FOR 1843]

•   •   •

Ah my beloved friend, how the foreshadowing of my improbable book stirs you into goodness & zeal—I have scarce so much zeal myself for it—I have cooled down wonderfully already since my first thought that way, & when I talked of it to Papa I fancied that *he* was a little bit cool & inclined to think that miscellaneous poems w.d not answer so well as I opined, without a poem of importance to make the introductions. In fact I was half inclined to give the matter up until next year again . . when your letter comes & relights me: & certainly my own view *is*, that a volume of miscellanies would answer & that a subsequent publication w.d appear with some advantage by my stirring a little now—& then, I have such a recoiling for good & bad reasons, from publishing poetry in the magazines—prose being altogether a different business, & engaged in with an altogether different sort of constituency! But after all, I am not earnest about publishing this year– Perhaps I may not do it after all. If you were to ask M.r Chorley, would it be necessary to *do the thing*—or could you ask as a matter of theory & hypothesis? As to *trusting* him, believing in his "*safety*," why of course I would & do. My only shrinking is from giving unnecessary trouble.

M.ʳ Kenyon & I talked a very little on the subject when he was here last, & he was a good deal surprised, he said, that Moxon sh.ᵈ have answered so decidedly. I myself however was by no means, surprised. I was Jeremiah the prophet all the way through, & had a second sight of the answer– M.ʳ Moxon told George that he *c.ᵈⁿᵗ* "push" a poem—that a poem w.ᵈⁿᵗ be pushed—& that all the poets, except Tennyson in his last publication, perished with him. Perhaps you are right as to M.ʳ Moxon: & there may be a larger worm at the root of his gourd than even unsaleable poetry.

I must interrupt myself to ask a question about a phenomenon. Did you ever experience a remarkable crisis of the intellect or hand, during which you have a tendency to spell every word wrong, to turn your *whiches* into *witches*– your *woulds* into *woods*, & to talk of the *pail* of the church? I do assure you that throughout this letter I have been on the brink of orthographical ruin—it has been an effort with me to keep pace with the 3.ᵈ class of a charity school in spelling. I positively wrote *improble* for improbable, or was about to commit myself with a lamentation upon the prospects of unsailable poetry.

To go back to my book—if it *be* a book, it will consist of your two ballads, 'The brown rosarie' & 'Romance of the Page,' & another unfinished ballad which shall be finished—& several poems of eight or ten pages to fifteen or twenty pages in length . . in brief, with all my thoughts in verse since my last volume went to press. I might make nearly as large a volume as the former one—but my wish is to compress it to a five shilling book – It w.ᵈ be more judicious in many ways, I think– Do not you? There can be no objection to Whittaker who did I believe publish the 'Chaucer Modernized' on his own account—but then, it w.ᵈ not do to force the poor man into a risk, or unless he embraces it willingly to consent that he sh.ᵈ undertake it. You are too kind in all things ⟨&⟩ wishes—ah yes!– may th⟨is year⟩ be happier than the last ⟨for⟩ you, dearest friend! Y.ʳ EBB

You do not say how you are. May God bless you. I will finish my letter another day.

.   .   .   [FEBRUARY? 1843]

Mr Cary's[1] report of the state of things at Oxford scarcely surprises me—and yet . . Carlyle's Hero-worship to be cast out!! Is it not the open confession that nobody there is a hero, or wishes to be a hero, or cares for anybody who *is*? I think so. As to Mr Newnam,[2] I had heard of his precedence in action to Dr Pusey, & indeed held in my hand, a book of his containing "the full sum" of Puseyism, before Dr Pusey began to fast. I also know his brother[3] who was a missionary with Mr Groves in India, after thundering over the university with "first class" talents,—returned with him to England, connected himself with the Plymouth brethren, & altho' detected by them in Arian views, triumphantly & in spite of controversy married a Plymouth sister, & settled at Bristol . . where I believe (at least I know nothing to the contrary) he continues to lecture. "*First-class*" *talents* I said: I was *told* so—I did not guess it. I heard him preach at the schoolroom at Sidmouth, where the Plymouth Brethren (you have heard of that sect) were in the habit of preaching, & where I occasionally went to hear them. His preaching was so very simple, that it seemed to me on the verge of being silly. One word faltered after another—words of two syllables—& sentences of two words—brevity without force—the very pith of commonplace. But he spoke the truth: & when his bride whom I never took for a bride (he was only ten days in winning her!) asked me what I thought of Mr Newnam, . . I answered that he seemed to know what truth was, better than he knew how to say it. Afterwards, I met him at a friend's house, & drank tea with him. A circle of women hung upon the articulations of his lips. He spoke very much as he preached—only he said 'yes' & 'no' a good deal oftener, those being his chief rhetorical figures in conversation. And then people asked me, what I thought of Mr Newnam? Why, what c.^d I think? He had a little half-smile in continuity, which I did'nt like,—he never said a word indicative of a thing beyond a commonplace. So I thought he was rather weak, & very dull, & by no means worth any thinking of!– Presently came the surprise. A friend of his, a fellow of a college, opened out the whole thunder-cloud to us. Mr Newnam of Oxford was a powerful man—but *this* Mr Newnam, *my* acquaintance at Sidmouth, was a Hercules to him —a *most* powerful man, . . a wonderful man. When he was at Oxford, he carried the first classes before him in a whirlwind,—& if he had breathed, the whole university w.^d have been scattered like dust. Equal to anything! Astonishing abilities! The professors bowed down to the skirts of his garment —the Dons were confounded in his presence—he was a hero without Carlyle!– You may imagine my confusion. I resolved never to call anybody dull, who was dull at tea time again.

M͞r Haydon has had the goodness to send me two admirable horses['] heads—& his studies for the Curtius, the Saragossa, & the Adam & Eve cartoon. The suggestions are delightful to me—& I lie here & dream dreams of these completions.

M͞r Kenyon—"Will I see him for a moment?" To be sure, I will– And so ends my letter–

> Ever your own
> EBB.

1. Henry F. Cary (1772–1844) was a translator of Dante and had been assistant librarian at the British Museum.

2. John Henry Newman (1801–90) (later Cardinal), whose name EBB consistently misspells, a leader of the Oxford Movement, published a retraction of his criticisms of the Roman Catholic Church in the *Conservative Journal* for February 1843; Edward B. Pusey (1800–82) was professor of Hebrew at Oxford and also prominent in the Oxford Movement.

3. Francis William Newman (1805–97), a classical scholar and lecturer in mathematics and brother of John Henry, held religious views opposite those of his brother. The Plymouth Brethren, founded in 1828, advocated antisectarianism and austere living.

[FRIDAY] [3? MARCH 1843]

* * *

My hopes had advanced the subscription beyond the £500. But I suppose that after just the first gathering from persons more immediately on the spot, there w͞d probably be an intermediate pause before persons at a distance could "come up to pole". Do, whenever you can write to me my dearest friend, let me know what number you have reached. No breathing being feels more anxiety than I do on the subject altogether—nor has *felt* more.

My dearest friend, it is not absolute obstinacy which drives me to America. I am not tempted to overstate the amount of talent in America . . far less to prefer the companionship of the poets there to those in my own country. But if you c͞d see the letters, the kindnesses

I have received from thence, you w^d not advise me to say 'no'– I confess I have not the heart for saying 'no'—the kindness has overcome
me– *You*, to whom everybody is kind,—who move worthily in an atmosphere of applause,—can scarcely guess how near the tears are to
the edge of the eyes, when kinder words than are said to you at
home, come from a strange country. Not that I complain, even to myself, of *un*kindness at home– On the contrary, I have always confessed
that for the most part both critics & readers have been as kind to me
here, as I had any reason for expecting. Still I c^d not say 'no' to those
kind Americans. To prove the reality of the kindness, the editor of
Graham's miscellany offers to me just four times over the remunera-
tion I sh^d receive here—two guineas for the briefest fragment . .
three guineas & a half for anything longer: the London magazines giving half a guinea for a closely printed page full– You will acquit me
of being influenced by the pecuniary consideration of this arrangement—& indeed to Mr Lowell[1] of Boston who said he was poor &
wanted my mss for nothing, I sent them on his own terms. I love the
Americans (altho' I never saw one of them in my life) I love them for
kin's sake & freedom's sake—& I am, besides, grateful to them for
being kind to me–

· · ·

My poor Flush. He was sitting on my sofa wagging his tail into
the very ecstasies of a tail (if you understand the metaphysics & phys-
ics of *that*) while he watched Arabel lacing on her boots. She said to
him "Flush, I cant take you out with me. I am going to the bazaar."
The tail stopped. Poor Flushie! He turned round & looked at me,—
significantly, as he always does in trouble,—and then began to cry!–
What do we mean by *understanding*?

May God bless you, my dearest friend.

Ever your attached
EBB–

'Montague, Eleonora Louisa,[2]
Was there ever such name between Paris & Pisa' . .
do you remember Leigh Hunt in the 'Feast of the violets'? Is she M^rs
or Miss Montague?—and do you know her personally?

Mr Kenyon calls Christopher North a 'glorious brute'—*I* call him
a "brute-angel". Both of us like him far better than you do. Oh

surely, surely, he is a great poet . . in prose! I am reading the *Recreations*—3ᵈ volume.³

Did you see, . . what I am reading just too late (but we must be benighted sometimes) in the number before the last of the Edinburgh Review, a notice of Maᵈᵐᵉ d'Arblay, very admirable in all ways, but chiefly interesting to you for the sake of the high estimate of your Miss Austen, who is called *second* to *Shakespeare* in the nice delineation of character.

1. James Russell Lowell (1819–91), American poet and editor of *Graham's Magazine* and, in 1857, first editor of the *Atlantic Monthly*.
2. Eleanora Montagu (1811–1903), English writer of poems and tales.
3. John Wilson, the *Blackwood's* writer, published *The Recreations of Christopher North* in 1842.

[WEDNESDAY] APRIL 26. 1843.

My beloved friend I have received your letter & the seeds & thank you for both—& the books can well be waited for. In the meanwhile you are in sad spirits . . or *were* . . . . & seem to go to Bath in a spiritual Box tunnel scarcely less gloomy than the actual one. As to the will & my literary executorship I smile at it instead of sighing, & think to myself how very little likely, according to all human probabilities, it is, that *I* should survive *you* & be called on to do more with your mss, than thank you, as I do now, most truly & tenderly, for such a proof of trust in me & affection for me. No, No, my dearest friend. By all that you say, you only persuade me further of the necessity of this journey & of the good it is likely to do you. You have life in you for thirty years & more, if God's will shᵈ be so,––& supposing that you are wise & serene & walk in the sunshine & open your heart to the south wind. Agitations & anxieties such as have shaken you lately, *will* leave, for a time, a trembling in the frame & sensibilities,—but after a while, these will pass . . and a new tide of calm & gentle feelings will flow back upon the sand. I look at your letter & think––"Ah! by this time, perhaps, she begins to be better"—& so I comfort myself. But let me have more comfort soon . . if you can with truth. I dont like, in the midst of all my wisdom, to think of you in low spirits . . so very depressed as this last little note makes out—so write to me & tell me, if you can, that you are reviviving [*sic*]. Write to me at any rate. Oh but I am sure to have plenty of letters during this journey, for the sake of my Public! –

* * *

I hear that M! Browning has two new tragedies, one of them near the press, viâ Belles & Pomegranates, & one near the stage, viâ M! Charles Kean[1]— & for this last I am sorry.

Not a moment more to write in! But I was under a vow to myself to write something to you today, & this is the something! May God bless you. Tell me that you like Bath *as a vision* . . . because I do. There is an attraction to me in the look of its mountainous streets & of the hills visible through the vistas of marble.

Ever your own
EBB.

* * *

1. Charles John Kean (1811?–68), the actor for whom Browning's *Colombe's Birthday* was probably intended. A second play, *A Blot in the 'Scutcheon,* was published in February 1843 as the fifth number of *Bells and Pomegranates.*

[THURSDAY] MAY 4– [1843]

Ever dearest Miss Mitford,

I *meant* to hear from you this morning, but I did'nt; & am only beginning to consider, now at three o'clock p.m., that I had no manner of reason for expecting such a thing. Your letter of yesterday was as water to the thirsty soul, & made me happy about you with the persuasion that you are getting on to be better & blyther, just as I c^d desire– Pure air to breathe—true friends to talk with—new & striking scenery to look at,—and old memories to consecrate & increase the present pleasure,––how c^d you not be better & blyther, even without Ben & Flush?– So now, if you please, I dont mean to be uneasy about you a bit more or longer—I give you notice of it!– You are with Miss Austen & Smollett . . to say nothing of Celia & Rosalind (you see how you make me invert the dignities of Shakespeare who taught me long ago to say Rosalind & Celia!) and Ps transfigured!– Altogether, that you sh^d remain another week at Bath, appears to me a wise step . . leading to enjoyment! I approve of it in spite of what you tell me about your presentiment of danger from arch-enchanting bishops at Prior Park,[1]. . for after all, I am not very much afraid that you will ever put your conscience in the keeping of the most fascinating of men. The good sense & clear judgment predominate in you too much—you are not a woman to go over in a rapture & a puff of incense into the belief of an infallible Pope—& therefore I am not afraid– For the rest I w^d not willingly speak with disrespect of Roman catholic Christians.

I have come into Papa's room, the adjoining room to mine, . . for the first time today—to have the windows opened & a little dusting done . . which will make me cleaner & more exemplary tomorrow– The consequence of living through the winter in one room, with a fire, day & night, & every crevice sealed close, . . you may imagine perhaps by the help of your ideal of all Dustfulness, latent & developped. At last we come to walk upon a substance like white sand, & if we dont lift our feet gently up & put them gently down, we act Simoom, & stir up the sand into a cloud. As to a duster or a broom, seen in profile even, ... calculate the effect upon us!–The spiders have grown tame—& their webs are a part of our own domestic œconomy,––Flush eschews walking under the bed. The result of which is that I am glad May is come, that I yield to that necessity at once– May God bless you—& give you health,—& gladness by its means! Write to me—do—! Your writing reeled from your pen in this letter! I never remember observing that it trembled so before. May God keep you, my dearest dearest Miss Mitford.

Yes, I have been in Bath twice—once when I was quite a child & we travelled *through* it & I did not stir from the hotel door—& once on our way from Herefordshire to Sidmouth, a few years since, when I was too weak & out of health to stir from the hotel window. We spent one night there on the latter occasion, & I gathered my impressions from my place at the window (. . of the York House) & in passing through the streets. So you see how right you were in telling me everything, & how much ignorance there is in me to disperse—& besides, if I knew the place by heart, I sh^d like to look at it through your stained-glass-idiosyncrasy, as you may readily guess. That my impressions, snatched up at random, & *your* impressions, sh^d have a shade of likeness, is delightful to me! As you found by my letter, & as I always said, Bath is the very ideal of a town to me,—worth a hundred Cheltenhams, notwithstanding those noble avenues which almost save Cheltenham! But as a *town* . . I choose Bath: it is a fine birth of its own hills . . marble of their marble, heart of their heart . . almost grand with their spirit. The Bath town-scenery is the noblest I ever saw . . apart from associations—and if I had to live in a town which was not London, I would rather live at Bath than anywhere, I think. Oh—the great nature stooping to look into the humanity, as those hills seem to me to do!—and the great human quarry eyed constantly by the Nature! how striking it all is! – Your description has refreshed & revived my impressions, & I stand close by you with open eyes!– Ah—but if I did so really, I should be looking at *you*—

Tell me if you found Mrs Trollope & whether she is recovering from the lakes. I am afraid 'the Widow' is not in the next New Monthly—making no sign in the advertisements.

· · ·

But I must tell you first that Mr Browning is said to have finished two plays, one for Charles Kean & the public, the other for himself & Bells & Pomegranates. I am sorry. He appears to me capable of most dramatic effluences & passionate insights—& it w^d be wise in him I think to spend this faculty upon poems which the sympathizing c^d read, rather than on plays cast to the mercy of the great unwashed who cant read right. And besides . . you will say, (altho' *I* have the grace to feel that I ought'nt to say it . .) acting a play of Mr Browning's, is like reading a riddle-book right through without stopping to guess the answers!– Something like . . perhaps. Yet after all, he is a true soul-piercing poet—and it is easier to find a more faultless writer than such a one—

Mr Kenyon met four & twenty . . . not fiddlers . . but harmonious spirits in different degrees, at your friend Mr Chorley's the other evening. The new German wonder M^r D . . . . . (I really am afraid to write him down, so little sure of him am I) raised thunderclouds & lightenings out of the piano forte . . and Moscelles, who is only a demi-god followed the miraculous with his heroic—and Adelaide Sartoris sang like a spirit—and Mrs Butler read Shakespeare.[2] And your Mr Chorley lives in an enchanted house in Victoria Square . . (a new square with tiny houses)—in a sort of golden . . not "vinegar bottle" . . but *vinaigrette* . . with ceilings & chairs of gold, & hangings of silken crimson– "It is like a jewelcase," says Mr Kenyon—and Mr Chorley lives like a ruby in the glory of it.

Poor little Flushie!—and Ben!—I like his letter . . . and that expressive . . "hardly" . . after the pause!

Tell me who is at Bath to see & admire you besides Miss James. I am so glad she is there—it is a comforting thought that you have a true friend near you after all—but do write to me for I am anxious. Do you see Mr Landor? Mrs Trollope? anybody else worth seeing?—any Ps.?

May God bless you, dearest friend. I never heard Mr Jay, & very likely sh.^d not admire him—but he is a good man with wide influence.

Ever your EBB–

1. Prior Park, near Bath, with its Palladian mansion and magnificent grounds, was at this time a Benedictine school directed by Bishop Peter Augustine Baines (1787–1843).
2. Adelaide Kemble Sartoris (1814–79), opera singer, and Fanny Kemble Butler (1809–93), actress, were daughters of the actor Charles Kemble.

[WEDNESDAY] MAY. 24, 1843.

My dearest Miss Mitford your letters are delightful, & mine sh.^d be grateful,—and will try to be so,—for the letter upon letter, . . . two at once, . . which I hold in my hands. If you ever *did* travel round the world (not that I think you ever will) and wrote to me at every stage, I sh.^d be as little likely to grumble, as at the voice of the lark you wrote about for the bazaar. No, no! you cant possibly send me too many letters. For now, I will confess to you!– I like letters *per se* . . & as letters! I like the abstract idea of a letter—I like the postman's rap at the door—I like the queen's head upon the paper—and with a negation of queen's heads (which does'nt mean treason) I like the sealing wax under the seal and the postmark on the envelope. Very seldom have I a letter which I w.^d rather *not* read—altho' very often do I write letters which I w.^d rather not write. Even people's stupidities emit a flash of liveliness to my eyes, between the breaking of the seal & the closing of the letter—and people's vivacities grow of course more vivacious in proportion. Perhaps this is almost natural considering my solitude, altho' it astonishes you: but certainly it will explain to you if nothing in the world could (which is an impossible hypothesis) how 'nine times nine' delightful and welcome the full measure of your letters must be. Who w^d not be delighted to have your letters? rich with life & colour & perfume as they are—dewy all over, with the breath of the south wind between the leaves? Well—triple the delight of everybody,—and you may guess at mine! Thank you my dearest friend!—thank you!—

I agree at once that you have proved your wisdom in coming back, by being better since,—and admit willingly, as Mr Kenyon does, that the weather helps to justify you abundantly. Also K's "passiveness", I observe from your description of it, had the occult element within side of it, of an irresistible activity. If I had been she, I w^d certainly have *pushed you on*—and perhaps I sh^d have been, and probably I sh^d have been, proved very wrong afterwards. But with that sort of passiveness at one side of you, & that untried difficulty before you, & that illness with its peculiar depressiveness, within you, I cannot certainly wonder that you sh^d dissolve your resolutions & turn homewards. As to Ben, he is a household god of himself, & worthy of all honor. No, I dont wonder at all that you sh^d prize him as you do— and it must indeed have been delightful to you to receive in such a welcome, a proof of such cordial attachment. I admire Ben afar off, & am grateful to him for his love to you— At the same time, whether he & Tom Thumb & a poney carriage will furnish you with the best means of travelling through Yucatan in August, I am not sure: because, you see, altho' the programme of it all sounds delightful, & this stepping leisurely from hillock to hillock, *is* the most perfect way of seeing the scenery & dreaming wayside dreams, yet I have fears that you may find it very expensive . . four or five times as expensive as the ordinary fashion is, . . & also liable to a thousand & one casualties which might end in serious embarrassment. You couldn't travel with a poney above twenty miles a day, . . I mean on successive days: and if you did so, do you calculate the multiplication of lodging & board,—and take into consideration the possible contingency of poor Tom Thumb's falling lame in Yucatan & leaving you to moralize upon solitude? Nevertheless there is time enough between now & August both for dreaming & reasoning—and indeed I hope my beloved friend, that we two may talk about it face to face here in London, before then—unless *you* have made "rash vows" against travelling except in August, with a Cæsar for patron saint of your *Augustalia*.

Of Mr Haydon's biography, I only have seen what extends to his twenty first or second year; but he promises to let me see the rest as he writes it, and I have no doubt of finding *you* in the midst of other notabilities. I was however wrong in telling you (and I think I did tell you) that Bentley had accepted his mss. I understood so from M.ʳ Haydon's expression to me; but it appears now that the said mss have not yet been offered to Bentley, and that the prospectus of the five successive volumes of four hundred pages each, is the writer's own theory on the subject.

Ah!—the popular poet writes verily most tender controversy!—& if this is the milk of human & Christian kindness, the cows thereof must have been fattened upon very bitter herbs! And then the Miss Mary Russell Mitford, *authoress*—forgive me, but I could'nt help smiling at the discretion of the missionary! Ah! he knew—or *she* knew— how "to come over you"—charming you with the voice of the Charmer most charmingly– Still & more gravely my dearest friend, & admitting all the miserable taste & judgment of this meddling zeal-without-knowledge, I will try to smooth your brow which M.ʳˢ Schimmelpenninck (O ye gods, what a name! & what a broad foundation for your theory about names!) did so well to admire, by suggesting that a very good & affectionate motive was probably at the bottom of the whole act, and that your missionary, in sending the Reverend Montgomery[1] to you, performed after all only an analogical act to the one K. contemplated, of 'sending for M.ʳ May.' Therefore do forgive, & take a brighter view of the whole action! Forgive "authoress" & all—everything & body except the Rev.ᵈ Robert's spirit of controversy, which, together with his faculty in poetry, I deliver over to you without a word about mercy. How much true heartedness & warm-heartedness may lie beneath an action of the straightest sect of the Pharisees to all appearance!– I plead for the unknown.

M.ʳ Kenyon has given to me a gift of flourishing ivy—& it is spreading so over my window that I sometimes think the god is holding up the thyrsus just below, telling me to have courage. Do you know I hear, now & then, *the rustling of the leaves against the pane*—oh, sweet rural sound! I think it is rain, & turning round, it proves to be the leaves. Then, when the scarlet runners & nasturtiums, planted in the same box, spring up to entwine their vivacity with the graver ivy leaves——these are my dreams for the future–

M.ʳ Eagles must be well worthy of knowledge & admiration, but I *shall* not see him . . not liking to say 'I *will not*'. I have no courage for it; and if I had, there are others with a stronger claim. I take it upon your showing that he is delightful—and that his wife is more amiable & good tempered than the common Gossip sayeth. M.ʳ Landor is an incarnation of contradictions; & I wᵈ not, cᵈ not, receive his estimate of any power or person after that wonderfully foolish eccentricity of his about Mʳˢ Hemans's "variety," not if he enunciated his criticicisms [*sic*] with a voice like Apollo's lute. Why didn't you answer "Yes, she was very various– She could sing three notes divinely". He might as well praise Rabelais for purity —or M.ʳ Browning as you suggest, for clearness– Still M.ʳ Landor is a man of fine genius, & not far (if far at all) from being the noblest prose writer of the day. His style is quite sculpturesque,—so pure & white, & full of ideality & grand suggestion. Do you know his Pericles and Aspasia? It will live with the language, & triumph in its life presently—but is too classical for *us*, in this first roar of the steam engine.

· · ·

Mary Howitt's last translation from Frederika Bremer's swedish, "The Home" charms me even more than 'The Neighbours' did. The Athenæum compares these books to Miss Austen's, but I shᵈ be afraid to tell you exactly how I wᵈ modify the comparison.

You are 'happy as a queen' on a brick floor,—and sleep better on the hard pillow than "at court!" Thank God that you are better!

Ever your attached
EBB.

1. Rev. Robert Montgomery (1807–55), popular religious poet, and minister of a chapel in St. Pancras.

[MONDAY] JUNE 19. 1843.

· · ·

I have written your message to M.ʳ Horne from whom I had just heard, . . he having the kindness to send me three copies, besides an order for getting for *you* tomorrow, five & twenty copies from the third edition![1]—& he is not at all better, I am sorry to say, . . so that I am gladder than I shᵈ be at all events, of his being likely to visit you & take refreshment from the airs under your bay-tree. Afterwards,—I hope it will be only afterwards, but he says to me, 'directly',—he is going down to his mother at Brighton, away from all the work & wisdom, dust & glorious tribulation of this London of ours, . . & there, will learn, I trust, to be better. From what I can understand, he overworks himself in mind, hands, & imagination. He seems to me to talk all tongues, from Spanish to Syriac—is a director in a South American mine company,—writes reviews in divers quarterleys,—& commissioner-reports for government,—& dissertations upon the folios of Albertus Magnus,—& tragedies, & comedies, & histories of Napoleon— & Orions in the interstices of all! – The body will fail & faint sometimes under such a load of soul-work, & *no* BODY can wonder at it. I am very glad for other reasons too, that he is going to see you. Tell me what your judgement is. When you have seen the man, & I, only the picture, you will have an advantage over me; & I expect to profit from it through your communicativeness. Tell me everything—do!–

Dearest Miss Mitford—I have seen my uncle Hedley! He has come from abroad with three of his sons, to settle one at Oxford, & two at school,—& then to return to his family at Lausanne,—or Paris. It was a terrible struggle for me to see him . . with the great gulf of these three years between the last time & this now, & such thoughts as w^d be present—but I was able to cry, . . & cried till I was half blinded, & disabled with a headache for five days. 'My dear child— my dear child!—' he said——he is very tender. The tears stood in his eyes & ran over. He knew & loved the Dearest in the world to me,— & felt, I am sure, what was in my heart in my silence——for it was impossible for me to *speak* even then.

Dearest Miss Mitford . . you cannot think how I have dreaded to see him, ever since March when I heard that he meant to come "in the summer." I dreaded it so much that I c^d not speak of it even to *you* . . & when I heard his voice down stairs my heart seemed to move away from its place:—& to look in his face, seemed impossible. But it is over now—I thank God for *that*. He is the only one of my uncles whom living I love—& he is not really my uncle . . not in blood— only by marriage & kindness. And what an "only" that last is!–

•   •   •

As to O'Connell,[2] he has not a cloven foot I believe,—but really I w^d as soon rank him second to Napoleon, as Wilberforce first among great men. Can you guess what Stormie said to your opinion of Napoleon O'Connell? "Second to Napoleon,"—said he!—"Why Napoleon is not to be compared to him!"

I *think so too.*

After all, great or little, what is he doing or about to do in Ireland? Displaying singular & unscrupulous ability—playing at ninepins with the souls of men? and what more? Not carrying the Repeal certainly! Perhaps (& that will be a just & happy result) destroying the Irish Church Establishment!– But considering the blind apathy in England & the blind fury in Ireland, what may happen before such a result, is frightful to imagine. His *power* is the only certain thing. Is he not amusing the world by causing the Irish Nation to stand balanced on one toe on the single air-hung rope—— "This can I do". It makes me giddy to look on.

There! Now I am to go down stairs for the second time—& I shall be in a chair out of doors presently, though I dont "sleep on a ground floor."

Oh! the perverseness of certain persons!–

> Your own
> EBB–

Say how your ankle is. You do not walk lamely? Tell me!–

1. Of Horne's epic, *Orion*, which he sold for a farthing, thus becoming known as "the farthing poet."
2. Daniel O'Connell (1775–1847), Irish politician and orator, elected to Parliament from Dublin in 1828.

[MONDAY] SEPT. 4ᵗʰ 1843.

• • •

As you speak of review-writing as a line of literature not objectionable to you, why not write for the Athenæum rather than another periodical? There can be no difficulty—and Mʳ Chorley is at the doors if there *could* be any difficulty—& half a guinea a column is their pay. The objection is to the residence out of London—but still if the convenience shᵈ be less, the degree of inconvenience does not amount to an obstacle—and you might not dislike the *variety* in composition; & the irresponsibility might have its attraction for you. What periodical did Mʳ Horne mention? Perhaps you wᵈ prefer a ground for more elaborate articles—essays in fact,—in the manner of the Quarterleys.?

I heard from M.ʳ Kenyon the other day that poor Miss Martineau's desease has given evidence lately of increase,—& that the slight hope of her friends, founded upon the stationary character of her symptoms, is painfully vanishing. It is with something like . . nay, it is altogether like a regret for a friend, that I think of this—so deeply have her letters touched me & induced upon me a sense of the sweetness & benignity of her character as a woman. M.ʳˢ Jameson is going down to see her, M.ʳ Kenyon says, almost immediately. She can *enjoy* still with a sensibility lively as ever, but suffers intensely in the pauses of morphine which suspends the pain. Three times a week she takes this morphine. *Why not every day,* one naturally & ignorantly wonders—! A great & admirable woman to perish so, pang by pang!– But we do not, need not wonder at *that!* The cross is the Hieroglyphic of our Human destination.

To pass abruptly to another subject, do you read the Chuzzlewitts,[1] & are you not (if you do) *irritated* . . to use a meek word . . with M.ʳ Dickens for his ingratitude to the Americans? I am irritated in the precise sense of the word. I move about my head & hands & feet as if there was no repose for me, . . I am vexed at heart with the "true & lawful" (perhaps) but certainly very outrageously ungrateful & forgetful Boz. To think of a man . . a man with a heart . . going to a great nation to *be crowned*—for they did no less than crown him . . his travels from city to city amounted to a triumph—& then to come home & hiss at them with all the venom in his body!– The last number of Chuzzlewitt, & one former number, are worse than malignant—& M.ʳˢ Trollope is charity herself compared to the Boz of them! Is it not too bad—quite too bad? I am as angry as if I were an American.

• • •

I am ever your
EBB

1. *Martin Chuzzlewit,* Dickens's novel satirizing Americans, was serialized in monthly issues from January 1843 to July 1844.

Saturday. Sept. 15 [*sic* for 16]. 1843.

Victory & joy my beloved friend! Flush is at home!– He was recovered last night.

To give you the whole history of the hunting out of the banditti to their dens, w^d be very long. My brothers, . . through a suspicious intermediatory,—Bishop of Oxford Street, who knows *you* & who seems to me to have a great many too many intimate friends who deserve hanging, (at the other extreme end from YOU my dearest Miss Mitford!) to be quite without pretension himself—, became acquainted with one of the three great Agents of the dogstealers, . . Taylor, . . an ostensible cobler, but bearing, I hear, the mystery of iniquity not merely in his hand but his countenance. When Alfred (Daisy) went to this man the day before yesterday, he said at first, . . "You will never see your dog, Sir, again". "And why?". "Precisely because of your handbills. You have been so ill-advised as to make the affair known; the police are on the alert: and in all such cases, the custom of the FANCY is to send off the dogs in question instantly, either abroad or into the country– It is a fatal step, to make a loss known to the police". Daisy however persisted manfully,—& having a card from Bishop & an imperative message that he (Taylor) was to find the dog, *upon his head*——"We will see, Sir, however," said the villain,—"what we can do. Leave me; and in two hours time I shall be in Wimpole Street with news of the dog—and if he is still in London & in the hands of the Fancy, you shall come with me & receive him at another place." This was the day before yesterday morning. At eight oclock in the evening when everybody was at dinner, Daisy was called into the hall to Taylor. "I have found the dog" said the wretch, "give me five pounds, & come in a cab with me to the place". Daisy had received instructions from myself to hesitate at no price whatever; but I unfortunately being low at the time in my finances & forced to borrow for the occasion, & he aware of this, he made some movement towards the dining room to get the money from Papa. Now Papa has an inveterate repugnance always to being what he calls "imposed upon",—& on this account, a good deal of our diplomacy, which went upon the HOPE *of being imposed upon in exchange for Flush*, was kept advisedly from him. At the proposition of "five pounds", he arose in indignation, got up from dinner to thunder thunderbolts against the agent of the Fancy, told him that he was a rascal, that he (Papa) w^d give not a farthing more than two sovereigns . . unless he gave *himself* (the agent) into the charge of the police; & that as to the dog, it & he might go!– The effect was immediate. Taylor smiled significantly at Daisy, & observed as he passed through the door, . . "You will never see your dog again".

My horror & distress when I came to hear of this, you may imagine. Papa said, 'Say nothing of this to Ba'—but the voices were loud,—& I had been listening all day for a whisper. My brothers told me that they feared to stir any more in the matter, as Papa had said that he w^d take it into his own hands. I never slept (or scarcely) for the second night.

Yesterday morning however, my resolution rose up into action, through hearing, as Henry did from Bishop, that the "Fancy"–people were capable of cutting the dog's throat if it did not bring them exactly what they calculated on receiving. I knew that Papa's plan was to proceed *by police*—& to leave the case pendent & my Flushie unenquired about for a few days, until the expectations of the right honorable "Fancy" came down to the two sovereigns. My despair overcame my sense of obedience! I sent down to Bishop, the *three sovereigns*, to persuade the other party to take *the two* & say no more about it. Is it a pardonable equivocation? Think . . of his throat being cut, poor little creature! It is not better to be imposed on a hundred times over?——— Imposition, I always think, disgraces the imposer, & not the imposed upon—although men, & particularly some men, are otherwise minded. Taylor came here and agreed to meet Henry at Bishop's with the dog—insisting besides on half a guinea more for his own share in the recovery—that is, for calling himself a cobler ("Boots neatly mended here!") when he is a dogstealer by trade. Henry agreed to everything, went down to Bishop's, & identified Flush who rushed up to him, kissing him eagerly, as Henry says, & then drank at a basin of water, which accidentally was in the room, as if the whole world's thirst were on his tongue. Taylor observed (the savage!—) "Yes! he is thirsty. And when you get him home you had better give him something to eat instantly, for he has ate nothing & drunk nothing since he has been with the Fancy"!– He said also with most marvellous coolness, "that they had been for two years on the watch for Flush, & that they had hoped to get hold of him the other day when he was out with the lady in the chair, as he had been several times lately." Conceive the audacity!—and the hardheartedness!! They must have guessed at my state of health, by the very movement of the chair,— drawn for a few steps & then resting!—and to calculate cooly on such an opportunity of taking away the little dog of which I was obviously so fond!– I said so to my brothers; & they laughed. "Hardheartedness! Why they w^d have cut your own throat for five pounds"!– And that is true.

Mr Taylor's parting consolation was to this effect. "Well Sir! If you lose your dog again whether in London or the country, come to me and I will recover him for you". Most marvellous audacity!—meaning of course . . (as you translate from Araminta) "If you lose your dog again whether in town or country, you may be sure that *I* am at the bottom of it".

The cab with Henry & Flush in it was at our door about eight oclock yesterday evening. Crow looking from a front window cried out "Flush is come"—and the minute afterwards I heard him gallopping up the stairs & felt his rapturous leaps & carresses upon my face & hands. Darling, darling little Flushie! He seemed bewildered, . . heartfull . . overfull of joy & wonder at finding us! I cried anew for pleasure,—and embraced & kissed him all over twenty times, dirty as he was, black as he was, palpably black with the soot & dust of their lothly dens. Then we gave him his favorite minced meat—and he refused to eat . . would not eat at all at first, from being so heartfull. It was only by degrees that the appetite developped itself from the loving nature! Yet his joy after the first hour, has broken out, only in fits. He lay on my pillow, & w.^d not be called down, . . & seemed grave & dispirited. He seems so this morning I think—& in the night he moaned & was restless. Perhaps he is not quite well from the terror & the long fasting—he is certainly thinner than when he went away. But oh! the joy of having him back! the joy on all sides! The raptures of the little creature were most affecting,—& his way of throwing himself at last into his old place on my pillow & refusing to move from it,—as if he were aware of enemies beyond, . . touched me very much. Oh, we shall take good care of him now! He never shall go from the house . . to walk in the streets, . . without a collar & chain; & he must learn to bear for the sake of safety, the discipline & restraint of the chain.

My dear Papa was delighted to come home & find Flush, & has not put me on an inquest for the means. I hear indeed that he asked Henrietta what I paid for him, & that she said "The reward of two sovereigns, I believe,—but really I know very little about it"—which was true, for everybody except Henry & me, had been out of the house all day. "Ah" remarked Papa—"two sovereigns! and I dare say, three besides". Which is true also—but I hope I shant be questioned. In fact the recovery of my Flushie has cost me somewhere about *seven* sovereigns, rather more than less!—but if it had been seventy instead, it w.^d not have spoilt my great joy in seeing him again–

Thank you my beloved friend for your kindest sympathy of this morning. I knew that you w^d be sorry. I love Flush twice over, you are aware . . for himself, once—and once for *you*.

Was the dog you lost, a spaniel? My dread was that the month of September w^d be fatal to Flush, & that he w^d be sent into the country on the strength of his drooping ears. Only people kept saying that he w^d be tried with a live rabbit before any such proceeding,—& he was sure to prove his absolute innocence of blood, whether of rabbit or mouse, if they tried him so!–

I am so glad you were "silly" like me—I save my reputation by it! To justify me to myself there was no need.

Here's a long letter—& from one who began by meaning not to be "very long". Sette's adventures (for three of my brothers like the three eastern princes set out different ways after a dog!) w^d take longer to tell—& how he met dark men in dark alleys; & how he drew a fallacious hope from the ultra blackguardism of a certain Jim Green who talked pure Alsatian,[1] & was just setting out for a dog-fight to meet "lots of dogstealers," prime men & his intimate friends.–

I have written enough today—& perhaps more than enough!— only you might care to hear some of the details of the 'victory', I thought, not merely for Flush's sake & my sake, but from your general *philodogery*. Oh, to transport the Fancy!! May God bless you my beloved friend.

Ever your attached
EBB.

What of Araminta?

We have had very animated good news from the travellers. I sh⟨^d have⟩ told you that in spite of my directions to keep clear of the police (I was so afraid of losing Flush in the uproar—so ready with all courtesy to the thieves, if they w^d but let me have him back!) ⟨. . .⟩ Henry had arranged for a policeman in plain clothes to follow his cab in another, & help him to secure the thief as soon as they had the dog. A difference in the hour, however caused this plan to fail.

---

1. Dialect of the inhabitants of Whitefriars, a section of London regarded as a sanctuary for criminals.

LONDON

Fame and
New Friendships
1843–44

In late 1843 and early 1844, as MRM settled into an unaccustomed leisure and EBB became involved in production of her new volume of poetry, the exchange of letters decreased somewhat in frequency. EBB's show contrasting sides of her personality. Although she had forcefully defended the public's right to information about celebrities (this in response to MRM's complaints about her privacy having been violated by published descriptions of the Mitford household), EBB was distraught at having to replace her personal maid. Her fears were unfounded, however, as the new maid, Elizabeth Wilson, remained with her and proved invaluable in the later move to Italy. By August, as she nervously awaited the reception of *Poems* (1844), just published by Edward Moxon (1801–58), EBB followed with interest—and with a wariness surprising in view of her later embracing of spiritualism—the increasingly popular phenomenon of mesmerism. With MRM enjoying a foreign-library subscription from EBB and contemplating a trip to Paris, the two avidly read the latest French novelists. Most striking at this time is EBB's replacing of male mentors with women role-models. In September she began a lasting friendship with the art critic Anna Brownell Murphy Jameson (1794–1860), whose professionalism and independence, as a self-supporting divorcée, she had long admired. She also corresponded with the journalist and political economist Harriet Martineau (1802–76) whose courage in the mesmeric

140

debates she envied (and whose well-known prickliness is graphically revealed in EBB's 28 September 1844 letter). She acknowledged her admiration of the French novelist Aurore Dudevant (1804–76), known as George Sand, in two sonnets in the 1844 volume despite warnings from conservatives like Henry Chorley that such public approval of the unconventional Mme. Sand might harm EBB's rising literary reputation.

[WEDNESDAY] DEC 27. 1843

My dearest Miss Mitford that you sh^d ever for a moment conclude from my silence, that I was tired of *you*, is an extravagance of conjecture I did not attribute to you!– The fact is I have *not* been well, & had a good deal of perforce writing to do notwithstanding; & then I did not like to write briefly to you with the news of my being unwell, & so buzz in your ear with a disquieting thought to no good end. I caught cold in a mystery. Fancy my catching cold through my hermetical sealing! I caught a very ordinary cold,—just such a cold as I might have caught if I had walked out in a December moonshine without my bonnet,—and I had a dry hard cough every time I opened my mouth to say even "yes" or "no" in a whisper,—and grew weak & unwell with it,—& moreover with a chest & bloodvessels made of glass, had very good reason to expect the catastrophe of spitting blood, with every breath. The catastrophe however has not happened—no sign of any rupture has appeared—and after some ten days of absolute quiet & silence I am recovering my voice & losing my cough. So now it is all over, or all *but* over, & I write of the past rather than the present, your kindness may lie down quietly on its sofa & go to sleep,—if it can—only its eyes are always too wide open for sleeping– Dear Mr Kenyon I have been obliged to refuse to see twice. It was impossible to talk. Even Flush had to be satisfied with pats upon his ears—and he—dear little thing,—quite seemed to understand, & was more unwilling than ever to leave the room. Well—& this is enough of me, I am sure. And if I say so much, it is because a cough is a matter of life or death with me—a hinge on which the door may turn either out or in. But it is shut now,—& in the course of being locked for the nonce.

•   •   •

Did you read the very powerful "Song of the Shirt" by Hood, printed in Punch, & now going the round of the papers? It is full of tragic sympathy & power—& despite your indisposition towards Hood, you will not touch the end of it unmoved. It was in the Athenæum of a week or two ago—

Also have you seen Wordsworth's Inscription for the grave of Southey? – I will send it to you if you have not,—and yet there is not much in it that is worthy of either of the great men. Is it possible for genius to grow old?—or to sink so deep in laurels as to be unable to stir a hand freely? But this poet's genius is not & never was, monumental & concentrative in its character—he never c^d say great things briefly,—and in that fact perhaps, lies the better reason for an obvious feebleness.

And yet again, how nobly he tolls his sonnets—he is concentrative enough in *them*: and he might have tolled a noble sonnet, one w^d think, over this grave.

Mr Kenyon left word three days ago that he was going to Devonshire in five or six,—& I hope I shall be able to see him for one half hour before he goes.

My sympathies like yours have been with the daughters, rather than with the step-mother, in the Southey case, be sure!– And although not agreeing with you that the poetry of Caroline Bowles[1] (the Birthday & the minor verses) is "meretricious",—nay, seeming to see in it much tender simplicity, freshness & moral sweetness, I do not class it or herself highly as poet & poetry, & am aware of the feebleness essentially,—the want of reach of mind & imagination. It is strange! But certainly I sh^d have fancied that with *you*, some portions of the Birthday . . the fishing scenes with her father in the sweet rural cheerfulness of their details—the passage about the clock—& various other points of the poem,—would have found ready sympathy & favor. Well—I never c^d have fancied that *I* sh^d be found pointing out these things to *you*, & that *you* sh^d call them "meritricious"! Oh no, my dearest friend!—not "meretricious" surely—that is, if I know the meaning of the imputation. She is a female half of Cowper—without his force, variety & originality—without in fact his genius— . . or his gloom. The Churchyard chapters indeed are some what too full of "the trick of sighing" —but then the subject exacted black bombazeen, & there was scarcely a way of escape. Her other works are serene & cheerful, I think. Oh—she is no favorite of mine. I speak without a prejudice "*for*"—either personal or literary.

The Christmas Carol strikes me much as it does you. I dont like the machinery—which is entangled with allegory & ghostery—but I like & admire the mode of the working out—& the exquisite scenes about the clerk & little Tiny; I thank the writer in my heart of hearts for them.

Dearest friend, I hope you received a little fish which I sent upon an embassy to represent me who was mute as a fish! Heart to heart, my dearest Miss Mitford, indeed! Wishes warm as the Yule log are with you at Christmastime & always.

Your most affectionate
EBB.

Thank you thank you for the seal! Ah—& I am ashamed to say that it has fallen somewhere—but it *shall* be found.

My book is not out of its MS yet—and I am very busy with it.

1. Caroline Bowles (1786–1854), Southey's second wife, whom he married in 1839. Her *Chapters on Churchyards* (1829) were vignettes of rural scenes often prompted by a name on a gravestone; *The Birthday* (1836) was a long poem.

[FRIDAY] MARCH 22. 1844

My beloved friend you will wonder what in the world has happened to me. I will tell you another day. Only I have been vexed, . . anxious, . . pained beyond common expression. The vexation began about my book, . . but it ends (*that* passing away) in a worse pain, . . the prospect of my parting from Crow. *You* will feel for me in this thing—I cried till I was faint with crying. Think of what this change will be to me, with my morbid feeling about strangers, & my bodily weakness. Well—to talk of it more, must be for another day.

Only I must say, that I do not blame her for leaving me—& that there has not been a harsh word between us, from the first day to this day—& no reason for it.

The vexation about the book, was a fit of despondency, after the exultation of the composition, . . to which I do not know if everybody is as miserably subject as I. My ms. of Eden[1] was as near the fire as ever ms approached—and only that M! Kenyon came into the room by a mere chance & took it away with him to read & pronounce judgement on, nothing c^d have saved it or me. To dearest Mr Kenyon my gratitude is inexpressible. He has saved me. My nerves were shattered to pieces; & he *set* them. Never was such a friend! And *I*, with so little courage left in me, that I could not even ASK him for help!–

All this, I write in the greatest haste,—& you will scarcely make out a great deal of sense from the midst of it.

Miss Martineau's letter, however, I enclose at last—but I received it back from Mr Crabbe Robinson (for whom Mr Kenyon borrowed it) only this morning. Also, I send a criticism on Orion, which Mr Horne "permits" me (under the circumstances, a command!) to forward "to Miss Mitford". I agree with you as to the combination of Douglas Jerrold's name & Sydney Smith's & Fonblanque's[2] . . decidedly,—& a little also as to that of Leigh Hunt's with Wordsworth's. Leigh Hunt is a true poet, to my mind; & I admit the article in the main—while I go with you in wishing that the two names (certainly on different levels) had not been joined together. It's like making a nosegay of a hollyhock & violet. But then Mr Horne w^d defend it on the ground of contemporaneousness . . as well as the ground of association by oppositions. He owns the parentage of the criticism on Tennyson.

•   •   •

I have a plan, . . if you will let me have it, . . of subscribing to a French library for you & arranging the conveyance—but it cant be for another six weeks,—at the end of which my next 'quarter' begins, & it can be done without anybody knowing a word of it—& the mythology of the mystery will be delightful for me to arrange. Be kind, & indulge me in doing it—& then, I shall pluck the fruit in being able to talk, & hear *you* talk of these esoteric mysteries, between you & me!

This is all written with something like the end of a poker . . not quite a poker, but its equivalent. May God bless you, my beloved friend! My M.S. is with Moxon at last—& the American edition is to come out at the same time, or rather before, in numbers of the *Home Library*,[3]—the Americans promising half-profits & undertaking the expenses. There will probably be two volumes.

What do you think of the engravings to the Spirit of the Age? how do you like Tennyson's head? And is not Southwood Smith's[4] very fine? And when do you come? last & chiefest! Your ever attached

EBB

•   •   •

1. EBB's leading poem, "A Drama of Exile," to appear in *Poems* (1844).
2. Douglas Jerrold (1803–57), editor and contributor to *Punch;* Sydney Smith (1771–1845), canon of St. Paul's, noted for his wit; Albany William Fonblanque (1793–1872), journalist and editor of the *Examiner,* also admired for his wit.
3. *The Home Library,* edited by Evert Duyckinck, was a projected series of prose and poetry by both American and English writers that ceased publication before EBB's volume could appear.
4. Dr. Thomas Southwood Smith (1788–1861) worked on sanitation reforms.

TUESDAY. MAY 7. 1844.

•   •   •

Crow *has* been very kind. She has come day after day, sometimes two or three days together, to dress me & arrange little things for me—shedding abundant tears when the time came for leaving me. She said, it was as great a deprivation to her as it c^d be to me,—she said *that* very kindly & earnestly. I earnestly hope she may be happy, poor thing,—and, so far, the business seems flourishing, & he is very attentive & apparently fond of her. She goes to her mother's to be confined,—& *then*, will come the full loss to *me*!

Wilson, the new maid, is very willing, very anxious, . . almost too anxious! very gentle, . . almost too gentle! a little failing in the vivacity & cheerfulness I like about me. I am afraid I shall never like her as well as Crow,––altho' she appears to be amiable beyond any finding fault with, & desirous of pleasing. Is that ungrateful of me? Perhaps so. My sisters say I shall like it all better presently. Perhaps so. But what I miss is,—the affectionate, gentle (always respectful) controul, which poor Crow used towards me,––the sort of half-nursing, . . & arrangeing of everything. She was with me when I was very ill & weak—& something of the gentle authority of nurse to patient, remained in her manner & ways—the "you must NOT have the window open in an east wind,"—& the like. Do you understand? I miss it all drearily. *Now*, I may have the window open all day, if it blows a hurricane,—unless my sisters come into the room & look that way! I may take double morphine draughts if I like! I may go to bed as late as I please,—& talk as long. It is a liberty I am not grown strong enough for,—& I feel the weight of it.

How querulous!—— ——

How childish! I am ashamed of myself almost, to write so to you. Only you do not despise me always, for even my foolishnesses.

·   ·   ·

Ever your attached
EBB

[TUESDAY] AUGUST 6th 1844

Ever dearest Miss Mitford I deserve a good scold upon the face of it. As a first defence I enclose the title page "which was to be", to prove how I acted upon your advice. Well! straightway Mr Moxon reprehended me. He could not make up his mind to "New Poems", . . he really could not!—and he did not see how "Poems" plain, wd suggest an idea of republication to people who read on the same page, "by so & so, author of the Seraphim &c." Therefore after all, "Poems" it is; and I hope that tomorrow or the next day I shall be able to send you, my dearest friend, the two volumes. Do keep yourself in the gentlest humour in the world. Keep in the sunshine, & think of your dahlias in full bloom.

You will partly understand how I wd not write until I had seen decided this weighty subject of the title page, . . and I have had other causes for delay, . . in some supernumerary matter to do for the work. Now I must thank you over & over again for your kindness in answering like an oracle to my questioning: and certainly, let Mr Moxon say what he pleases, I am of opinion that 'New Poems' wd make an excellent title, comprehensive, definite, unobjectionable in every way. Your opinion has at any rate thrown out the 'Drama of Exile', if it has not thrown in the 'New Poems':—and 'Poems' agrees with your antipathies, whatever else it may disagree with. For the rest, I humbly doubt whether a drama in the Greek form, may not have as much right to call itself 'drama', as one in the Shakespearean form. The Greeks had the name first, so please you. Lo!—the first sign of my beginning to quarrel with my critics! Indeed I am nervous– I cant help being nervous! Now that the active part is done, in which I was bold as a lion, this hard part of passive endurance seems (in prospect) ten times more overcoming.

Tell me the whole truth, my beloved friend, truly, therefore kindly! The truth is very important to me for the present & for the future. Try to put aside for a moment your affection for me, . . and judge of these poems, as if they were the work of another hand & heart than your friend's. I am grateful to you for much already—let me be grateful for *the truth* . . now. We can love each other, you know, all our lives afterwards . . there will be time enough!–

M.[r] Kenyon has come back from Southsea & the Isle of Wight, in full bloom of kindness & good spirits. I am so glad he has come back . . & miss him so,—when he is away! This, of course! Think of such a lamp being put out in my darkness, for a whole fortnight!–

Do you think I sh.[d] send a copy of my book to M.[r] Merry? Does he care for poetry? Tell me. You know he has sent me his various little polemical treatises—and perhaps he might expect me to respond in verse. I have a high respect for him on certain grounds; but if he sh.[d] not care for poetry, & w.[d] not expect any 'presentation' of the sort, why I w.[d] not trouble him with it,—& so increase the great necessary expence of giving copies. Direct me what to do. I am going to send one to Wordsworth, as tribute . . and to Leigh Hunt, as gratitude—and to Landor, as unworthy return for some gifts of his.

Here is Flush, rejoicing like Bacchus himself, among the grapes! eating one grape after another, with exceeding complacency, shown by swingings of the tail. "Very good grapes, indeed!" What a fancy for Flushie, to take! Just because Papa has sent me this little strip of a branch, he in his sympathy of possession must have his share!– Grapes indeed!

After all I did not see M.[r] Horne. He wrote to tell me that my refusal quite "affected" him, . . & that to call the disappointment "bitter" was the coldest word. *I*, in a fit of remorse, unsaid my refusal, & told him to come. *He did not come.* There was so much to do at last, that he could not—or at least did not. I have not seen him. He told me that I sh.[d] hear from him from Prussia, & I have not heard since. Have you seen the second edition of the "New Spirits"? I wish I could see it! I want to know how he retorts on his reviewers & to what extent. It is dangerous ground to move on,—& I did all I could to dissuade him from planting his foot on it. Unless there is *a fact* with which to oppose criticism, all the ohs & ahs in a man's breath, only prove that he is struck somewhere, & that the wound hurts. I am very sorry that he sh.[d] have assumed that position before the reviewers—but the fact is, I *believe,* not that he wished to sell an edition by an intentional indiscretion . . but that he suffered real & miserable vexation under the various attacks made upon him, & could give it vent in no more efficient manner. To judge by his letters, his spirits appeared to me quite depressed,—whether by the thunder of the critics, or by the cold drizzle of the individuals called "New spirits." To think of Dickens' being dissatisfied! Poor M.͕ Horne! He appeared to me far more *thrown* by this last adversity than he ever was by the death of his Katy.[1] I speak so, you know, simply from the evidence of his letters.

Tell me now about Paris . . what do you think of doing? & when, of going? Here is August—and if you mean to go, you sh.ᵈ assuredly. . . . *come to London*. Oh—the selfish spirits of this generation! We are all thinking of ourselves from morning to night. & you know if you DONT go to Paris, you will come to London for six weeks . . two months . . how long!– Am I not to muse of it, from morning to night—more especially as I have done my book, & have nothing to do but to idle & think wickedness . . ?

May God bless you, my beloved friend!– This is all written at railroad pace,—all the steam up!

Oh, but I must not forget to observe what I forgot to mention last time I wrote, when I wrote of M.ͬ͢ Hemans's memoir by M.͕ Chorley, & the letters in it, . . that *one* fervid letter[2] there quite bore me away, . . your's upon Rienzi, . . & set me wishing for a multiplication of such,–as full of eloquence & life.

But with *one,* I shall be contented at present . . *for* the present.

Write it to your

> ever affectionate
> EBB–

1. Catherine Walter, whom Horne was thought to have courted, died the preceding January.
2. A footnote added by Chorley to one of Mrs. Hemans's letters quoted MRM on her excitement at seeing her *Rienzi* performed in 1828.

[FRIDAY] SEPT. 20. 1844.

My ever dearest Miss Mitford, you will think harm either of your own letter or of me for being so slow in having the fire struck out of me by it to illustrate your theory. But neither of us is to blame. The letter was faultless; & I would have responded to it in a moment, (I felt all the impulse) only that there were previous claims which forced me to write till I was tired. Now at last I come to you,—sighing for pleasure as Flush does. How kind of you to feel as you do about my letters. It is just *so* with me & yours. My bell rings whenever you pull the string. There is a singular *sympathy in dyspathy* between you & me which brings together closer than a simple sympathy would. And then *I* who care for 'pen & ink', do not value your letters *only* for their influence on myself, but because my creed is that they will be hereafter a part of our literature,—that your letters will be as popularly known as your Villages!– It's a doxy of mine!

Dearest friend, I am going to tell you my news. Miss Martineau is better, & likely to be better,—and the means . . can you guess the means? . . why you are to look for the means, to MESMERISM.[1] Is this not great & wonderful news?—yes, & joyous news? She says that until June, she was believed to be insensible to the influence, (which you know many persons are) but, then, she became sensible to it. The bad symptoms receded—she recovered appetite, sleep, & so much strength, that, after a seclusion of four years & a half from the external air, she is now able to go downstairs every day & lie on the grass flat beneath the sky, without any fatigue. Her own maid magnetizes her twice a day—and the learned say that she will recover. This, she says, she can scarcely believe possible, but she is better already than she used to think possible,—and, in brief, she evidently *hopes*. At first, when the improvement was not yet a certain thing, she desired to keep the whole secret, lest she sh^d injure the cause of Mesmerism. But now her expression is "Everybody may know it." Well,—it is wonderful news certainly,—& to *me*, who heard it without any sort of preparation, (for she had never breathed a syllable about Mesmerism to me), it came with such emotion, that I could but think of it the night after instead of sleeping over it. That the agency sh^d be found available in cases of epilepsy & nervous affection, we may all under-stand,—but how in such a case as *her's*, where disease had produced (as I suppose it had) change of structure, there sh^d be a change back again under that influence, I wonder & am astonished at. Also, my impression had been always, that mesmeric patients were of the weaker class as to nerves & mind. But Harriet Martineau!—— It is wonderful! And if the restoration takes place, what a sensation in fa-vour of the mysterious agency, will rationally be excited everywhere!

Who will dare to doubt anymore the existence of the agency—as my own father has done hitherto? What will M.̣ May say,—he, who used to talk of hysteria? The phenomena of hysteria are morbid symptoms in themselves, & not *correctives* of morbidity.

You will be very glad, I am certain. *I* was so glad, that I thought as a secondary thing of what w.ᵈ otherwise have gladdened me much, . . & which *did* gladden me much, . . her opinion of my poetry. I told you, I think, that she was "sworn" to tell me the whole truth of the new volumes,—& the silence struck me as so very ominous a sign, . . a whole month's silence! . . that when the letter came I was half afraid to open it. But there was no need for fear,—except for my head's turning round. She speaks far beyond the utmost edge of my uttermost hope!—talks of the "immense advance'['] on the other volume,—& says (best of all) that the "predominant impression with her is the *originality*." I am very much pleased of course—very much! It is fair to add that she agrees with you in a preference of the smaller poems,—& though with kind words for the Drama, that she observes upon a general impression of monotony as its effect on the mind. Altogether I am far more than satisfied,—more than pleased. I will let her find fault with the paces of my hobby of Rhyme, & not complain. It's a letter as extravagant in generosity, as could have come to me from Three Mile Cross!

Then I have heard from M.ʳˢ Jameson,—a very kind letter! I hope she did not fancy that I wanted her to write me compliments. *That* was not my wish. I heard from M.̣ Kenyon that she thought of writing,—& then, she did not write—& then, I wished she might do it, . . hoping to have a critical discriminating opinion from her, which might benefit me. But she has written in very general kindness, such a letter as I am of course glad to receive, but should not choose to ask for. Do you understand?

Oh yes! I am delighted to hear everything of George Sand, & I did not know all you tell me, . . not the legal process, for instance. For the rest, I have read somewhere not long ago of a visit paid to her by a gentleman who apprized her of the fact of her works having been translated in Germany. "*Without* the immoral parts"? she asked him scornfully, . . whereat her daughter looked aside & blushed. Also I have the impression that this said daughter is married, & older than represented by M.ʳˢ Jameson. Does not M.̣ Chorley in his 'Manners & music' speak of having seen George Sand in man's clothes at the Paris opera,—& of another vision of her in a steamer in a like costume, where she was smoking herself into an atmosphere of cloud, & reading the bible? Oh—& there is an account of her certainly in "Les Catacombs," by Jules Janin,[2] a collection of vivid papers which were full of interest to me & will be to you. Do send for them. Those supplements are tiresome—and, I think, they occur everywhere. It is extraordinary how little sense of order the circulating booksellers are endowed with. Everywhere, their catalogues are a compilation of supplements. I have just read Coningsby. It is very able, & yet scarcely efficient, . . if I do not write contradictions. It has no story, & not a great deal of character: and is powerful as an exponent of the Young England political views, without being specific. Still a master-mind lives in the book, & the reader feels it everywhere. But I sigh for the Contarini Flemings,—& the atmosphere of pure imagination which he, D'Israeli, has left above him. A man of assured genius he must be confessed.

I confess besides that Balzac is a painful writer. And what you observe about nature & art, is, to be sure, so very true! We have all seen skies which no painter w^d venture to paint,—*could* paint without the imputation of extravagance,—have we not?

Your Flush is worthy of the god Bacchus,—so leave them in high converse! As for mine, his principle is to eat & drink everything he sees me touch,—& a good deal besides. I have fancied lately that the "least touch" as your Irish hero w^d say, of toasted cheese, hot with mustard & cayenne, assisted my digestion. Think of the heroic effort it must have cost Flush, to approach this high argument. He coughs & sneezes, & then resumes the charge. He considers it a personal affront if he is not allowed to eat everything left on the plate. But what he really & after all cant do, is to *persuade me that he likes it*. In *that*, he fails utterly, like M^r O'Connell on the balcony.

Because, you see, you are forced to admit his failure, . . his being unequal to the circumstance. They have him in the Pictorial Times, with an umbrella over his head instead of a halo,—& this is very much as, according to my doxy, he will appear to posterity. A great man, nevertheless—! a great man of the steam engine age! of this "wondrous Mother-Age", as Tennyson calls it, that has such a wonderfully ignoble looking family.

Napoleon!—ah yes—Napoleon! Do you know it struck me before, how differently it w^d have been with Napoleon! No man, better than Napoleon, understood the heroic poetry of situation. He was always equal to his position, whatever *that* might be, . . Austerlitz,

Moscow, Fontainbleau. Napoleon was cast in the heroic mould, & fell naturally into the heroic gesture. His very grey surtout does not dress him out of the heroic! He is as statuesque as Hercules, though in boots!

•　　•　　•

I am ever your affectionate
EBB–

1. The famous "cure" in the case of Harriet Martineau's pelvic tumor and the role of mesmerism versus orthodox medical opinion were to become causes célèbres with Martineau's defense of her mesmeric experiences in a series of letters to the *Athenæum* in November and December.
2. Jules Janin (1804–74), French journalist and drama critic.

SEPT. 28. 1844 SATURDAY

Certainly my dearest friend I do agree with you & Mrs Jameson in disagreeing with Miss Martineau on the subject of the letters. You know how strong my impression was from the first,—& the more I have thought of it since, the more settled has been my opinion. I told her generally, in speaking of the Essays on the sick room,[1] that I differed from her on certain points, without specifying, I think, what they were. And, in fact, when a person like herself prints an opinion, one is bound to take for granted that she has considered it too well to be likely to be easily shaken in it. But I firmly (on my side) believe that she is not only quite wrong, but quite inconsistent to the whole tenour of her life & writings, in the particular wrongness. I never felt much more firmly persuaded of anything than of this,—as you knew before. Still I *wonder*,—in being given to understand that a simple difference of opinion, c^d make her cold to anybody. There might have been, as you say, a little sharpness in the argument used against her,—and Mrs Jameson may have felt hurt at the want of confidence involved in the precaution about the letters, to the extent of irritation & the desire of retort. We cannot judge of this,—not knowing! Assuredly there must have been something painful to her habitual correspondents, in the nature of some sentences in the Essays,—do you not think so? If YOU had written them, assuredly *I* should have been hurt. I could not have helped it. And now I will tell you what happened once to me (not long ago) with respect to Harriet Martineau. You know that she has written to me occasionally since last autumn, when she began the intercourse by the kindest note imaginable about my poetry. I answered it with a warm appreciation of a kindness & honour which had touched as well as surprised me from such a quarter; & she wrote again at long intervals, I always answering her letters. Well,—at last, just as my books reached her, & before she had even cut the leaves, I had from her the most singular letter I ever received. She intimated in it that I had done myself harm with her by flattering her,—that I had flattered her more than was becoming to a Christian woman to flatter or be flattered,—that Miss Sedgewick[2] had done the same, . . had persisted in doing it in the face of her remonstrances,—had in consequence been rejected from her correspondence, . . & that, thereupon, Miss Sedgewick had "changed her hand" & called bad names instead of good. The infinite surprise with which I read this letter, . . the *humiliated* surprise . . for there are charges which humiliate nearly as much as if they were convictions, . . you will understand without difficulty– With all my faults, I am not accustomed to see myself reproached for this of falseness,—and then I had been so utterly unconscious of "flattering" Miss Martineau, that I feel sensitively it w^d have been an act of presumption in a stranger like myself & with an unestablished reputation, to take the liberty of praising her to her face, even according to my honest view of her powers & gifts. I cannot believe that I did more than express in a general manner my sense of what she was & my grateful sense of her condescension to me—& if I expressed it warmly, the warmth came from my heart certainly, & had nothing in it of phosphoric falseness. I told her so in reply. I thanked her for speaking to me of the impression, since she entertained it—and I respected a virtue which I c^d not however help feeling was, at that moment, somewhat austere towards me– From the other emotion of humiliation, I did not speak to you of it *then*. I really felt abashed. Can you understand? I thought everybody w^d think as even Papa did, "WHY WHAT CAN YOU HAVE BEEN SAYING?" And really, really, I am *true*! I write the truth (as it appears to me) even to strangers who send me books, & perhaps expect nothing but thanks & praise. I write the truth (as far as I can perceive it) even to friends, whom I love dearest & most blindly. I seek the truth myself, & seek it earnestly– I am not fond of using too strong language, & of dealing in the common commerce of compliment– And yet, you see!—— Well—I c^d not help thinking it rather hard, & undeserved——but there was a nobleness on her part, even in the hardness; and her letter about the books has overcome, in good measure, the painful impression, & left me grateful for her sympathy.

But you will understand how I felt exactly. What sh^d *you* say if I were to reply to one of your letters of generous excess, by warning you off with a charge of flattery, & an example of treachery? Only I never wrote to her . . never, . . I c^d take a great Styx oath, . . as *you* have written to *me*,—and, again, there is not the *love* in the other quarter, as between *us* . . you & me, . . to justify such "excesses." But I c^d take a great Styx-oath that I never spoke *to* her, as warmly as I have spoken *of* her, to you & others. That is sure.

• • •

Papa is absent,—gone to Cornwall, to examine a quarrey in which he has or is about to have, shares,—& not likely to be at home until the middle of next week. I inherit his bedroom during his absence; and my room is, by his desire, being made so clean & perfect by the whole generation of sweepers & cleaners, that it will not know itself again, they say. Then, I am to have a green double door instead of the cloth curtain, which will save me from the footsteps on the staircase, & from Flushie's barking out the consequences thereof. I am well pleased with the green double door. And I am going (perhaps) to have a blind for my open window, with green trees on it, which will be as rural as Mademoiselle de Scudery in "pays tendre".[3]

Thank you for telling me of Ainsworth's Magazine. As to Mrs Jameson, she is extravagant in speaking so of me,—& the whole world may see how—and I sh^d have received any critical opinion or reproof from her gladly & gratefully. Reading her letter made me ashamed for a minute—as if I had asked for a complimentary letter!– But you know precisely how I feel, & how I *felt*, in wishing her to write at first, & there is no need of more words.

Did you see any clairvoyance in your cases of trance? Perhaps not,—as you do not say.

• • •

Yes,—but to leave out a line in a sonnet! *That* is as wrong as to put a weak one in, . . is'nt it?– Are you in earnest, . . do I understand you rightly, . . that you advise me to send my books to Ma^dme Dudevant? I am half ashamed to confess how often I have thought of doing it, myself—but every time I shrank back– *Could* I have courage? *Might*

I have courage? Do you know that in general I have rather a dislike to sending about my books as a gift to persons whom I admire,—it is so like thinking them worth their acceptance,—and asking for praise in return. Except to Carlyle, I have sent to nobody, without a specific reason for it. I have not sent even to Joanna Baillie,—to whom perhaps I sh.ᵈ have done it. M.ʳˢ Jameson told M.ʳ Kenyon that she had bought the Seraphim & intended to buy the new volumes—therefore I felt it allowable to express my respect for her while I spared her an expense. M.ʳ Serjt. Talfourd sent me his 'Ion', when nobody had ever heard my name,—not even *you*!—and it was right to recognize that early attention.

Ah—you tempt me with George Sand! And M.ʳ Kenyon is going to Paris directly, early in October, & might take the books. Suppose you send her 'Belford Regis' or another work, & let me slip mine into the shade of it? Suppose we join *so* in expressing, as two English female writers, our sense of the genius of that distinguished woman? if it did not strike you as presumption in me to put my name to yours as a writer, saying *"we"*. We are equally bold at any rate. M.ʳ Kenyon told me I was "a daring person" for the introduction of those sonnets. He had heard an able man say at his table a day or two before, that no modest woman would or *ought* to confess to an acquaintance with the works of George Sand. Well! are you inclined to do it? Will you? Write & tell me. I would give anything to have a letter from her, though it smelt of cigars. And it would, of course!– Answer me directly—for I have taken a fancy to the plan in writing of it. She w.ᵈ know *your* name! Think of it!–

Once, I had a romantic scheme of writing my whole mind to her of her works. *That* was when I first read them,—and I lay awake all a night in a vision of letters anonymous & onymous—but it passed away,—& I considered how little good it could do.

May God bless you, my beloved friend! I write you to death when I begin.

Ever your attached
EBB–

• • •

1. Her *Life in the Sickroom* appeared anonymously in 1843 and rumors attributed it to EBB. Harriet Martineau took a strong position against any publication of her letters.

2. Catharine Sedgwick (1789–1867), American author of *A New England Tale* (1822) and other fiction.
3. Madeline de Scudéry (1607–1701), whose novel *Clélie* described an allegorical Arcadia.

Three-mile Cross
Nov. 28, 1844.

My dear Love,—I should like to have known Madame d'Abrantes,[1] that is, if she had not been too rich and high a lady; for my adoration of Napoleon, which increases every day, is so borne out by the testimony of one who had such opportunities of knowing him, that it is a most satisfactory and comfortable thing to read all that she says on that subject. Think how he would have enjoyed Balzac! I am sure he would—just as we do. By the way, old Mr. Robert (the excellent translator of "Notre Dame") says he does not think Balzac would suit the taste of the English. The fact is, that there is great peculiarity in the manner as well as matter of Balzac; and it is necessary to learn the character of his style, fine as that style is, just as it is necessary to master a difficult handwriting before enjoying the letters of a correspondent. Also I doubt whether Balzac be not too good for the taste of English novel-readers. Every now and then I find people talking of poor Miss Pickering, as I should talk of Miss Austen or of Scott—persons of sense and education, and high station. And the taste for Mrs. Howitt's translations of Fredrika Bremer (always begging your pardon) seems to me an indication of the same sort.

By the way, if I were not so old and stupid and lazy, I should like to try my own hand at translating Balzac, and see if I could not put one of his novels into such English as should give some faint idea of his French.[2] This is not so vain as it seems; for I should try, by the closest adherence to his vivid and colored language, to produce an almost Chinese copy[3] of this great original; and any person tolerably familiar with prose composition might do this by taking proper pains. Such a translation, giving to it great labor, might, I think, succeed. I do not mean merely *sell,* but might do justice to the manner of the author. This, however, would require an experienced English writer.

•   •   •

Ever yours,
M.R.M

1. Laure Permon (1785–1838), wife of Duc d'Abrantès, a general in Napoleon's army. She wrote extensive memoirs (1831–36) of the Napoleonic era.

2. MRM did translate some of Balzac's tales for publication by Rolandi in 1846.

3. MRM, who was proficient in French, voices her vanity and her modesty. A Chinese copy would be a slavish imitation.

LONDON

A New Correspondent and a Crisis

1845

The early months of 1845 proved a crucial period for EBB. Her health improved, the reception of *Poems* (1844) established her reputation in England and America and she finally met the poet who had so long interested her. On 10 January Robert Browning, just returned from Italy, wrote to acknowledge her compliment in "Lady Geraldine's Courtship" (his poetry, she had written, showed a heart "blood-tinctured, of a veined humanity"). Intrigued by his startling self-introduction ("I love your verses with all my heart . . . —and I love you too"), EBB entered into a correspondence that soon became her major preoccupation. Conscious of MRM's critical view of Browning, EBB skirted the subject of their sudden intimacy and kept to safer topics such as the queen's visit to the Duke of Wellington at Strath-fieldsaye near Reading and the depredations of MRM's maid Jane who had "half-stripped" the house of clothes and linens. Some confidences to MRM continued, however: memories in the [22] January letter of her adolescent "inward life," so like the heroine of Balzac's *Modeste Mignon;* lingering self-reproach recorded in 8 February for refusing, against her liberal principles, to contribute to the Anti-Corn Law cause (the "Leaguers"); distress expressed in [26 May 1845] at the visit of a relative associated with the Torquay tragedy. Particularly revealing is her description in 26 February 1845 of a regular caller (and would-be suitor?), George Barrett Hunter (?–1856?), an Independent minister she had known since 1832. His jealousy of her success contrasted sharply with the encouragement offered by Browning (who was at this time helping with revision of her 1833 translation of *Prometheus Bound*), and the seeds of her major poem *Aurora Leigh* (1856), with its exploring of a woman's need for both art and love, may have taken root as she pondered the contrast. By 20 May EBB had allowed Browning to call on her—an event reported, with studied casualness, to MRM. Shortly thereafter he visited her regularly twice a week.

[WEDNESDAY] [22] JAN. 1845.
Ever dearest Miss Mitford–
     In the first place, . . to show how we strike electric sparks by coincidences, . . I put down 'Modeste Mignon'[1] to take up your letter. I read my French abomination at breakfast & dinner & tea time, . . so as to forget myself & be delighted to find that I have eaten a little more than usual in my trance (deeper than the mesmeric) & happy state of physical unconsciousness. And at breakfast, came the post, . . or at the very earliest period after breakfast, . . when even Mignon could not beguile me further into muffin. And your first words are . . for I read the yellow paper first, . . are still of Mignon, Mignon. It is a decided case of flint to flint—& of electricity by coincidence.
     Well—and I am delighted with the book just as you are—nay, *more* charmed than you say you are, . . because charmed beyond the point of pleasure produced by mere artistic power in the writer. The truth is . . let me whisper it into your ear—that if I were to write my own autobiography, or rather, (much rather!) if Balzac were to write it for me, he could not veritably have made it different from what he has written of Modeste. The ideal life of my youth was just *that*, . . line for line . . colour for colour—and one expression especially startled me with its identity to my own experience, . . I mean when he speaks of *"la satieté par la pensée"*. I have felt it to a degree, that when face to face with my own mind (& if *that* is an Irishism, why so is the Greek *know thyself!*) the doubt has again & again occurred to me whether it was quite an exceptional experience on my part, or comparatively a common one. The process of castle-building, everybody, I suppose, more or less, has been an adept in—but that consistent living of another synchronal life in the ideal, cannot be equally

so—Madame de Genlis describes in her autobiography something like it—but Balzac's Modeste realizes my own experience of it over again. And that "satieté par la pensée".!– *There*, lies the test of the morbidity—for it is morbid—it is dangerous! & worse romances than poor Modeste's is likely to be, (I have only read a third of the book) might come of it, . . where the foundation of principle is not strong to the exceptional degree also. Do read that part about the ideal life over again, . . & think of me. I was Modeste without her beauty. I used to move about at one time in a dream,—happy beyond the realities of life (perhaps)—until the satiety came,—& another thing, . . the *remorse*. For as there is satiety for life 'par la pensée', just as for real life . . so is there remorse for it besides. Let those who have imaginative daughters, beware of that 'safe plan,' as it is said to be, of keeping them in seclusion—let them beware of their love of solitude & habits of silence. They may be drinking deeper of life among the sheep, that [*sic*] they ever w.d think of doing in the city. Such girls will not run away with M.r A or M.r B—no, nor with their father's footman by an illusion. They may be above that—but scarcely safer than that. At least, life in the mind is *not nothing*. It is as operative in its effects on the character as exterior life, . . & then, *who can controul it*? What friend's counsel,—& what mother's tear?

So much more, I could write of this! I believe that, in my own case, poetry was my safety valve, . . & that without it, the disease within (we must call it a form of insanity) w.d have manifested itself fantastically some day. I hope not worse than fantastically—but the imagination at play with loaded pistols, is a dangerous thing, & we must not be too confident of ourselves.

See how frankly I write to you. Do not think too badly of me in exchange. It proves the power of this romance that it should set one's self in the sight of one's self livingly & vividly, as it has done with *me*! And then, as you say, such beautiful writing! Such subtlety, both in words & thoughts! He is a great writer. As to Bernard, Balzac leaves *him* behind thousands of miles, to my apprehension. My dearest friend, praise Charles de Bernard[2] as you please, but dont name him with Balzac!—that post is not tenable.

For the rest, I agree with you that Delavigne is not a man of genius, (precisely what I meant to say of him!) & that Victor Hugo is. I agree altogether. But if you see no genius in that magnificent scene of pure passion in Pippa Passes, which you were one of the first to point out to me, we differ again & widely. Faults, & obscurities & perplexities of diction, Browning has undoubtedly—but it appears to me as clear as this sun of noonday, now shining on my paper, that he is a man of genius in a true sense. You are not, I think, quite right in what you say of his having been cried up & applauded. He has had very little of the 'rank popular breath' for him; & the critics have shown him (from the Athenæum downwards) no superfluous courtesy. Those who esteem him, are of a small circle, but generally esteemed themselves for their insight into imaginative poetry . . a fit audience of few. Be sure of one thing—that the world will not let die that scene which you pointed out to me in Pippa Passes—to go no further! We shall see—that is, we shall see some things—& other people will see other things. My opinion is that Browning's name will stand, when the springtide comes!

•   •   •

Today I have had a curious intimation & question by letter, . . whether, in the case of an *official application from the Leaguers*, I should object to writing them a poem for their grand Bazaar? – I hesitate how to answer. My sympathies go strongly with the body,—& I am flattered at the idea of its having occurred to anybody in their relation, that my poetry was worth having!—love & vanity go *so* far! But then, I am not sure, first, whether cornlaw matters are the best in the world for the matter of poetry, . . & secondly, whether it is not & whether it might not be considered by some of my friends, undesirable to take such a prominent post in the political ground, harp in hand & petticoat down to the ankles.

But I am writing ungenerously—I feel I am. *Not like a Godiva!* It is a righteous cause, & I know it to be righteous– It is not mere partyground. I believe I ought to do it, if they ask me. Tell me if I ought not. Tell me your whole thought. Of course it is wholly dependent on the official invitation—I w^d not think of meddling otherwise. But if I am asked—ought I to say 'no'—unless Papa says 'no'—? I could not vex *him* of course. Tell me your whole thought—& tell *nobody else*. It sounds whimsical, . . but the real truth is, as far as I can learn, that Leeds with its roaring commerce & dense smoke-canopy, is one of the strongholds if not *the* stronghold of my poetry, which all you refined people call 'mystical'. They seem to like it there, as well if not better than anywhere else. Strange!—is it not?

And now I shall write no more today. If the Queen is right queenly, she will do herself the honour of going to see you from Strathfieldsaye —(or how is it spelt?) We shall see—as I say of Robert Browning's genius.

Your most affectionate
EBB.

•   •   •

1. Balzac's novel, incorporated into "Scènes de la vie Privée" in his *La Comédie Humaine*.
2. Charles Bernard du Grail de la Villette (1804–50), French novelist and protégé of Balzac, best known for his *Gerfaut* (1838).

Three Mile Cross,
Autumn, 1844. [*sic* for January 1845]

What a very cheap thing childish happiness is! You will be astonished to hear what (besides a sharp feverish attack and writing to you) has occupied my last week—very much astonished. This, dearest, is the fact. I found that the Queen's visit[1] to Strathfieldsaye had strongly excited the interest and curiosity of the little children here, and I determined they should see her and have a holiday. Everybody expected that she would return by Reading (indeed the unlucky mayor sent me word, so late as yesterday morning, that "he had no conviction of her not returning through his town,"—a very grand diplomatic message); and it was only on Wednesday afternoon that I finally ascertained that she would go back by Wokingham, as she came. I then arranged to take all the children (two hundred and ninety) in waggons lent by the kind farmers, as far as Swallowfield Lane, the point where her Majesty turned off from the Basingstoke Road into the Cross Lanes which lead to Wokingham; that they and their schoolmasters and mistresses should meet at nine o'clock at my house, to have delivered to each of them a pretty hand flag of pink and white, made by Jane (who has fitted up three yachts and was flag-maker-general to the Isle of Wight); that we should then march in procession to the lane, the children riding in waggons decked with laurel and large flags of the same colours: which was done accordingly, I leading the way with Mrs. Amott and her children, the clergyman's family, and some other gentry, followed by a body-guard of great boys, who seeing me walk would not ride (was not that pretty of them?), and meeting there eight or ten carriages containing all the gentlemen's families of the parish.

We had chosen our place well, for the Queen was escorted to that point by her noble host, who took leave of her just in front of our waggons, which looked between the laurels and the pink and white flags like so many masses of painted-lady sweet peas. The party made exactly such a pause in parting, and afforded such a little incident as allowed to everybody the fullest and pleasantest view of those they came to see. After this we all returned, I the last, this time, with Miss Lay—still walking, though I had got into Mrs. Praed's pony chaise to see the sight. We all returned—carriages, waggons, body-guard and all—to my house, where the gentlefolks had sandwiches and cake and wine; and where the children had each a bun as large as a soup-plate, made doubly nice as well as doubly large, a glass of wine, and a mug of ale. All this seems little enough; but the ecstasy of the children made it much. They had been active from four o'clock in the morning. They had been shouting and singing all day. They did sing and shout all the afternoon, for I had made it my particular request to the schoolmistresses and masters that there might be no scolding or keeping in order—flinging ourselves upon the children's own sense of right. And well did they justify the trust! Never was such harmless jollity! Not an accident! not a squabble! not a misword! It did one's very heart good. Of course we took care of the mistresses and masters also; and their pleasure in the children's pleasure was very good to see—the sympathy all through. To be sure it was a good deal of trouble, and Jane is done up. Indeed, the night before last we none of us went to bed. But it was quite worth it—one of the few days of promised pleasure which in spite of Seyed, Emperor of Ethiopia, do sometimes keep their word. It rained I believe, somebody said so; but nobody minded it, the children least of all. I shall never forget their delight.

The Queen looked pale and ill—simply dressed—smiling and well-behaved; the horses going at a foot pace, and the glasses down. Prince Albert is decidedly handsome. Our Duke went to no great expense. One strip of carpet he bought, the rest of the additional furniture he hired in Reading for the week! The ringers at Strathfieldsaye (and the church is so near the house that William the Fourth, when Duke of Clarence, who had a genius for blundering, when visiting poor Lord Rivers asked if it was not the dog-kennel!)—the ringers, after being hard at work for four hours, sent a can to the house to ask for some strong beer, and the can was sent back empty! Also a poor band, who had been playing till the breath was out of their bodies, begged for a little dinner, and received such a piece of bread as is laid on a napkin for dinner and such a piece of cheese as is sent round on a napkin after dinner. The Duke is a *just* master—as Johnstone, his gardener, said to me once when I idly asked if he were a *kind* one—and not a very bad landlord; but he has no open-heartedness. He is without that high sense of what is due to his own position which made Napoleon, with all his spirit of order, so truly magnificent. It was a fine balance in Napoleon, which made him equally displeased at Madame Mère's economy and Josephine's debts. The Duke looked relieved beyond all expression when he had made his last bow to his royal visitors; his whole countenance said plainly, "Thank God it's over!" and no doubt he felt so. There was only one most extraordinary thing in our children; Sir Robert Peel passed us, going to town by railway, just at the top of the village, and Jane says that they hissed him! Is not this most remarkable? All our gentry are Conservatives. Now that my dear father is dead, we have not a Whig in the parish. But they said, "There goes Sir Bobby," and they hissed him!

[M.R.M.]

1. Queen Victoria and Prince Albert made the visit 20–23 January 1845.

TUESDAY. JAN. 28. 1845.

* * *

Delightful it was for me to hear of your avatar with the two hundred & ninety —though I grudge the honour a little to the Majesty who appeared so ignorant of the best means of honoring itself. To think of the queen's going to Sir John Cope's old house, as "an object," instead of your garden! The pity & disdain with which I read it in the newspaper, you w^d have smiled to see. Poor, foolish queen. The Hanoverian wits, to say nothing of royal wits in general, are apt to have a 'divine wrong' in such matters—they cannot see or understand. Rogers has his poetic 'claims allowed' at Buckingham palace, just because he is Rogers the banker, & has 'a taste' & a fine house to show it in. Oh this world! & these kings & queens of the world! I

mean these kings of Bokhara & these queens of England! for in
France & Prussia the crowns go together with more civilization. And
now I have talked enough high treason for one morning.

Mrs Jameson has come too in the midst of it. We have been talking of Lady Byron—& she has been desiring me to 'keep my mind
open', while I was thinking of the difficulty of shutting up my temper. Evidently she knows the mystery—she is Lady Byron's friend,—
& she considers her to be more than justified. Can it be possible, I
say to myself (& to you) that anything in the world can untie this knot
& justify Lady Byron.? The question is a first gesture in the struggle
to keep one's mind open. Do *you* think it can be possible? I wish I c^d
think & believe so. Yet, of Marie Antoinette[1] & Lady Byron I have
dreamt daggers all my life—& if even, in the one case, it sh^d prove to
be most murderous wrong, why I must suffer the remorse of it. She
is not a mathematician, says Mrs Jameson—–not scientific . . not cold
& perfect—on the contrary the poetical element is the chief thing in
her—the imagination is the strongest element. Can you conceive *that*
of Lady Byron? It has reversed my image of her, whether it has or has
not opened my mind. She, Mrs Jameson, has been breakfasting this
morning with Rogers & in company with Hallam[2]—& she tells me that
she is quite "sick" of the perpetuity of the everlasting talk about mesmerism. There seems to be, according to her account, enough of
"damnable iterations", & no conclusion in any sense . . no end of it.
Between scoffers & enthusiasts, there is no middle. She believes to a
certain point, but resists the clairvoyance. I wish I could do the same–

•   •   •

My dear, dearest friend, . . how we do meet in coincidence &
similitude!– Well—I never sh^d have taken you to be a dreamer in the
emphatic sense of Modeste Mignon & me—& even now, delighted as
I am with the similitude (& I quite clapped my hands over your letter)
I cannot make out how it could have been precisely so—*you* in the
midst of that thick, gay country neighbourhood—& *I*, living from one
end of the year to another without the sight of a face beyond my own
household, . . nay, isolating myself even from *that*, except during the
evenings, in my little room at the top of the house! You never could
have lived such a life—surely never,—*you* who glorify the social spirit
in the very inner movements of your mind. The house we lived in,
lay in a hollow of hills, —& from one of the hills I used to gaze away
my sight on a white ribbon of a road which unrolled itself along the

green distance, & was called the London road. I used to think that it
tied us to the world—that white ribbon—& that if an angel w^d take it
up in his hand, & draw us nearer, how my heart w^d beat with a
strange emotion!

Ah—if I had known *you,* when I was at Lyme Regis, not many
years ago! To think of my having walked down those steep streets,
built as if the whole town had tumbled down a cliff, & was struggling
up out of the sea again . . without a thought, except of the picturesqueness of the situation!–

My dearest friend, we are always disagreeing, just because we
agree so *deeply.* Now I forgot to tell you about Mrs Jameson! I do *not*
think that she is pedantic. She does *not* seem to *me* to speak in sentences. It strikes me still that she wants impulse a little—& what the
French call *abandon*: but this does not seem to *me* to arise from over-
carefulness as to what she shall say, or how she shall say it—I think
it does not. I like her very much—but I have not fallen in love with
her at first sight, as you know, I did with *you.* But to fall in love at
first sight once in a life, may be as much as is necessary.

For the matter of corn law rhymes, you decide generously & dis-
creetly . . which is the perfection, I suppose, of good counsel. We
shall see. I think it very likely that the lady who wrote to me, belonging to some 'Ladies committee', might be speaking quite wildly in
what she said, . . & that beyond her own particular unanimity, nothing more may be thought of it by anybody. I answered slightly & cau-
tiously, that I could not say a word on the subject without knowing
what was expected from me, & who expected it,—& whether it w^d be
in my power or not, to do what she suggested. Indeed I by no means
understand the sort of thing likely to be required of me—nor do I (on
reconsideration) much expect to hear of *anything* being required of me
seriously. There are writers infinitely better qualified—& they need
not go further than their own Corn law rhymer, Elliot.[3] Also I suspect
my female correspondent with her foot in the ladies' committee, to
be a wandering Pleiad, gone astray through a fancy for me, from the
probable views of majorities male & female. I do not know her personally—but the thing may be so: and not a word therefore have I
said to mortal ear about the hint delivered to me, except to *your* ear.
If I learn more to any intent & purpose, I shall of course speak to
Papa—so as to be sure of not vexing him—but really I dont expect to
learn more. The probabilities are against it.

Talking of the subject of verses, I must tell you who are so tenderly kind & quick of sympathy, that the good accounts of the poems continue,—& that Moxon told M! Kenyon the other day, of the second edition being at hand, & of his intention of proposing to me a cheaper & more popular form for the work. That is good news, (—is it not? . .) past any prudent expectation! Six months have not passed since the publication—indeed *five* have not—& the second edition & the cheaper form both sound very well. Of course I am pleased. Why should'nt I be pleased? Dont forbid the bans for my being pleased . . if you please.

.   .   .

Now this positively is the last of me for today.

Hic jacet
your most affectionate
EBB.

What a Duke to be Napoleon's victor! For shame!–

1. EBB meant to write "Marie Louise," as she later told MRM. Empress Marie Louise (1791–1847) was Napoleon Bonaparte's second wife, and is coupled for EBB with Lady Byron as a wife who betrayed her husband's memory.
2. Henry Hallam (1777–1859), historian and father of Arthur Hallam, the subject of Tennyson's *In Memoriam A. H. H.*
3. Ebenezer Elliott (1781–1849) denounced the Corn Laws in his *Corn-law Rhymes* (1828).

[SATURDAY] FEB 8– 1845–

My dearest friend & temptress . .

All the week is unrolled, day after day, & not a word from you to say when you will come! I w^d not teaze you for the world (as me-thinks, I always make a point of saying when I am in the crisis of tormenting you!) but you are to be pleased to remember that I am a mortal being, & made of Adam's rib (only a degree better than the raw material of Red-Clay Adam himself) & that though I can make one parenthesis after another in a manner unknown to purists, I *cant* bear to be tantalized by such words as . . "I must come next . . . .

this week", & a silence afterwards. Have a little mercy, . . do– Dont suspend me on the point of a needle over the plains of Paradise—take a stitch one way or the other—& dont let it be a stitch in my left side. And after all . . I w.ᵈ *not teaze you for the world*!

Well—I want 'an opinion' from you too, previous to the decision. I had quite concluded in my own mind, that the fantasy about the Corn Law Bazaar was the fantasy of an individual, & that I sh.ᵈ hear nothing more of it—when lo! this morning, came an official invitation from the Leeds' Ladies committee, backed by the authority of the London General Council, signed by a secretary . . all in form & precision, . . asking me to do the poem. Of course I am pleased in one way . . I do not pretend to be otherwise than pleased. And yet I am in doubt—for it appears rather more than doubtful whether Papa will let me do it or not. My own feeling is quite *for* it—: but *he,* after smiling a little over the note, begins to murmur about its involving me with the party, and about its being far better for the farmers, to have a fixed duty. Now *I,* you know, am leagues before the rest of my house in essential radicalism, . . & by no means believe in the ruin of farmers being dependent on the preservation of duties on corn, or even in the desireableness of *saving* a farmer & landed proprietor at the expense of the great body of the population. The people ought to have free trade in corn, & they will have it, . . without duty & restriction . . whether I write a poem on the actual grievance or not. And if I did write the poem, it w.ᵈ not be a mere party-poem—it w.ᵈ be an exponent of the present *Grievance* (admitted by liberals of every class)—just as the 'Cry of the Children' was an exponent of the Factory Grievance. The League unites so many sympathies among men who differ otherwise, that I do not at all see how I implicate myself with a political party in doing this deed . . if I did it.– I w.ᵈ rather not narrow the sphere of my poetry by wearing a party badge either in politics or religion—& I perfectly see the undesireableness of *that.* But to refuse to give or rather to refuse to attempt to give, a voice to a great public suffering, when I am asked to do it . . & when I recognize the existence of the suffering . . should THIS be refused?– Oh— I w.ᵈ not vex Papa for the world—& I see that he is not, so far, much inclined to give a joyous sanction. And what do you think he said . . "Miss Mitford w.ᵈ not do it, if she were asked". 'Yes'—I said, 'she would—I have reason to know she w.ᵈ' 'No–' he said—'if it came to the point, she never w.ᵈ implicate herself with that party. You had better think it well over before you write them an answer'! I did not like to repeat particularly what you HAD said,—because, that I sh^d have had talk with you on a subject I never mentioned to *him* or anybody, might have struck him as strange—while the fact was, that I believed (after the first doubt I confided to you) in no fact but a fantasy on the part of an enthusiastic woman, . . & that, as a fantasy I answered it, & then dismissed it from my mind. The actual invitation coming, quite astounded me, . . & has given me courage even to *wish* to do the thing. And now do write to me directly, & let me be able to tell Papa that *you* w^d consent, in my position,—*(if really you would!)* & that an association with the people in order to the removal of an admitted grievance, is not the same thing as an implication with a party, & the wearing of a badge. His whiggery as opposed to my liberalism at full length, makes a difference, of course, in the mode of viewing the question—but then, it seems to *me* that, even on the ground of whiggery, a good deal may be said on the side of *Consent.* See how Lord Morpeth has attended these great meetings—& other whigs of an approaching calibre.

Well! I wish you were here to talk it over.

. . .

I am always your most affectionate
EBB–

[TUESDAY] FEBRUARY 11. 1845

Ever dearest friend

Do you know I half lamented on Sunday that I had written for your counsel on Saturday in relation to the Bazaar. And here is my reason!– Every feeling within me was pulling one way (in favour of the application) & every friend without me, the other way, & against the application—and as I saw there was nothing for me but to yield, why there was a sort of comfort in having no voice with me & in the necessity being as large & strong as possible. Papa was against it, which, if he stood his ground, was enough of course to decide the question. And then, I enclose to you the letter dearest Mr Kenyon wrote to me on the same side. And then all my brothers . . whom I had a regular quarrel with, by the bye, because they took up the argument on wrong grounds altogether, & abused the League & laughed

at the ladies' committee, & at the idea of my verses doing good at
all,––a woman's verses!––oh, think of the impertinence of it,––& how
I was like a very Pythia for rage, . . the divine inspiration apart!– And
then, to close the scene & clench the whole series of arguments, M!
Kenyon came, & told me that he had seen M! Chorley, & that M!
Chorley declared it w^d ruin me for ever if I attempted such a thing,
. . that my poetical reputation was at a crisis, . . & that from the moment I trusted it into the air of that region, it w^d fall flat, . . that nobody w^d read or buy me any more, as a matter of principle, . .
nobody! & that my utility, from that hour, w^d be circumscribed,
shackled, undone,––that the act w^d be fatal to me as a writer! Well!––
and so, I half regretted asking you for your counsel––& seeing that it
was necessary to execute myself, I wished it done with as sharp an
axe as possible, . . & as quickly. *Your* thoughts . . I knew them! They
were my own. Still, your letter made itself welcome,––& after all, it
could scarcely make me feel surer than I was before, & am at this moment, that in refusing I have *not* acted as generously as I ought to
have done, nor from as high motives. I am not satisfied with myself––
not at all. What was the folly called 'my poetical reputation,' in comparison with the duty to which I was invited? *I* too, who have always
professed & desired to sacrifice nothing to poetical reputation . . . .
not even my own views of Art & composition! Indeed I am displeased
with myself. And the trouble & labour I had in writing my answer to
the Committee, would have proved to me my own self-displeasure, if
I had not previously been aware of it. And yet, what could I do? How
could I act contrary to the advice of all around me, & especially
against my own father's? I felt it was not possible. Also I might perhaps have circumscribed my future means of utility, . . if ever so little
at present. Only again . . that argument, which is the least ignoble of
all at first sight, . . is nothing after all but the doing of evil that good
may come, or that another evil may *not* come . . : it is pitiful expedi-
ency––to say the best of the best!

I enclose you dear M! Kenyon's letter. What he says about his
fossil-republican-cousin, relates to a saying of mine that I was in politics of no extant party, but a sort of fossil-republican. He comforts me
by the suggestion that I might have written some fiery stanzas tending
to rick-burning ––but I should'nt, I think. And I have written my 'ungracious' refusal––yes, most ungracious––! in which, however, I have
tried to assure them that in essential points, & where the principle is
concerned & not the form, I would not falsify the trust they repose in

me. Is'nt it pitiful of me,—now, is'nt it? ought'nt I to be ashamed of myself? I *am*, my dearest friend, I *am!*– My only consolation is, a resolve to write something with a League-object, though out of the League-livery—THAT, I *will* do. I am chafing against a bit, like my Prometheus.

And by the way, what do you think I have chosen for an employment lately?– You know my opinion of that miserable production called my translation of Æschylus's Prometheus, & which sh^d be rather called the blot on my escutcheon. Well! To prove my truth of selfreproach & efface the blot, . . I have been translating the whole over again. I began with the first Greek line & ended with the last, not referring at all to my former misdoing, & have completed a version, which however faulty in many respects, is not faulty in the way of the preceding one, . . in being as cold as Caucasus on the snow-peak, & as flat as Salisbury plain. It has more poetry, at least, & is nearer Æschylus: & I have had great pleasure in doing it, & in feeling that I have done something to retrieve my own disgrace as a poet by my own hand. Perhaps I may print it in a magazine——but I do not know. I have not made up my mind. I did it for conscience' sake, more than from any other motive. Now I may sleep at nights, & Æschylus's ghost not draw the curtains . . . "all in his winding sheet."

· · ·

And pray why should'nt Eugene Sue have a "bearde" as well as Beelzebub in the old mystery plays? And why should'nt Balzac have a beard? And a beard too for Frederic Soulié & the rest? Charles de Bernard & George Sand cant be bearded I suppose, the more's the pity, . . except by the beards being tied on like their pantaloons, . . which is not impossible on second thoughts.[1] But dont you know, my dearest friend, that the full bloom of the beard is as common as boots in Paris streets; & that from the king's sons to Paul who isn't the apostle, everybody is bearded like a pard —? And why not, pray? I like it. I admire it. I like it both on picturesque grounds,—& on . . on . . (what shall I say?) on humanitarian or anthropological grounds. For Nature having produced a woman with a smooth chin & a man with a bearded chin, it is surely primâ facie, absurd, to make both faces equally smooth—& to scrape & scarify one chin to the level of the other chin. Shaving is abominably unnatural—beards are the most natural things in the world. Certainly I agree with you that where a fashion in dress & bearing is universal, the individual who resists it is foolish & affected in the act. *That* I agree in altogether. But where as in Paris, the practise of beard-wearing is common, I applaud, & wish Good speed to the beards. I sh.^{d} like very much to see a little pointed well-smoothed & perfumed beard, a Vandyke beard, on the face of any of my male friends . . always provided that there were plenty of rough ugly beards out in the streets to justify the grace. I like it in itself—but affectation & the singularities which express it, I do *not* like.

Tell me how Jane is. Let me hear—do—of your plans.

• • •

Your attached
EBB

1. EBB was under the misapprehension that Bernard was a woman.

WEDNESDAY. [19] FEB. 1845.

What I was going to say of men, or rather of a man, . . was just this of Mr Hunter. It might be amusing if it were not so vexatious, to hear him talk as he does—talk *at* you, (viz at me) as he does. Ever since my last book has brought me a little more before the public, I can do or say or wish to do & say, nothing right with him—and on, on, he talks epigrams about the sin & shame of those divine angels, called women, daring to tread in the dust of a multitude, when they ought to be minding their clouds. All this, not a bit in joke—but gravely & bitterly. Every new review he sees, there is a burst of indignation—and the League-motion, obliquely entertained as it was, wrapt me in a whirlwind. You know . . & I tell him, . . the feeling is all to be analyzed into contempt of the sex. It is just that, & no less. For a woman to hang down her head like a lily through life, and 'die of a rose in aromatic pain' at her death, . . to sit or lounge as in a Book of beauty, and be "defended" by the strong & mighty thinkers on all sides of her, . . this, he thinks, is her destiny & glory. It is not the pudding-making and stocking-darning theory—it is more graceful & picturesque. But the *significance* is precisely the same,—and the absurdity a hundred times over, greater. Who makes my pudding, is useful to me,—but who looks languishing in a Book of Beauty, is good for nothing so *far*.

Angry as all this makes me, I am *not*, as you are perhaps aware, a very strong partizan on the Rights-of-Woman-side of the argument—at least I have not been, since I was twelve years old. I believe that, considering men & women in the mass, there is an *inequality* of intellect, and that it is proved by the very state of things of which gifted women complain,—& more than proved by the manner in which their complaint is received by their own sisterhood. At the same time, the argument used by men in this relation, should go no further than the fact,—and it is cruel & odious to see the yearning they have, not to meet the weakness of women with their manly protection, but to exaggerate that weakness, in order to parade their protection. I know that woman (many of them) encourage this tendency by parading their weakness—and it is detestable to my eyes, in an equal degree, on both sides of sex.

I have been expecting to hear from you—& I am wondering whether I shall have to wait to monday before I see you. Happy day, whenever it comes!–

       •   •   •

And, however I hate, I cannot express one thought more, or one indignation. For M.͞r Hunter is here, between me & post time; & he comes so far (from Brixton) that I cannot refuse to see him. May God bless you! Try to read me—& bridge the differences . . the gaps.

Your ever attached
EBB.

[Wednesday] February 26. 1845.

Ever dearest friend I thought it would be so– The roads, for the rest, are too bad—and Monday will be the best day for both of us. I am better a good deal, & shall hope to be tolerably vocal by the time you come, and Monday comes. "Benedetto sia' &c. But I need not bless it. It will bless *me*.

       •   •   •

But poor, poor M.͞r Hunter—you must'nt be too severe on him. If I had not been vexed I would'nt have mentioned him at all,—I would'nt for the world, mention him to Papa,—but one's temper will bubble over sometimes when it has boiled too long. And really it *is* hard, to hear him talk, & to read him when he writes. But it is'nt what you say—oh no—he is not jealous of me—of *me*! It's a sort of masculine rampancy which w^d have a woman under the feet of a man that he might stroke her there like a hound. He says, my dearest Miss Mitford, as coolly as possible upon every possible opportunity . . *"before you were spoilt"* by so & so!——not in joke—not a bit. He thrusts all sorts of red hot scorns at me . . and when I try to get rid of the subject of literature altogether, I am sure to have it doubled into a ball of conversation & thrown back upon me, full of little pins about female writers & so on. And then, everyone who praises me, he anathematizes. For instance, in the New Monthly Magazine of last month, in a paper 'on Puppies' written by I dont know whom, the phrase occurred . . . . "We half adore Miss Barrett; &, like herself, can admire George Sand". Well—Arabel took up this magazine, & in a sisterly fit of boasting, put it into his hand when he was sitting here by me—. "Ah!" he said—"it's just so! just as I thought. An honorable thing this is, to be sure, to have one's name bandied about in connection with an abandoned woman, by all the rakes in London!"– Did you ever hear a more gracious interpretation or more comfortable commentary? I laugh when I can,—& sometimes have half a mind to cry—because though you attribute to me my beloved friend, qualities which are the mere accidents of a dream of the affections, yet I do believe that you are right in thinking that I am not pedantic & spoilt by any little praise permitted to me. How could I be, with such a safe dead weight to pull me back . . which I feel *most* after a moment of elation? You might as well open the window for a bird with a broken wing, as expect me to fly away from a sense of the position which becomes me. You praise me for being cheerful—& so I am, I thank God, in a very good measure—but then, there are seasons of effort & of reaction:,— & also, much of the possibility of being cheerful comes from the faculty of throwing oneself beyond oneself, and living as *we* can do, for hours together, in art & fiction & poetry. For the rest, there is at my side a vacancy & a silence which strike on me sometimes as freshly as ever, and sometimes as despairingly. Ah—when questions like that League question——but I have no right to sadden you. You are so kind to me my dear dearest friend—so kind—so full of sympathy— and then, when you think me bright, how often it is that I am basking in *your* sunshine. I sit close to you, and afterwards "I smell of Anacreon".

But for dear Mʳ Hunter, you are not to infer any disparagement of him from what I said. He is just *a man* & has a man's instincts. With the most indubitable degree of regard for me, he has his own ideal of a woman, & would set me straight whenever (which is every moment) I dont lie level to it. As to sympathy, we must not talk of it in such a state of things!—sympathy is a word out of place. But do not say anything of all this when you come, to anyone here—for I never complain of dear Mʳ Hunter, save when taken unawares in a moment of confidence like this. He has high qualities & faculties, and is not to be blamed for his man-nature. Be sure that it is natural to men to have such views, whether they develop them or not. I assure you he quite detests America ever since they began to praise me there. The fever, in its external form, began with my prose papers in the Athenæum, & has been at its height since the poems.

· · ·

I am very, very much better. I am coming into blow, I think, for Monday. May God bless you, dearest friend! I hope Jane is better. If your Flush keeps Valentine's day, he is more of a Pusseyite than mine, . . who scorns the cats.

Poor Sydney Smith– Poor Yorick! He jested with the melancholy of death,—and said that he had lost flesh enough to make a respectable curate of,—& that he remained very thin, considering he was *stall-fed.* If you laugh at *that,* it is his epitaph, you laugh.

Your ever affectionate
EBB.

· · ·

[TUESDAY] MARCH 18, 1845

Ever dearest friend– How my Love for you has been pulling at my sleeve these two days, to write . . & write! But I have been so low, & weary, & tired of life. It is as much as I can do to stand up against this bitter wind, without smoothing down my petticoats– Still—I am not ill in the strong sense . . mind! I am weak—my heart is disordered; & I feel all day long as if I were lying on the edge of a fainting fit—do you know what THAT is? Yesterday, I went to bed at four o'clock—& even the ninth volume of the 'Juif' would not animate me as it should.

•   •   •

Ah—M! Chorley. But you know, I cannot exchange him quite for M! Browning. M! Browning & I have grown to be devoted friends I assure you—and he writes me letters praying to be let in, quite heart-moving & irresistible. In the summer I must see him—& M! Chorley too. I shall like to see *both*. And then for Hyeres & everybody!–

You see what M! Chorley says of Paracelsus! You see it is not merely a dream of mine!—he is full of genius.

And then he writes letters to me with Attic contractions,[1] saying he *'loves'* me. Who can resist *that*—?–

But do not talk of it if you please, although it is all in the uttermost innocence, . . as testifies the signature

of your most affectionate
EBB.

•   •   •

1. Browning's most recent letter, of 11 March, noted she failed to understand his feeling for her because "the language with which I talk to myself of these matters is spiritual Attic, and 'loves contractions' as grammarians say."

MONDAY. [26 MAY 1845]

Ever dearest Miss Mitford, your letter is thrice welcome——or rather four times,—because thrice welcome it w^d be under any circumstances—& I wanted to know this time, how you were, & whether all the diablerie performing about you of late, had done any harm to your spirits. What a capacious idea of thieving that girl must have had!– And how strange it seems that all this wickedness, which must have taken its time in ripening, should have continued without a suspicion on your part!—only I am foolish for saying so, because YOU *could'nt* suspect a person & live with her,—I know you could'nt. Association brings trust with you—& you cannot help it. As to the unfortunate sinner, although it makes one's blood run cold to think of her blasphemous lie, yet I can understand something of the madness that drove her to it,—the protest against humiliation & disgrace, in the presence of the mother of the man she loved! It is comprehensible—is'nt it? God was less to her, at that moment. But how awful to stand by & hear!–

And as to the prosecution, you are surely, surely right about it, & will not have to regret it—it will be a "twice blessed'['] mercy, . . to giver & taker. But can you not recover many of these stolen goods? all the linen for instance, & things of the sort which c^d not easily be made to vanish into the earth—? Do tell me. Tell me too if you have a clue to a maid yet? & if you w^d like me to enquire for one here? I know of one young woman who w^d take ten guineas a year, & who is skilful enough in dressmaking, I fancy—but you will tell me.

Ah—Mr Haydon!– His letter made me more than smile. Is'nt it excellent, the indignation at the "great fact" of a poet who has 'thoughts too deep for tears', condescending to put on another man's "inexpressible"?[1] It quite tickled my fancy . . to use the common phrase. Also, it was not unamusing to know that He of the Lakes did really come plump down on both his knees before our queen's fair majesty, & that a lordling or two were found ready to pick him up. I never heard that particular. And now only fancy what harm Mr Haydon does himself by talking after this fashion at Mr Serj^t Talfourd's & elsewhere—think how he *kills* himself by it! And after all, it is'nt consistent doctrine for a man who talks of the "divine right" by the hour—now, is it?

I am writing to you in a pre-occupied mood today, my very dear friend,—for my aunt Hedley is to be here tomorrow or the next day; & I *dread it through all my being. I shall see everything over again,—& feel it.* I love her,—but would give . . oh, so much! . . to be able to defer this meeting. I am a coward, you see—& rankly so. I have a dread of mental pain, which grows & grows in me, to my own consciousness—& really I fancy sometimes that I c^d be content to be separated from all life & its emotions, so as to avoid the pang of all. This is morbid—but then, I am morbid altogether—and this east wind has shaken me, & 'jangled' my nerves—& this expectation about the Hedleys, which has been on the fringe for several weeks now, creaks at the least breath. Oh—I shall be better after I have seen her, you know! It is nonsense—foolishness . . weakness, at best.

M.ʳ Kenyon has not returned yet,—but will, I suppose, at the end of this week, or the beginning of next—-and oh!—did I tell you in my last letter that I had seen lately *(now I beseech you to keep my counsel & not tell M.ʳ Horne—& not tell M.ʳ Chorley!)* M.ʳ Browning? He said in his courtesy more, in the way of request, than the thing was worth,—and so, I received him here one morning, & liked him much. Younger looking than I had expected—looking younger than he is, of course—with natural & not ungraceful manners,—& full of his art, which he is destined, I believe, so worthily to sustain. He is kind enough to promise to read my new Prometheus for me,—& we shall be good friends I hope. You & I differ about his genius,—& also on the dignities of pen & inkishness in general—but a poet is something after all, ... EVEN if (to quote from M.ʳ Haydon's idea of the pro-foundest degradation) in another man's inexpressibles!– Alfred Ten-nyson is in London, or has been lately,—& likes it beyond all places, I understand—his soul rejoicing in Polka & Cellarius²—& in going home to smoke,—& otherwise professing an intention of writing no more, because he has written all he has to say. Do you like *that*? No—no—no!– I do not like it for one—I even like it so little, do you know, that I feel quite sorry to have told you.

Thank you, thank you, for letting me see the pencilled lines by poor Clare!³–How strangely melancholy, that combination is—of men-tal gifts & mental privations! Poor Clare!–

•   •   •

Pray for your ever affectionate
EBB.

1. On the occasion of his first court ball as poet laureate, Wordsworth appeared in borrowed "clothes, buckle, and stockings."
2. A kind of waltz named for the Austrian dancing master who brought it to Paris in 1840.
3. John Clare (1793–1864), the ploughboy poet of Northamptonshire who was con-fined to a mental institution. A friend of MRM's visited him there and brought back the "pencilled lines" mentioned by EBB.

LONDON

Courtship and
Decision
1845–46

In the summer of 1845 EBB was well enough to see MRM again at Wimpole Street and to arrange a picnic for the Barretts in MRM's garden. The need to keep this innocent enough affair from Mr. Barrett's notice indicates his increasingly autocratic behavior and helps explain EBB's secrecy about her growing involvement with Browning (the course of which she confided only to the pages of her notebook, in poems later published as *Sonnets from the Portuguese*). By summer's end, when doctors advised a winter in Italy, Mr. Barrett adamantly opposed the move and, emotionally explaining the change of plan to MRM, EBB shows herself beginning the process of disengaging herself from her father's domination. At year's end, demurring at MRM's request for a poem on grounds of pressing commitments (including the writing of "A Runaway Slave at Pilgrim's Point" for the Boston *Liberty Bell* and the rewriting, never accomplished, of her 1842 *Athenæum* essays), she struggled with the momentous decision to escape to Italy with Browning. Meanwhile, her fame continued to spread, by way of Edgar Allan Poe's dedication to her of *The Raven and Other Poems* (1845)—eventually published without the "abusing preface" mentioned in [1 December]—and, less gratifyingly, by way of the setting to music of her "Cry of the Children" by MRM's friend, the vocalist Henry Russell (1812–1900). Current scandals in France became subjects for discussion in early 1846 as MRM once again made plans for a visit to Paris. Two of these causes célèbres discussed in [21 February 1846] were the case of the imprisoned author of *Mémoires de Marie Capell, veuve Lafarge* (1841), accused of murdering her husband, and the casual affairs of the actress Élisabeth Félix (1820–58), known as Rachel, whom EBB contrasted with George Sand. In late June as MRM, having canceled her Parisian trip, was about to visit EBB again, both were deeply shocked by the suicide of Benjamin Haydon. Humiliated at having his latest exhibition outdrawn by a performance of the American midget Charles Sherwood Stratton (1838–83), known as "General Tom Thumb," Haydon, after sending EBB his journals and a portrait of MRM for safekeeping, had shot himself in his studio.

WEDNESDAY. [4 JUNE 1845]

Ever dearest Miss Mitford, I am concerned that you sh^d still be unsettled; & . . in the matter of the *deficits*, . . will you let me know if I can send you anything as friend to friend . . ? Will you love me enough to let me know it? It w^d be a dear proof of your affection to me, . . if you w^d give that proof, . . & I sh^d have such a pleasure . . *Now, will you?*

• • •

I had heard nothing of the Tennyson marriage,[1] & if he has found a princess dowered with 'fine gold', under 'a silken coverlid,' . . why so much the better,—at least so I hope!– She must condescend to the smoke, —& perhaps to the polka——but the smoke is said to be so essentially Tennysonian that he could'nt be supposed to rhyme without it. As to my friend, Mr Browning, you made me smile a little at your anxiety about the influence of this cloud-compelling Jupiter among my clouds. You seem to think that, between us, reasonable people have no chance of ever seeing the sun! Well—I will take care, as you tell me!– And then you know I have other faults *besides* the fault of obscurity . . (& Mrs Jameson had the boldness to tell me to my face the other day that she did not think me obscure!!) & Mr Browning may show me how to correct *these* . . seeing that I recognize him for a master in art, 'after his kind', however to your astonishment. And for my 'Prometheus,' if my former attempt was anything but a disgrace, as a poetical rendering of Æschylus, & if my present one is

not in some degree worthier, . . . (for I do not praise it, mind . .)
then, I am ignorant of Æschylus, & of myself, & of the first elements
of poetry as an art, . . & "grope as the blind". Your M.ʳ Blackstone[2]
is probably of an elder school, & talks, as M.ʳ Boyd does, of scanning
this & the other English verse, & abjures the gross improprieties prac-
tised out of Dryden & Pope—&, in fact, that any one, . . who could
praise my first translation *as a poem, knowing the poetry of the original,*
. . sh.ᵈ prefer it to my new one, c.ᵈ not very much surprise me. In my
own mind, it is legitimately qualified to be used as a cramming book
by young students,—for "this & no more!"—& is for the rest, dead,
& prostrate, stiff & cold . . "corps morte" in a full sense, . . & the
work of a mind imperfectly possessed of its own wide-awake powers.
I could not speak my mind then . . my own mind! how much less,
Æschylus's?–

•   •   •

Yes—I did not suppose M.ʳ Browning to be younger,—& only observed that he did not look older, if so old as I *expected*——which
comes, as you say, of the slightness of form & figure. You are a little
wrong, I believe, in fancying that his personal friends only hold him
in estimation as a poet– His poems pay their way . . which is something in these beggarly days—& my brother hears him talked of
among the lawyers . . far on the outside of M.ʳ Serj.ᵗ Talfourd—and
then, I really must remind you, dear friend of mine, that Pippa Passes
made an impression on yourself. As to M.ʳ Horne he has never seen
nor thought of asking to see M·S. from my hand. He is too much occupied for such misdoings. Have you heard from him?—and has a
note from the viola accosted the ear of your Hayward Grace? I expect
him to go down in a flash of lightning one of these days, with a heart
ready blown to offer in his right hand, & the left hand extended for
your mediation.
      You will see that I am not so depressed, without my saying it—
& indeed the meeting with M.ʳˢ Hedley is over, . . & I was able to cry
well & be quiet afterwards, . . & now I shall enjoy her presence &
society. The worst of me is, just now, that I have left off sleeping 'for
the nonce' . . & without Frederic Soulié[']s[3] expedient of sowing up
my eyelids, I really cant *see* where it's to end. Oh—but *that* is jest—
& you are not to mind it! I have not murdered sleep . . & shall be in
a deep doze before long, there's no need for doubting. And in other
ways I am growing better & stronger as the sun shines, & walked into

Papa's room yesterday, & shall try to get out in the carriage perhaps before the century ends, . . & people begin to say that I look better.

•   •   •

Not a word more. Love me my beloved friend! And write & say if I can do anything, supply you with anything[—]gowns . . collars &c—now do!–

Am I not your own affectionate
Ba—?

1. Tennyson finally married Emily Sellwood in 1850 after a ten-year rupture in their engagement.
2. The Rev. F. C. Blackstone (1795–?), translator, and friend of MRM and Thomas Arnold.
3. Frédéric Soulié (1800–47), French sensational novelist and dramatist whom MRM and EBB read avidly. One of his characters has his eyelids sewn up.

SATURDAY MORNᵍ [21 JUNE 1845]

It makes my heart leap my beloved friend to think of you as coming so soon. Would it be quite the same thing if you were to come instead on *thursday* —by the way? Answer freely—only *at once*. And, to keep you in countenance, here am I going to speak out freely in a matter for which perhaps you will reprehend me. But I appeal to your known goodness & indulgence my dear dear friend, & open my heart to you, & entreat you (taking courage from the imagination of your smile) to *forgive me if I do not see Mʳ Chorley*—though of course YOU shall see him, & he is as welcome as the air to this house. Now here is my case. I am weak & morbid—be it so! I confess fully . . if you give me your absolution afterwards & leave me to the free enjoyment of my favorite sins. But it is not all weakness & morbidness—& to prove it—listen to me!–

Here is the summer, & for the last fortnight or longer (except for the want of sleep . .) I have been growing & growing just like the trees—it is miraculous, the feeling of sprouting life in me & out of me —& now I begin to sleep again & to look altogether like another person. But to get on & make progress such as I hope to make this summer, I *must* be quiet—& if you did not but know the effect of seeing one person, or of talking to people I am accustomed to see, on the whole night's rest after, you w^d say as all my medical advisers have always said . . that *"repose was my life."* Well then—just now is the turning point of the summer; & besides I am in the most peculiar circumstances you can fancy . . & persecuted on all sides, beyond your fancy, by letters & messages, & entreaties in each & all, of people who want to come in "for one moment." As a statistical fact I will just mention to you that *forty* of our relations are at this time in London,—everyone of them with an especial claim in his or her right hand—& male cousins (to boot) constantly in this house, & never seeing me!– Add to these my friends—infinitely more zealous, to do them justice—& the whole flock of sighing Aramintas! *Now a line must be drawn*—or my sepulchre must be prepared—do you not see the necessity? I confided to you *as a secret & in my trust in you*—that I had indeed . . after a struggle . . seen Mr Browning—but then, writing about poetry & criticism, in a correspondence we had, had made us personal friends, in a manner, before he came—& I honour his genius, & c^d not refuse a request he thought it worth while to press so kindly on me . . when the circumstance of his *living seven miles out of London* made him exceptional, in itself,—& when he promised, in all faith, that the fact of his having seen me sh^d never escape his lips. Mr Kenyon too, whose friend he is, will not betray it—& *you* will not, I know——, but, you know, it w^d be too ludicrous to administer such qualifying oaths of secrecy to one's visitors all round,—& I neither could nor would do such a thing. I see the ridiculous side of it too quickly—if there were nothing else. No—.

· · ·

Ever dearest Miss Mitford's

gratefully affectionate
EBB.

THURSDAY [10 JULY 1845]

Ever dearest kindest Miss Mitford,

I write to throw at your feet a burden of thanks & praises from many whom you made happy & grateful yesterday. My brother Alfred said to me expressively . . "Miss Mitford won every heart of us"—& *that's* true—for he does not often fall or rise into enthusiasms. How kind of you,—how good of you—how I thank you! Only all pic nics are spoilt to the general mind in comparison, from this time forth for ever—nothing after Whiteknights & your garden, being found commonly dreamable. Everybody came home in a sort of 'tipsy jollity' & a full bloom of recollection—& *you* were in each—your name, & that of your cottage & your colossal strawberries in proportion to the joys. And to show that it was'nt all a dream, here are only the flowers!——

Will you ask your gardener, by the way, to look in the garden for a pin of one of my brothers, . . a coral pin, I think . . which, planted there, is not likely to sprout up into a coral grove. And also will you understand that as soon as we can get an order for the post, we will send you our debt about the tickets. Acquit us in the meantime of dishonesty prepense—just as I do your lady of the Browning traditions, of intentional exaggeration—though . . while I receive part of the gossip into belief, I assuredly, like a second Jove, "dispense the rest in empty air". Do you think that a man can want money, who is travelling . . now to the east, now to Russia . . spending four years in Italy—(for if it is true that he was an attaché when under age, *that* was years ago—) since from 1836 to 40, he was abroad, & again last year, & would be in the east now, he says, except for his anxiety about his mother's health. Also he reproaches other poets for that very thing of which his friend accuses him—a want of masculine resolve to work like common men, when they want money like them. "How can work do dishonor to any man?" he has said—"& what is there in poetry to disqualify one from ordinary duties". So that the charge is altogether unlike & contrary to the nature of the man, which is eminently masculine & down right—strikingly so I think! Not an inch of gold lace or broidery in what Chaucer would call the "full yerdë long". So I quite, quite disbelieve. You know my dearest candid friend, it['] s quite possible to be a "visitor & family friend", without knowing very accurately, & without *talking* very accurately. His family may regret perhaps that he does not, by means of his talents, climb the woolsack rather than Parnassus Hill —*that* sort of regret is possible enough!—but I feel quite confident that if his position had required him to work, he is the last man under sun to shrink from it—I would throw down my silken gauntlet to maintain that point. That your informant *can* be wrong, the tradition about the *age* proves—for here's a fact——Paracelsus was published in 1835—& *not* the first work of its author. Now it was well understood that Paracelsus was the production of a young man several years above twenty. No—you were more right at first, be sure. And in fact, if Paracelsus was produced at twenty, with all that curious learning & profound thinking, it is the most wonderful work produced by man—*that*, I should say. But no— he was young—only not quite so young as that, I believe—in fact, I am confident. And I remember facts enough to justify much confidence.[1] It is true that M! Browning senior, is full of refinement, book-refinement,—without the son's genius. He (the father) was at school with M! Kenyon. The sister is considerably younger than her brother,—"by many years", he has told me—& I hear that *she* is something more than a girl. So you see! Mind you dont talk of my mysteries of Eleusis before M! Horne when he comes—or indeed before *any other person*—for, if you do, my beloved friend, you will bring me to bane. Also *I trust to you*—heart to heart . . & gossip to gossip.

•   •   •

I am your ever affectionate
Ba—
SHALL *it be?*

Talking of Eleusinian mysteries, did you understand that the escapade yesterday was unknown to the High priest here?—to Papa, I mean?—— Very wrong! Yes—*that* is true. *You must not mention it!* A little over-strictness sometimes *drives* into temptation.

1. At this time, Browning was 33; his sister was less than two years younger. He had visited Italy briefly in 1838 and spent four months there in the autumn of 1844.

[SATURDAY] [13? SEPTEMBER 1845]

Ever dearest Miss Mitford if I have not written the details you desire to know, instantly, it has been because really I am scarcely in possession of them yet, it being undecided between this next week & the week after, on which day I am likely to sail. I will tell you however what I can . . & if it is not much, blame the stars who are shining so doubtfully just now 'tra si e no'!

For the last two or three years I have been so much better & stronger in the summer & thrown back so hardly in the winter, that the wisdom & necessity of getting nearer the sun if I ever meant to live again, in the sense of ordinary life, was quite obvious to me. Last autumn when my brothers went to Ægypt, I was on the verge of desiring to go with them– But in this present summer, better & fitter for travelling than I ever found myself, & exhorted besides by my aunt Hedley who saw with her eyes how the change came with the sun, & how, from a feeble colourless invalid, I strengthened & brightened as the season advanced . . she, seeing it day by day!, . . I took the courage necessary for contemplating a winter passed in the south somewhere—& Malta, I thought of first. Well, then, Papa wished me to see Chambers & have his advice—& I sent for him, & was examined with that dreadful stethoscope, & received his command to go without fail *to Pisa by sea.* He said that it was the obvious thing to do—& that he not merely advised but enjoined it—that there was nothing for me but *warm air* . . no other possible remedy. He thought me comparatively well in certain respects—& that the malady on the lung was very slight & likely to be without results if the right precautions were taken—although I should be careful, as relapse was too possible. The weakness, he said, came from the action of the cold on the muscular system covering the lungs, & on the vascular system of the lungs, which were both very weak & sensitive to changes of temperature—and he also observed that the general nervous system was shattered & impaired. You see there is nothing for me in England during the winter, but to be shut up as I have been:—& the cold kills me & the seclusion exhausts me . . & there is no possible alternative here. Also, the cold cannot be shut out so effectually as not to operate injuriously,—*for,* said D! Chambers, 'You are not to think this, merely nervous weakness—though you are very nervous! it is in great part from the muscles covering the lungs being affected by the cold air . . & nothing but warm air is a remedy to it!' He left me in great spirits about myself & about what Pisa is to do for me—& I have since heard nothing but good of the place & climate. The sea is to do good too, I understand . . & I am not fearing it in any way. At the same time I am in very doubtful spirits—very agitated & full of sad thoughts . . from many causes on which I cannot enter now. You shall hear from me my ever dearest Miss Mitford, before I leave England——& over the Alps, my letters shall fly by as many a drove as shall be reasonable on considerations of postage. D! Chambers named *May* as the earliest time on which he c^d allow me to think of leaving Pisa—& in the meantime, all who have any kind regret to lose me, must consider that they lose only the sight of my bodily weakness & exhaustion in the sight of me stretched out on that sofa . . & what is *that* worth, to the kindest? Whereas during my absence I shall be perhaps out of doors every day in an Italian sun . . every day that it does not rain . . & able to think of my friends with gladder if not with fonder thoughts. So do not regret me my very dear kind friend—do not. And (but for the parting & my nervousness now,) I should have liked you to have seen me once so as to be able to think of me 'after my own likeness' a little, & not as you have been used to see me lately. M.ʳ Kenyon has just been persuading me that he never saw me looking so well in his life before!——which if not precisely true, means at least that I am looking much better & more like what I used to be, . . though still tottering & trembling about the room, & growing white with an exertion. And I cannot take the usual means of growing strong, you see— & Chambers persists in desiring that I sh.ᵈ live chiefly on milk & vegetables, & eschew the "strong meats & drinks" of the strong . . which proves that he has some fear of me in the face of his hopes.

•   •   •

And now, no more– Only you shall hear again. Oh no, no,—your affection for me *should not* draw you into such a toil . . even if it were possible for you to go to Italy, which I know it is not. Besides I shall be 'back again in a moment' you know. Ah—but to write lightly when my spirits are as they are . . you do not guess how! May God bless you–

Your EBB.

It is all uncertain about my companions. I hope for too many brothers & sisters perhaps & it is all unsettled. You shall hear.

[MONDAY] [27 OCTOBER 1845]

I upbraid myself for not writing to you my ever dearest Miss Mitford—but I have had no heart to write . . no heart . . it is just the word!—for mine has been tossed up & down by sadder thoughts than the mere non-recovery of health could bring me. Let us leave the subject– I cannot talk of it. *I should have gone infallibly*, if it had not been for the apprehension of involving others with me in a series of difficulties . . which (as to *them*), would have constituted my condem-

nation in my own eyes. As for the good to be derived, I see it as you
see it—& perhaps everyone else sees the same. It is not the *sight*
which is awry—not the power of seeing– I want only the sun—I faint
here for lack of the sun: & it is proved to me that I should be in as
good health as the rest of the world, if I could have the two things
together, warmth & air. But this shutting up you see, which is necessary to prevent the tendency to organic disease of the lungs, shatters
the nervous system—& the alternative of either evil is inevitable
while I live in this climate. I feel like a bird in a cage . . inclined to
dash myself against the bars of my prison—but God is good, & coun-
ter-motives have been given to me in moments of the greatest bitterness, sufficient for encouragement. So I live on—"bide my time"—
only without the slightest expectation, my loved friend, of the results
you speak of from the quarter you look to—no!– In fact, nothing
should ever induce me to appeal again, on any personal ground whatever, to that quarter. It is from no want of frankness . . this reticence
to you!—& you will be the first to understand the respect of my silence. So let us leave the subject for what is pleasant—for I shall see
you . . shall I not? Any day, this week even, I shall be delighted to
see you—any day after tomorrow, tuesday. Begin from wednesday, &
go on. Only it is too bad to think of bringing you so far through the
cold—but I let your kindness have its way. Only again, I suddenly
think that you may be retained by prudential motives—because one
of my brothers has been ill with fever of a typhoid character (not absolutely typhus) & though now convalescent, & able to leave his bed &
take soups & strengthening things, I know what a sound typhus must
have ⟨in⟩ your ears. Yet the medical men have been of opinion
throughout that no harm was to be apprehended for visitors at the
house—& my other brothers who sate up, night after night, with the
poor invalid hav⟨e⟩ been & are perfectly well—— I tell you in any
case.– Judge for yourself . . & in the case of the least fear, do not
come. You will find me (if you do) still off the sofa, & able to walk
about—only not looking quite as flourishing as I really did in the summer—a little fagged (as must needs be) with all the heart-bruising!–
And I shall struggle not to sink this winter,—& if it is a mild winter
. . ah, well! all this is with God. And the *wound* is apart from it, ...
apart from the mere *health*, & to be unaffected by it. May God help
me! my reeds have run into me from all sides almost . . yet still I
cling!–

•   •   •

Well—you will write in any case–

> And I am ever
> your affectionate EBB.

MONDAY. [1 DECEMBER 1845]

•   •   •

What is this Reading bazaar? for the hospital . . or to what end? But I ask questions when I should be giving answers, . . the reason being that I scarcely know how to give my answers. Dearest Miss Mitford . . the gladness & pride I should feel in letting my name or the work of my hands lie by yours even for a moment & in a little thing, it cannot be needful for me to tell you. *That* is obvious . . you can want no professing of it nor proving of it. But the truth is . . that, having been idle past all belief & imagination, I, at the present moment, know not to which side to look, to do the work pressed upon me. I have been completely upset of late . . all through the autumn & the latter part of the summer . . & people invoke me from America, as if I might be dead . . or what besides?– I have to write for the anti-slavery people at Boston, . . & to prepare the prose papers printed in the Athenæum (which will be rewriting them, or worse!) & to make additions & complete a volume of prose miscellanies for the American publisher who undertook my poems & calls for those. And I feel now heavy & stupid with past idleness. How I shall complete these engagements & answer heaps of unanswered letters, I cannot tell—& if I were to promise to do your ballad, my bond would be worth nothing at all.– You see!– And then I have been thinking that I should do you no good by promising & keeping even,—that your Reading people want *you* & not *me*,—& that any story you chose to give them, would sell as quickly & well as if Alfred Tennyson put a Locksley Hall to the end of it! Your name would do the whole—now consider that it would. And it you take another view, tell me & let me look round again & make a struggle,—since I would not for the world disappoint you in the matter of a straw—so think & tell me.

• • •

Now I have something to ask– Do you know Mr Russell your member, mighty in railroads? —& if you know him, see him, & speak to him, would you object to ask him some day to give the weight of a word in behalf of my brother Alfred who is anxious to get employment on the great western railroad? I mean in the way of clerkships, & the like—& I do *not* mean, ever dearest Miss Mitford, that you should take trouble or suffer yourself to be annoyed to the extent of a fly's buzzing in the matter. Only *if* . . you understand all the 'ifs'. Alfred wants occupation, & young men rush to the railroads for occupation from every side. Mr Russell is chairman, he says—but I merely speak as I am bid, & without in the least expecting that you can do anything– I promised Alfred to ask you, & keep my word *so*.

I hear that somebody in America (Edgar Poe) has been dedicating a book to me & abusing me in the preface. Is'nt that pure justice—& an original way of administering it? Mrs Butler has *again* decided on *not* returning there. Mr Kenyon dined in company with her the other day at Mr Procter's—& she was in great force & eloquence.

• • •

Your ever affec.^{te}
EBB

Saturday. [21 February 1846]

• • •

For Ma^{dme} Laffarge, remember that she had to represent her situation . . which is to my mind . . most intensely painful for all its commonness . . enough to drive any woman frantic. She speaks out— had to speak out at the trial . . where that letter of hers was produced . . the dramatic letter . . in which she made *(invented)* a position & a lover for herself to escape the legal dishonour. Oh dreadful! You must not blame her for speaking, in any wise, since others had spoken for her, poor wretch. And in writing that letter, she seemed to me to follow a blind instinct. What woman, with a sense of shame in her, would not rather go with her lover to the end of the world . . let it be sin twenty times over, . . than give herself to a master by *law*, unsanctified by the testimony of her affections—? The lover not being there, she invented one. A blind instinct of her despair, it seems to me,— in a situation full of horror– God keep us from such marriages, here in England.

I hear that Dumas has been writing a romance called 'Monte Cristo', which is as popular as ever 'Les Mysteres de Paris' was, . . & a little longer . . being somewhere in the *fourteenth* volume now. Also George Sand has published a book called 'Le pêché de Monsieur Thomas' or, some name like it. The book you name, I never heard of. For the rest, all these romances of ours are never read in Paris by unmarried women, nor by the married . . except in an *aside* very strictly kept . . & with a sofa-pillow close by for security!—this I heard the other day—*Balzac* for instance is never named in female society—his works are considered "licentious". The women are none the more virtuous for such precautions—quite otherwise than virtuous, in fact: but *vice is not talked of*—the sepulcher is kept both silent & white. So, in regard to the theatres . . (except the classical great theatre,—) . . "on va, mais on n'en parle pas" —that is, the married women go . . in their silence . . bien entendu . . but the unmarried not at all. Mademoiselle Rachel's character is trailed in all the mud of Paris—she is *"devergondée"*, they tell me. Her lovers seem to out-number Ma^dme Dudevant's . . which is saying . . . . what, is it not saying? And thus, she who was at first received by the Faubourgh St. Germains circles, among the most excluding of the exclusives, has utterly destroyed a social position which was of such peculiar brilliancy for a French actress. For the actors & actresses, as well as painters & musicians, have more difficulty in making way in Paris, than they w^d have here in London . . they are not tolerated, socially speaking, except under express conditions—I am surprised to hear it. The *literary* artists have a social 'status' of their own, you are aware—but it is not so with the others.

•   •   •

I am your affectionate & grateful
EBB–

[EARLY MARCH 1846]

Ever dearest Miss Mitford, how wonderfully the winter does forget itself & seem inclined to go on dreaming of summer into summer back again. I have been down stairs several times, & with no disadvantage—& perhaps some day when it is not damp, besides being warm, I may get out into the carriage . . or walk a little in the street . . who knows? In the meanwhile, not a word do you say about the arrowroot. Is it good, bad, or indifferent? Will you have some more?– I have ordered some oysters for you. And now I am going to talk of Mʳ Russell & the 'refrain' –

I have considered my ever dear kind friend, & certainly it does seem to *me*, that the natural refrain of that poem should be the first line repeated.

'Do you hear the children weeping, o my brothers?'

or if a reference to the machinery is absolutely desirable why there are the four lines ending

'O ye wheels (breaking out in a mad moaning)
Stop!—be silent for today.'

It does seem to me that it would be difficult to graft in your refrain on the body of the poem—but I yield to reasonable remonstrance, if necessary, & leave it in your hands. The probability is that Mʳ Russell will not care for either my thoughts or my rhymes. Your goodness has the habit, I know, of running miles before ordinary probabilities.

·   ·   ·

Ever your affectionate
EBB

TUESDAY. [30 JUNE 1846]

Do come, ever dearest Miss Mitford, & fear neither aunts nor cousins, whom you will escape by just a day. I write this hurried line to say my 'Do come', & no more. Long before & much more in detail I should have written, but the shock of poor Mʳ Haydon's dreadful death overcame me for several days. Our correspondence had ceased a full year & a half I think; but the *week preceding the event*, he wrote several notes to me, & by his desire I have under my care boxes & pictures of his which he brought himself to the door. Never did I anticipate *this!*—never did I imagine that it was other than one of the passing embarrassments so unhappily frequent with him. Once before, he had asked me to give shelter to things belonging to him, which, when the storm had blown over, he took back again. I did not suppose that, in this storm, he was to *sink*—poor, noble soul!–

And be sure that the pecuniary embarrassment was not what sank him. It was a wind still more *east*. It was the despair of the ambition by which he lived, & without which he could not live. In the selfassertion which he had struggled to hold up through life, he went down into death– He could not bear any longer, the neglect, the disdain, the slur cast on him by the age,—& so he perished. The cartoon-disappointment—the grotesque bitterness of the *antagonism of Tom Thumb*, which he recurred to in one of the notes he wrote to me at the last—these things were too much:—the dwarf slew the Giant. His love of reputation, you know, was a disease with him—&, for my part, I believe that he died of it. That is my belief.

In the last week, he sent me his portrait of *you*, among the other things. When he proposed sending it, he desired me to keep it for his sake,—but when it came, a note also came to say that he "could not make up his mind to part with it" . . he would *lend* it to me for a while. A proof (with the rest) that his act was not premeditated. A moment of madness—or a *few* moments of madness! who knows?

I could not read the Inquest, nor any of the details in the newspapers.

Oh—certain I was, that you would be shocked beyond words.

On thursday then, my very dear friend! Come as early as you can—, & be sure that my affectionate thoughts will leap on to meet you.

As ever your
EBB–

LONDON, PISA,
AND FLORENCE

Marriage and Travel
1846–48

On 12 September 1846 EBB married Robert Browning in a private ceremony at St. Marylebone Church, and a week later left with him for the continent, accompanied by her maid Wilson and her pet spaniel Flush. Her letter of [18 September 1846], written on the eve of departure and eloquently justifying the decision, shows that she had given MRM no inkling of the state of affairs even at their last visit late in August. Perhaps MRM guessed the truth; at any rate she sent an assuring message to Orléans and the correspondence continued as before, except that letters were necessarily written over greater intervals with EBB's echoing her new state of marital felicity. A miscarriage in March kept her and Browning in Pisa (their first stop in Italy) until April when they moved on to Florence. A 20 August [1847] letter reports the latest on favorite topics: Tennyson's new poem *The Princess* (in which the "Commonwealth" is an all-female university) and his taking the hydropathic cure for depression; and Harriet Martineau's return from a Palestinian tour. News was especially welcome to Three Mile Cross as increasing lameness curtailed MRM's beloved country walks and crowded garden teas. In 1847 she began a satisfying correspondence with the young art critic John Ruskin (1819–1900) who published his first work *Modern Painters* (1843) under the pseudonym "A Graduate of Oxford" (and hence is referred to hereafter by EBB as "your Oxford student"). While the Brownings visited Fano and environs during the summer of 1848—remarkable testimony to EBB's improved health—MRM was able to enjoy a rare vacation at a cottage on the Thames.

FRIDAY [18 SEPTEMBER 1846]

My dearest friend I have your letter & your prophecy, —& the latter meets the event like a sword ringing into its scabbard. My dear dearest friend I would sit down by your feet & kiss your hands with many tears, & beseech you to think gently of me, & love me always, & have faith in me that I have struggled to do the right & the generous & not the selfish thing,—though when you read this letter I shall have given to one of the most gifted & admirable of men, a wife unworthy of him. I shall be the wife of Robert Browning. Against *you*, . . in allowing you no confidence, . . I have not certainly sinned, I think—so do not look at me with those reproachful eyes. I have made no confidence to any . . not even to my & his beloved friend Mᵣ Kenyon—& this advisedly, & in order to spare him the anxiety & the responsibility. It would have been a wrong against him & against you to have told either of you—we were in peculiar circumstances—& to have made you a party, would have exposed you to the whole dreary rain—without the shelter we had – If I had loved you less—dearest Miss Mitford, I could have told you sooner.

And now . . oh, will you be hard on me? will you say . . "This is not well".?

I tell you solemnly that nothing your thoughts can suggest against this act of mine, has been unsuggested by *me* to *him*– He has loved me for nearly two years, & said so at the beginning. I would not listen—I could not believe even. And he has said since, that almost he began to despair of making me believe in the force & stedfastness of his attachment. Certainly I conceived it to be a mere poet's fancy . . an illusion of a confusion between the woman & the poetry. I have seen a little of the way of men in such respects, and I could not see beyond that with my weary, weeping eyes, for long.

How can I tell you on this paper, even if my hands did not tremble as the writing shows, how he persisted & overcame me with such letters, & such words, that you might tread on me like a stone if I had not given myself to him, heart & soul. When I bade him see that I was bruised & broken . . unfit for active duties, incapable of common pleasures . . that I had lost even the usual advantages of youth & good spirits—his answer was, "that with himself also the early freshness of youth had gone by, & that, throughout his season of youth, he had loved no woman at all, nor had believed himself made for any such affection—that he loved now once & for ever—he, knowing himself——That, for my health, . . he had understood, on first seeing me, that I suffered from an accident on the spine of an incurable nature, & that he never could hope to have me stand up before him. He bade me tell him, what, if that imagination had been true, what there was in that truth, calculated to suppress any pure attachment, such as he professed for me? For his part, the wish of his heart had been *then*—that by consenting to be his wife even so, I would admit him to the simple priviledge of sitting by my side two hours a day, as a brother would: he deliberately preferred the realization of *that dream*, to the brightest, excluding me, in this world or any other."

My dear friend, feel for me. It is to your woman's nature that I repeat these words, that they may commend themselves to you & teach you how *I* must have felt in hearing them—I who loved Flush for not hating to be near me . . I, who by a long sorrowfulness & solitude, had sunk into the very ashes of selfhumiliation– Think how I must have felt to have listened to such words from such a man. A man of genius & of miraculous attainments . . but of a heart & spirit beyond them all!——

He overcame me at last. Whether it was that an unusual alikeness of mind . . (the high & the low may be alike in the general features) . . a singular closeness of sympathy on a thousand subjects, . . drew him fast to me—or whether it was *love simple* . . which after all is *love proper* . . an unreasonable instinct, accident . . 'falling', as the idiom says . . the truth became obvious that he would be happier with me than apart from me—and I . . why I am only as any other woman in the world, with a heart belonging to her. He is best, noblest—— If you knew him, YOU should be the praiser.

I have seen him only & openly in this house, observe—*never elsewhere*, except in the parish church before the two necessary witnesses. We go to Italy . . to Pisa—cross to Havre from Southampton . . pass quickly along the Seine, & through Paris to Orleans—till we are out

of hearing of the dreadful sounds behind. An escape from the winter
will keep me well & still strengthen me—& in the summer we come
back . . if anyone in the world *will* receive us– We go to live a quiet,
simple, rational life—to do work "after the pattern in the mount"
which we both see . . to write poems & read books, & try to live not
in vain & not for vanities–

In the meanwhile, it is in anguish of heart that I think of leaving
this house *so*– Oh—a little thread might have bound my hands, from
even working at my own happiness– But all the love came from *that
side!* on the other—too still it was—not with intention . . I do not say
so—yet too still. I was a woman & shall be a wife when you read this
letter. It is finished, the struggle is ————

As to marriage . . it never was high up in my ideal, even before
my illness brought myself so far down. A happy marriage was the hap-
piest condition, I believed vaguely—but *where were the happy marriages? I*, for my part, never could have married a common man—and
never did any one man whom I have had the honour of hearing talk
love, as men talk, lead me to think a quarter of a minute of the possibility of being married by such an one. Then I thought always that a
man whom I could love, would never stoop to love me– That was my
way of thinking, years ago, in my best days, as a woman's days are
counted—& often & often have I been gently upbraided for such romantic fancies—for expecting the grass underfoot to be sky blue, &
for not taking M! A or B or C for the "best possible" whatever might
be.

We shall not be rich—but we shall have enough to live out our
views of life—& fly from the winters in Italy.

I write on calmly to you– How little this paper represents what
is working within in the intervals of a sort of *stupour.*

Feel for me if not with me my dear dear friend– *He* says that we
shall justify by our lives this act,—which may & must appear to many,
. . as I *say* . . wilful & rash. People will say that he is mad, & I, *bad*—
with my long traditions & associations with all manner of sickness. Yet
God judges, who sees the root of things – And I believe that no
woman with a heart, could have done otherwise . . much otherwise–
You do not know *him.*

May God bless you—I must end. Try to think of me gently—
& if you can bear to write to me, let me hear . . at Orleans—Poste
Restante.

Here is the truth—I *could not* meet you & part with you now, face to face.

•   •   •

Your most affectionate
EBB

Wilson goes with me, of course. And the last commission she has is to settle with Rolandi[1] for you. God bless you—

1. The foreign-book circulating library subscription that EBB was providing for MRM.

[Florence] [Friday] [30 April 1847]

Have you thought me vanished from the world, my dearest friend, that I have yet made no sign in recognition to your last welcome letter? I hope so, rather than any thought of neglect or forgetfulness, . . which must always be amiss, remember, when attributed to *me* by *you*. The truth is very different indeed. Your letter found me unwell, & at the brink of a crisis from the effects of which I scarcely have recovered at this moment though we came to Florence nine days ago and I hope in two more days to be able to get into the galleries & see a little of the wonders of our beautiful city here. So ill I have been,— not from the old causes nor in the old way—(my chest indeed has made itself forgotten lately, the air of Italy agrees so well with its requirements) but from a *new* cause, & in a way you will guess when I tell you that I had treated myself improperly for a condition of which I was unaware & brought on a premature conclusion as might, I suppose, be expected. Then, as it was of *five months date*, of course the trial to the constitution was great; and the exhaustion has been very great, though I bore it all with more vigour than anyone w^{d} have thought possible in me, & rallied more quickly. Still it is nearly six weeks since the event, and the strength has not all come back yet— and Tantalus & I may lie together in a myth, I on a sofa, as thirsty as he,—within a stone's throw of the Venus & the Raphaels. Having been very headstrong in the beginning (refusing to give ear to my husband's entreaties about seeing a physician in that good time which would have saved everything) I determined to make up for it by obedience & submission at last; & D.ʳ Cook let me travel to Florence on condition of resting absolutely, afterward—so I rest, & resist all temptations of the devil & Michael Angelo. It is but fair to poor dearest Robert, whom I frightened out of his wits nearly, & quite overcame in his spirits—& who has been lavishing on me for these six weeks, even an *excess* of the ordinary overflowings of the deepest & tenderest nature in man– He has nursed me, comforted me, loved me—the words fail me, (as *he* never did) when I try to describe what he has been & is to me. If marriage was a little oftener what I have found it, how different the world would be, & how much happier, women! Well!—but I must hasten to tell you that we were in haste to leave Pisa for Florence because M.ʳˢ Jameson gave us tryst at the latter place, two days after our arrival. She was to come last saturday—but on friday night when Robert & I had just finished coffee, & he was at the piano playing to me, as I lay prostrated on the sofa, Shakespeare's favorite air which the antiquaries turned up, a voice at the door said "Upon my word! here's domestic harmony!" & in walked M.ʳˢ Jameson & her niece, that moment arrived from Rome. They had come a day sooner, to keep Shakespeare's birthday with us (friday was Shakespeare's birthday) & with a bottle of wine from Arezzo to drink deathless memories withal—and we had a merry supper accordingly & welcomed our guests gladly, &, as our guests, they remained in this house for a full week, till seven o'clock in the morning of this present writing, when it is friday again & we have lost them.

•　　•　　•

For Pisa, we confess that never was deeper dulness & nowhere a completer system of cheating . . , that we were cheated in house & board, as perfectly as Italians can cheat . . "Pisani traditore" says the proverb: but we were happy, happy, happy at Pisa & grew quite pathetic on having to leave it. And I never went to the top of the Leaning Tower, & left most of the churches unseen . . because so much was put off to the last & at last I was ill—it was very provoking. Here I have just had a moment's vision of this beautiful Florence as in entering it we passed the bridges & glanced up & ⟨down the⟩ dear yellow Arno, shot between the double range of marble pala⟨ces. We⟩ are settled in an excellent apartment, & mean to be well & strong, ⟨if⟩ God will let us, & enjoy everything to the heart of it. In the meanwhile I will pray you to write to me & tell me that you have lost your rheumatism (do tell me *that*) & are in good spirits! Tell me all you choose to tell me—for no little detail, though it only relate to your shoestrings, will find me indifferent. At Pisa Robert read to me while I was ill, & partly by being read to & partly by reading I got through a good deal of amusing French book-work, & among the rest, two volumes of Bernard's new ["]Gentilhomme Campagnard." Rather dull I thought it, but clever of course—dull for Bernard. Then we read "Le Speronare" by Dumas—a delightful book of travels. Even Robert who took your view of the trial & swore he never would read a book of Dumas' again, was charmed with the Speronare (being beguiled into a glance at a page of it) admiring the vividness & vivacity, & the *bonhommie* besides the grace of style. But Robert & I had ⟨tre⟩mendous combats about the trial—and I am not tired . . I will take up your gauntlet in turn . . I dont see things as you & he do, about poor Dumas, and I will confess to you, dearest Miss Mitford, that I read with a certain admiration & sympathy of a man's brains being actually torn out & pulled for & tugged for & struggled for by a pack of newspaper hounds. There was something to me almost grand in that charge of having written only twelve volumes in three months—only forty eight volumes in eight months—of having folded his arms & written only forty eight volumes besides translating Shakespeare! —almost sublime in those attending certificates of medical advisers & friends, "Vous allez crever mon cher ami"—if you dont take breath a little on the coast of Africa or at some royal marriage. Nay, I forgive him that folding of the drapery, about his marquisates, it is so French & Dumastic. He wanted to brave that as he could write a multitude of books, so he could double his identity. The "moi, Alexandre Dumas, Marquis de P_____"[1] . . . . well, I for my part, could only laugh outright & forgive him with all my heart.

· · ·

your ever affec^te
EBB.

1. Dumas could not properly claim a title although his grandfather was the Marquis de la Pailleterie.

Florence—
[Friday] August 20– [1847]

I have received your letter at last my ever dearest Miss Mitford; not
the missing letter, but the one which comes to make up for it and to
catch up my thoughts which were grumbling at high tide I do assure
you. No, I never had the letter you speak of . . the answer to mine—
and if I had not heard now, I should have written, so uncomfortable
did the long dismal unusual silence make me. Unlucky woman that I
am, to have missed that letter . . yet lucky to have this!—and scarcely
ever does it happen that I lose a letter, scarcely ever. I hear from &
write to my sisters once in every ten days . . sometimes oftener; and
neither they nor I have had to complain of a lost letter between us.
But yours certainly is lost, and I am glad almost now to think that it
is. Better lose a letter than a remembrance of yours! so much better.
Dearest friend, let me begin by talking of your rheumatism– What!
you have rheumatism after all the heat in England this summer, of
which we hear– I hoped that it w^d have been the merest history by
this summertime!—and it is terrible to listen to accounts of your being
lame to such an extent, & so restrained in your healthy exercise. I do
not like to advise you; but if I were you, as advisers say, I would turn
to the water cure straightway. It is a legitimate case for the water
cure, and if I were you I would try it.

•   •   •

Nearly all my friends of both sexes have been draining off into
marriage these two years—scarcely one will be left in the sieve—and
I may end by saying that I have happiness enough for my own share
to be divided among them all & leave everyone contented. For me I
take it for pure magic, this life of mine. Surely nobody was ever so
happy before. I shall wake some morning, with my hair all dripping
out of the enchanted bucket. Or if not, we shall both claim the
"Flitch"[1] next september, if you can find one for us in the land of
Cockaigne, drying in expectancy of the revolution in Tennyson's
Commonwealth. Well! I dont agree with Mr Harness in admiring the
lady of Locksley Hall. I must either pity or despise a woman who
could have married Tennyson, & chose a common man. If happy in
her choice, I despise her. That's matter of opinion, of course. You
may call it matter of foolishness, when I add, that I, personally, would
rather be teazed a little & smoked over a good deal by a man whom

I c^d look up to & be proud of, than have my feet kissed all day by a Mr Smith in boots & a waistcoat, & thereby chiefly distinguished. Neither I nor another, perhaps, had quite a right to expect a *combination* of qualities . . such as meet, though, in my husband, who is as faultless & pure in his private life as any Mr Smith of them all . . who would not owe five shillings . . who lives like a woman in abstemiousness, on a pennyworth of wine a day, never touching a cigar even. But now for poor Tennyson, of whom you are not the first . . alas! . . to tell me these sad stories——is it sure of Tennyson that if he had been happy, if for instance that very woman of Locksley Hall had not embittered his life & cast him out into solitude, the bad habits in question w^d have taken root & grown? There, is a doubt sufficient to condemn her out & out before the world, God & her soul. *I* think so, at least. Do you hear, as we do from Mr Forster, that his new poem is his best work? As soon as you read it, let me have your opinion. The subject seems almost identical with one of Chaucer's– Is it not so?

We have spent here the most delightful of summers, notwithstanding the heat . . and I begin to comprehend the possibility of St Lawrence's ecstasies on the gridiron. Very hot, it certainly has been & is . . yet there have been cool intermissions,—and as we have spacious & airy rooms, & as Robert lets me sit all day in my white dressing gown without a single masculine criticism, & as we can step out of the window on a sort of balcony-terrace which is quite private & swims over with moonlight in the evenings, and as we live upon water melons and iced water & figs & all manner of fruit, we bear the heat with an angelic patience & felicity which really are edifying. We tried to make the monks of Vallombrosa let us stay with them for two months—but their new abbot sai⟨d⟩ or implied that Wilson & I stank in his nostrils, being women . . and San Gualberto the establisher of their order had enjoined on them only the mortification of cleaning out pigsties without fork or shovel. To have a couple of women besides, was (as Dickens's American said) "a piling it up rayther too mountainious". So we were sent away at the end of five days– So provoking! Such scenery, such hills, such a sea of hills looking alive among the clouds. *Which* rolled, it was difficult to discern. Such pine woods, supernaturally silent, with the ground black as ink . . such chesnut & beech forests hanging fr⟨om⟩ the mountains!—such rocks & torrents, such chasms & ravines! There were eagles there too ⟨and⟩ there was *no road*. Robert went on horseback, and Flush[,] Wilson &

I were drawn in a sledge . . (i.e. an old hamper . . a basket wine-hamper, without a wheel) by two white bullocks, up the precipitous mountains. Think of my travelling in that fashion in those wild places at four oclock in the morning! . . a little frightened, dreadfully tired, but in an ecstasy of admiration above all! It was a sight to see before one died & went away to another world–

• • •

This Florence is unspeakably beautiful, by grace both of nature & art,—and the wheels of life slide on upon the grass (according to Continental ways) with little trouble & less expense. Dinner, "unordered", comes through the streets & spreads itself on our table, as hot as if we had smelt cutlets hours before. The science of material life is understood here & in France. Now tell me, . . what right has England to be the dearest country in the world?– But I love dearly dear England, and we hope to spend many a green summer in her yet. The winters you will excuse us . . will you not? People who are like us, neither rich nor strong, claim such excuses—. I am wonderfully well, and far better & stronger than before what you call the Pisan "crisis"– Robert declares that nobody would know me, I *look* so much better. And you heard from dearest Henrietta? Ah, both of my dearest sisters have been perfect to me– No words can express my feelings towards their goodness. Otherwise, I have good accounts from home of my father[']s excellent health & spirits . . which is better even than to hear of his loving & missing me. I had a few kind lines yesterday from Miss Martineau who invites us from Florence to Westmoreland – She wants to talk to me, she says, of "her beloved Jordan". She is looking forward to a winter of work by the Lakes, & to a summer of gardening— The kindest of letters, Robert has had from Carlyle— who makes me very happy by what he says of our marriage. Shakespeare's favorite air of the "Light of Love", with the full evidence of its being Shakespeare's favorite air, is given in Charles Knight's edition.[2] Seek for it there. Now do write to me & at length, & tell me everything of yourself. Flush hated Vallombrosa & was frightened out of his wits by the pine forests. Flush likes civilized Life, & the society of little dogs with turned up tails, such as Florence abounds with. Unhappily it abounds also with *fleas*, which afflict poor Flush to the verge sometimes of despair. Fancy Robert & me down on our knees combing him, with a basis of water on one side!—— He suffers to such a degree from fleas that I cannot bear to witness it. He tears off his

pretty curls, through the irritation. Do you know of a remedy? Direct
to me Poste Restante, Florence . . Put *via France* . . Let me hear . .
do!

•   •   •

EBB–*Ba*

1. Cf. the proverb "He may fetch a flitch of bacon from Dunmow," said of one married a year without quarreling with his spouse. Among friends who were "draining
off into marriage" was R. H. Horne, who had recently married a young nonheiress,
Catherine Foggo.

2. Probably *A Pictorial Shakespere* (1838–41) by Charles Knight (1791–1873), editor
and publisher of a popular edition of Shakespeare's plays.

[FLORENCE] [SUNDAY] MAY 28 [1848]

So you have been in danger from the poney which took bread from
K's hand! There's a treacherous poney! Dearest Miss Mitford, how it
touches me to think of the fright you have had, you who I fear, I fear,
are not at the strongest as to nerves & health just now! I catch my
breath at the image of the kicking creature & of you petrified in the
carriage . . unable to move . . and K's courage, well rewarded by your
safety.

•   •   •

And now, I must tell you what we have done since I wrote last
little thinking of doing so? You see our problem was, to get to England as much in our summers as possible, the expence of the intermediate journeys making it difficult of solution. On examination of the
whole case, it appeared manifest that we were throwing money into
the Arno, by our way of taking furnished rooms, while to take an
apartment & furnish it, would leave us a clear return of the furniture
at the end of the first year in exchange for our outlay, & of all but a
free residence afterwards, with the priviledge of making it productive
by under-letting at our good pleasure. For instance, rooms we paid
four guineas a month for, we could have the whole year unfurnished
for ten or twelve, . . the cheapness of the furniture being besides
something quite fabulous, especially at the present crisis– Laying
which facts together, & seeing besides the all but necessity for us to
reside abroad the colder part of every year, we leapt on our feet to

the obvious conclusion you have before you!—and though the temptation was too strong for us to adopt quite the cheapest ways of the
cheap scheme, by the dense economy of preferring small rooms &c,
. . though in fact we have really done it magnificently, & planted ourselves in the Guidi palace, in the favorite suite of the last count, (his
arms are in scagliola on the floor of my bedroom, . .) though we have
six beautiful rooms & a kitchen, . . three of them quite palace rooms
& opening on a terrace, . . & though such furniture as comes by slow
degrees into them is antique & worthy of the place, we yet shall have
saved money by the close of this year, . . while, for next year, see!
We shall let our apartment & go to England, drawing from it the prod-
uct of *"furnished rooms"*!–

●   ●   ●

What I claimed first, in way of priviledge, was a spring-sofa to loll
upon, & a supply of rain water to wash in! and you should see what a
picturesque oil-jar they have given us for the latter purpose. It w^d just
hold the captain of the forty thieves. As to the chairs & tables I yield
the more especial interest in them to Robert. Only, you would laugh
to hear us correct one another sometimes– "Dear, you get too many
drawers, & not enough washing stands. Pray dont let us have any
more drawers, when we've nothing more to put into them." There
was no division on the necessity of having six spoons—some questions
pass themselves. Now do write to me & be as egotistical!– At last we
have caught sight of Tennyson's Princess & I may or must profess to
be a good deal disappointed. What woman will tell the great poet that
Mary Wolstonecraft herself never dreamt of setting up collegiate
states, proctordoms & the rest, . . which is a worn-our plaything in the
hands of one sex already, & need not be *transferred* in order to be
proved ridiculous? As for the poetry, beautiful in some parts, he never
seems to me to come up to his own highest mark, in the rhythm especially. The old blank verse of Tennyson was a divine thing, but this
new, . . mounted for certain critics, . . may please *them* perhaps better
than it pleases me. Still the man is Tennyson, take him for all & all,
& I never shall forgive whatever princesses of my sex may have ill-
treated him.–

●   ●   ●

your ever affectionate
Ba

Taplow
July 30, 1848.

I have taken so much of your advice, my very dear love, as Mr. May thought right—that is to say, the part that regarded change of air and change of scene. He said that the sea, in my particular case, would be rather bad than good, and advised a short journey, where I could have my pony chaise among interesting scenery, and not beyond reach of him. Accordingly here I am, about twenty miles from home—in a pretty house, with our rooms opening on a garden full of trees and flowers, which goes down to the Thames (we have our own private stairs and landing from the little terrace), and the beautiful old bridge just below. A prettier English scene does not exist. I have already driven to Orkwells, the beautiful old hall of the Norreys, part of which is just as it was in the reign of Henry the Sixth—and that part the most important—the banquet-hall, with its dais and music-gallery and long range of painted windows—the open galleries, buttery hatch, porch and gables, with the exquisite carving of their fretted roof as delicate as a lady's fan. Then I have been (where I have permission to go every day) through Lord Orkney's noble woods to Cliefden Spring—a woody acclivity (of I am afraid to say what height) on one side, and the bright river on the other—the actual

"Cliefden's proud alcove,"

where Lady Shrewsbury held her lover the Duke of Buckingham's horse, while he fought with and killed her husband. Then to Burnham Beeches—a piece of forest scenery hardly to be matched in England, whether as regards the ground or the magnificent trees. Then to the vaults at Lady Place, where the Revolution of 1688 was hatched, and which looks just fit for such a holy conspiracy, standing, as it does now, with the old mansion taken down, in the midst of its romantic lawn. All these I have seen, and to-morrow I am going to Dropmore; and I am more improved in health and strength and spirits than I had thought possible.

One reason why I was so much better here is, that I have only one female friend (and that a very favorite one) within reach—half of my worries proceeding from a quantity of tiresome visitors. Some I have seen this summer who are not tiresome—the Miss Goldsmids, Sir Isaac Goldsmid's daughters. The eldest is a very remarkable woman[1] and she spoke of Mr. Browning with great interest, as having been at the London University with her brothers. Also Mr. Ruskin spoke of some vintage verses of his as singularly true to nature; and his praise is worth having. He is a most charming person, but was, when I last heard of him, laid up at Salisbury. I fear for his health, and so does his mother.

Ah! my dear love, I have nothing but fear for France. As to Lamartine, I never did expect any good from him; except "Les Girondins," I always detested his writings—so weak and wordy and full of vanity. And "Les Girondins," they say, is untrue beyond the usual untruthfulness of history—a mere party pamphlet. When he was in London a few years ago Mr. Rogers asked him, with strong interest, to give him some details about Béranger, "the greatest French poet." "Ah! Béranger," said M. de Lamartine, "he made advances to me, and, of course, wished for my acquaintance; but he is a sort of man with whom I do not choose to have any connection!" Think of that! Mr. Rogers told the story himself, with the greatest indignation, to the Ruskins, and they told it to me.

•   •   •

Ever most faithfully yours,
M. R. Mitford

1. Probably Anna Maria Goldsmid (1805–89), of the wealthy family who were friends of MRM.

FLORENCE.
[THURSDAY] AUGUST 24– [1848]

•   •   •

What a lovely nest you must have found on the river-bank, & how you must have enjoyed the scenery & the freshness, the new drives & new impressions—(I am quite pleased & satisfied . . you could not have chosen better, certainly. .) the old friends & old resources being carried with you in a manner, so that you combined all things.

As for ourselves, we have scarcely done so well—yet will,—having enjoyed a great deal in spite of drawbacks. Murray, the traitor, sent us to Fano as a "delightful summer residence for an English family," & we found it uninhabitable from the heat . . vegetation scorched into paleness, the very air swooning in the sun, and the gloomy looks of the inhabitants sufficiently corroborative of their words, that no drop of rain or dew ever falls there during the summer. A "circulating library" which "does'nt give out books", and "a refined & intellectual Italian society" (I quote Murray for that phrase) which "never reads a book through" (I quote M.ʳˢ Wiseman, D.ʳ Wiseman's[1] mother who has lived in Fano seven years) complete the advantages of the place—yet the churches are beautiful, and a divine picture of Guercino's[2] is worth going all that way to see. By a happy accident we fell in with M.ʳˢ Wiseman, who having married her daughter to Count Gabrielli with ancestral possessions in Fano, has lived on there from year to year, in a state of permanent moaning as far as I could apprehend. She is a very intelligent & vivacious person, & having been used to the best French society, bears but ill this exile from the common civilities of life. I wish D.ʳ Wiseman, of whose childhood & manhood, she spoke with touching pride, would ask her to minister to the domestic rites of his bishop's palace in Westminster —there wᵈ be no hesitation I fancy, in her acceptance of the invitation. Agreeable as she & her daughter were however, we fled from Fano, after three days—& finding ourselves cheated out of our dream of summer coolness, resolved on substituting for it what the Italians call 'un bel giro'. So we went to Ancona . . a striking sea-city, holding up against the brown rocks & elbowing out the purple tides—beautiful to look upon. An exfoliation of the rock itself, you would call the houses that seem to grow there—so identical is the colour & character. I shᵈ like to visit Ancona again when there is a little air & shadow—we stayed a week as it was, living upon fish & cold water. Water, water, was the cry all day long: & really you shᵈ have seen me (or you shᵈ not have seen me) lying on the sofa, & demoralized out of all sense of female vanity, not to say decency—with dishevelled hair at full length . . and "sans gown, sans stays, sans shoes, sans everything" . . except a petticoat & white dressing-wrapper. I said something feebly once about the waiter; but I dont think I meant it for earnest, for when Robert said "Oh, dont mind, dear", certainly I didn't mind in the least. People *dont*, I suppose,—when they are in ovens, or in exhausted receivers. Never before did I guess what heat was—that's sure. We went to Loretto for a day—back through Ancona, Sinigaglia . . (oh, I forgot to tell you—there was no fair this year at Sinigaglia– Italy will be content, I suppose, with selling her honour!) Fano . . Pesaro, Rimini, to Ra-

venna; back again over the Apennines from Forli. A "bel giro"—
was'nt it? Ravenna where Robert positively wanted to go to live once,
has itself put an end to those yearnings. The churches are wonderful:
holding an atmosphere of purple glory—and if one could live just in
them, or in Dante's tomb . . well! otherwise, keep me from Ravenna!
The very antiquity of the houses is whitewashed, and the marshes on
all sides send up stenches new & old, till the hot air is sick with them.
To get to the pine-forest which is exquisite, you have to go a mile
along the canal, the exhalations pursuing you step for step—and, what
ruffled me more than all beside, we were not admitted into the house
of Dante's tomb "without an especial permission from the authori-
ties". Quite furious I was about this, & both of us, too angry to think
of applying: but we stood at the grated window & read the pathetic
inscription as distinctly as if we had touched the marble. We stood
there between three & four in the morning and then went straight on
to Florence from that tomb of the exiled poet– Just what we should
have done, had the circumstances been arranged in a dramatic intention! From Forli, the air grew pure & quick again; and the exquisite,
almost visionary scenery of the Apennines, the wonderful variety of
shape & colour, the sudden transitions, & vital individuality of those
mountains . . the chestnut forests dropping by their own weight into
the deep ravines, . . the rocks cloven & clawed by the living torrents
. . and the hills, hill above hill, piling up their grand existences as if
they did it themselves, changing colour in the effort—of these things
I cannot give you an idea—and if words could not, painting could not
either. Indeed the whole scenery of our journey . . except where we
approached the coast . . was full of beauty. The first time we crossed
the Apennine (near Gorgo San Sepolchro) we did it by moonlight—&
the flesh was weak, & one fell asleep, & saw things between sleep &
wake—only the effects were grand & singular so, even though of
course we lost much in the distinctness. Well,—but you will understand from all this, that we were delighted to get home—*I* was, I assure you. Florence seemed as cool as an oven after the fire . . indeed
we called it quite cool! and I took possession of my own chair & put
up my feet on the cushions & was charmed, both with having been
so far & coming back so soon.

·   ·   ·

Thank you for the news of our authors—it is as "the sound of a
trumpet afar off," & I am like the war-horse. Neglectful that I am, I

forgot to tell you before that you heard quite rightly about M! Thackeray's wife who is ill *so*. Since your question, I had in gossip from England, that the book "Jane Eyre" was written by a governess in his house, & that the preface to the foreign edition refers to him in some marked way. We have not seen the book at all. But the first letter in which you mentioned your Oxford student caught us in the midst of his work upon art. Very vivid, very graphic, full of sensibility . . but inconsequent in some of the reasoning, it seemed to me, & rather flashy than full in the metaphysics. Robert who knows a good deal about art, to which knowledge I of course have no pretence, could agree with him only by snatches—and we both of us, standing before a very expressive picture of Dominichino's (the David—at Fano) wondered how he could blaspheme so against a great artist. Still, he is no ordinary man—and for a critic to be so much a poet, is a great thing. Also, we have by no means, I should imagine, seen the utmost of his stature.

*   *   *

your most affectionate
Ba

1. Nicholas Wiseman (1802–65), Roman Catholic prelate and author, was papal envoy to England in 1848.
2. "L'Angelo Custoda" by Giovanni Barbieri (1590–1666), called Guercino. It was the subject of Browning's poem "The Guardian-Angel: A Picture at Fano" published in *Men and Women* (1855).

Motherhood and the Italian Scene
1848–50

In late 1848 and early 1849, as they awaited the birth of their child at Casa Guidi—now their permanent home—the Brownings avidly followed Italian and French politics. They had watched from their apartment opposite the Pitti Palace the celebrations following the first signs of democratic reforms by the grand duke, Leopold II of Tuscany, only to see him revert to conservatism and be driven into exile a few months later along with Pope Pius IX ("Pio Nono"), on whom EBB had pinned even more extravagant hopes for the cause of Italian freedom. She turned her hopes instead toward the newly elected French president Louis Napoleon whose liberalism could help Italy as well as France. These events and her reactions to them are recorded in *Casa Guidi Windows: A Poem, in Two Parts* published in 1851. On 9 March 1849, EBB gave birth to a healthy Robert Wiedemann Barrett Browning (called Wiedemann in early letters, then "Penini" or "Pen"), an event followed within days by word of Mrs. Browning's death in England. Recuperating for the summer in Bagni di Lucca, EBB met the Irish-born novelist Charles Lever (1806–72), admired by MRM for *Charles O'Malley* (1840). Back in Florence she had a brief but memorable acquaintance with Margaret Fuller (1810–50), the American essayist and editor who had married the Marquis Angelo Ossoli. An old acquaintance from Torquay surfaced: Theodosia Garrow (1825?–65), a minor poet now married to Thomas Trollope (1810–92), son of MRM's friend Frances Trollope and brother of the novelist Anthony. An unlikely new acquaintance was "Father Prout," pseudonym of Francis Sylvester Mahony (1804–66), defrocked Jesuit, journalist, and poet. The pattern of mingled joy and pain continued into 1850. Mr. Barrett's refusal to accept Henrietta's marriage to a cousin, William Surtees Cook (1813–77), reopened an old wound for EBB. EBB's prominence among contemporary English poets was recognized when her name was proposed for the laureateship in 1850 at which time her husband's just-published *Christmas-Eve and Easter-Day* failed to impress the critics. An idyllic vacation of three months was spent in Siena while EBB recovered from a July miscarriage and from the news of the Ossolis' drownings in a shipwreck off New York on 19 July, a tragedy worsened for EBB by memories of Bro's death. Nevertheless, EBB brought out another edition of poems in the fall and her comments in 24 September [1850], about clearing away "feeble rhymes" and "dingy mistiness," show her advance in self-criticism and technical proficiency. She was also forthrightly critical of MRM's choices for a book of poets (published in 1852 as *Recollections of a Literary Life*), outgrowth of a periodical-editing project by which Chorley had lured MRM out of her long retirement. With books in preparation, both women were keenly interested in the publishing terms won by the novelist Elizabeth Gaskell (1810–65), author of *Mary Barton* (1848).

FLORENCE.
[TUESDAY] OCTOBER 10. [1848]

My ever dearest Miss Mitford, Have you not thought some hard thoughts of me for not instantly replying to a letter which necessarily must have been, to one who loved you, of such painful interest. Do I not love you truly? Yes, indeed— But while preparing to write to you my deep regret at hearing that you had been so ill, illness came in another form to prevent me from writing, my husband being laid up for nearly a month with fever & ulcerated sorethroat. I had not the heart to write a line to anyone . . much less to prepare a packet to escort your letter free from foreign postage: and to make you pay for a chapter of Lamentations without the spirit of prophecy, would have been too hard on you . . would'nt it? Quite unhappy I have been over those burning hands & languid eyes . . the only unhappiness I ever had by *them* . . and then he would'nt see a physician; and if it had'nt been that, just at the right moment, Mͬ Mahoney the celebrated Jesuit & Father Prout of Fraser, knowing everything as those Jesuits are apt to do, came in to us on his way to Rome, pointed out that the fever got ahead through weakness & mixed up with his own kind hand a potion of eggs & port wine . . to the horror of our Italian servant who lifted up his eyes at such a prescription for a fever, crying "O Inglesi, Inglesi!", . . the case would have been far worse, I have no kind of doubt. For the eccentric prescription gave the power of sleeping, & the pulse grew quieter directly. I shall always be grateful to Father Prout . . always. The very sight of someone with a friend's name & cheerful face . . his very jests at me for being a 'bambina' & frightened without cause, . . were as comforting as the salutation of angels. Also, he has been in Florence ever since, & we have seen him every day—he came to doctor & remained to talk. A very singular person, of whom the world tells a thousand & one tales, you know, but of whom I shall speak as I find him, because the utmost kindness & warmheartedness have characterized his whole bearing towards us. Robert met him years ago at dinner at Emerson Tennant's,[1] & since has crossed paths with him on various points of Europe. The first time I saw him, was as he stood on a rock at Leghorn, at our disembarkation in Italy. Not refined in a social sense, by any manner of means, yet a most accomplished scholar & vibrating all over with learned associations & vivid combinations of fancy & experience—having seen all the ends of the earth & the men thereof, & possessing the art of talk & quotation to an amusing degree. In another week or two he will be at Rome:—

•   •   •

As for me, I am well too, but had the wisdom two days ago to upset myself out of, yet in company with, one of our lolling-chairs . . falling forwards (as I knelt in the chair which fell backward) on my forehead with a violence, which protected the rest of my body happily, at the expence of breaking the giddy head, the cause of the mischief. Here's the end of keeping in the house for months together, to avoid shakings & strainings! One falls out of an easy chair into the arms of destiny. I *hope* however that there is no worse harm than a week's disfigurement & an hour's headache—but the shock stunned me & could'nt have happend *at a more unfortunate time*. Nobody was ever born to be happier & unhappier than I—the "mingled yarn" is black & white. Poor Robert is very vexed—only really I feel well this morning & may have escaped, through God's great mercy, the particular evil.

How graphically you give us your Oxford student! Well! the picture is more distinct than Turner's . . & if you had called it, in the manner of the master, [']'A Rock limpet," we should have recognized in it the corresponding type of the gifted & eccentric writer in question.[2] Very eloquent he is, I agree at once—& true views he takes of Art in the abstract . . true & elevating. It is in the application & connective logic that he breaks away from one so violently.

• • •

We are expecting our books by an early vessel, & are about to be very busy, building up a rococo bookcase of carved angels & dæmons. Also we shall get up curtains, & get down bedroom carpets, & finish the remainder of our furnishing business, now that the hot weather is at an end. I say 'at an end', though the glass stands at seventy. As to the "war," *that* is rather different—it is painful to feel oneself growing gradually cooler & cooler on the subject of Italian patriotism, valour, & goodsense; but the process is inevitable. The child's play between the Livornese & our Grand Duke, provokes a thousand pleasantries. Every now & then a day is fixed for a revolution in Tuscany, but up to the present time, a shower has come & put it off. Two sundays ago, Florence was to have been 'sacked' by Leghorn, when a drizzle came & saved us. You think this a bad joke of mine, or an impotent sarcasm, perhaps; whereas I merely speak historically. Brave men, good men, even sensible men, there are of course in the land, but they are not strong enough for the times or for masterdom. For France, it is [a] great nation; but even in France they want a man, & Cavagniac is only a soldier. If Louis Napoleon had the muscle of his uncle's little finger in his soul, he w^d be president . . & king; but he is flaccid altogether, you see; & Joinville stands nearer to the royal probability after all. "Henri Cinq" is said to be too closely espoused to the church—& his connections at Naples & Parma dont help his cause. Robert has more hope of the *republic* than I have:—but call ye *this* a republic? Do you know that Miss Martineau takes up the "History of England" under Charles Knight, in the continuation of a popular work?[3] I regret her fine imagination being so wasted. So you saw Mr Chorley? What a pleasant flashing in the eyes! We hear of him in Holland & Norway. Dear Mr Kenyon wont stir from England, we see plainly. Ah—Frederic Soulié!—he is too dead, I fear. Perhaps he goes on, though, writing romances, after the fashion of poor Miss Pickering!– *That* proves nothing. I long for my French fountains of living literature, which, pure or impure, plashed in one's face so pleasantly. Some old French 'memoires' we have got at lately!– Brissot's for instance. It is curious how the leaders of the last revolution (under Louis seize) seem to have despised one another. Brissot is very dull & flat. For Puseyism, it runs counter to the spirit of our times, after all, & will never achieve a church.

You talk delightful scenery in your last letter, & I dont wonder at the old trees haunting you. Is K. quite strong again? I hope so. Oh that you may be stronger your own dear self. My brothers & sisters,— the whole house except Papa who stays at home, . . are enjoying the neighbourhood of Windsor, where they are settled for two months. May God bless you! Robert's regards go with the love of

your ever affectionate
Ba

1. Sir James Emerson Tennent (1804–69), politician and travel writer.
2. Turner's painting "War: The Exile and the Rock Limpet" (1842) showed Napoleon meditating beside a rock pool.
3. Her *History of the Thirty Years' Peace 1815–45* (1851) was part of Knight's "shilling volume" history series.

FLORENCE.
[TUESDAY] JANUARY 30– [1849]

My dearest Miss Mitford, since we have taken to reforming in this Tuscany, everything of course goes to ruin, & among other things, the arrangements of the post office. I did not get your letter for days after the right time—which must account for most of the apparent delay in replying to it!—and now let me say first, how anxiously I read what you write about your health, & how gladly I venture to hope that really you are making progress in spite of all. Is it not so, dearest Miss Mitford?

•   •   •

But can this which I have just heard of you from M! Kenyon be true . . that you are meditating an excursion to Paris? Oh, I never shall believe it till I have your own affidavit of having actually been there . . though one may understand how the temptation of a Napoleonic dynasty may draw such as you. If you go, remember the Hotel de la ville de Paris, close to the Madelaine church. We were there, & found it the pleasantest & quietest of residences for the quietly inclined, & singularly cheap—we paid only seven francs the four & twenty hours, for a suite of rooms . . dining room, drawing room, & three bedrooms—small, but full of elegance & comfort—dining out at the traiteur close by, but finding excellent coffee, eggs & French rolls at home, for which & attendance, of course there was some extra expense.

•　　•　　•

It sounds scarcely credible to some of my husband's friends, that, for these two years we have been together, he has never spent one evening from home—rather "domestic," is it not?, . . for a "good for nothing poet," such as dear M.! Chorley & you write verses upon & make mouths at? Here are theatres, concerts, operas, going on night after night,—& never yet have I succeeded in persuading him . . . . . still, if it shall please God that I get happily over the trial before me, there will come a respite perhaps, from sofas & armchairs, and I shall go with him to see a play of Alfieri's & hear music of Rossini's: for quite a reproach it sounds to be so long in Italy & to live on as if the only neighbourhood were a frog-marsh, however enjoyable may be the home-evenings by the blazing pine-wood, & over the little supper tray's Montepulciano & roasted chesnuts. I am very well . . really better than most women are apt to be in a similar position, & likely, say the learned, to suffer less at the crisis, from the very peculiarities of temperament which hitherto have been my bane . . so that altogether I do venture to hope that the *fall* has done no harm—God grant it!— the thought occurs uncomfortably now & then. One thing is certain, . . that it did not affect the vital principle—for I had not felt the dear second life until a full fortnight after the accident, & I felt it at the usual time– Therefore nothing is to be feared for the *life*. The opium is being steadily diminished too—and nothing can be more favorable than the medical opinions—& I have no misgivings, no fatal presentiments for myself—the only feeling with me being (I mean the only *personal* feeling) a sort of impression that a cup filled runs over, & that my happiness as a wife is too great to bear other kinds of happiness

to be superadded—also that a life, overladen with gifts, drops naturally in the course. God be praised in all cases.

. . .

For my part I detect in myself spasms of an unnatural & ghastly
sympathy with ancient forms & princedoms. Our poor, conscientious
tender-hearted Grand Duke gives me the heartache to hear of—&
Powers[1] the sculptor was saying the other day that he would'nt last
long under the sovereignty of the people . . he had too weak a frame
for it. Meantime, church-affairs are in a still more curious state than
political—the papacy is essentially *down*. The Florentine populace has
sent away its archbishop under a hail of potatoes & apples . . & now,
they are (by my fay) about to elect another, of their own liking . . yes,
& the favorite candidate is not in orders—but what of *that*, I wonder?
where's the objection to *that*? He'll sing this Te Deum to their "Ev-
viva la republica", which is the principal point. Singular, is it, that our
English Puseyites should take up the worn out formulas of these Roman Catholics, precisely as the latter discover the fact of the wearing
out. Our books are come, & our rooms look perfect in comfort. Somebody has lent us Jane Eyre– As interesting, but *much over-rated*, it
strikes us both—& how it could be doubtfully with any, a *woman's*
book, surprises me a good deal. Yes, the intermixtures (talking of
women) in Constant's memoirs are curious enough, but unpleasant.
Louis Napoleon has a great position, & is likely to have a greater—at
least I am perfectly prepared for the revival of the Empire in France –
We shall see. The Orleans family, on the other hand, may have an
excellent chance of catching back the crown in the rebound. I believe
in France, but not in the French republic. My uncles & aunts are staying quietly at Tours, & there's nothing, I should think, to fear. Father
Prout remains at Rome.

. . .

your ever affectionate
EBB

1. Hiram Powers (1805–73), American sculptor, best known for "The Greek Slave"
(1843) on which EBB wrote a sonnet (*Poems*, 1850).

FLORENCE.
[MONDAY] APRIL 30. [1849]

I am writing to you . . *at last*, you will say, ever dearest Miss Mitford,
. . but except once to Wimpole Street, this is the first packet of letters
which goes from me since my confinement. You will have heard how
our joy turned suddenly into deep sorrow by the death of my husband's mother. An unsuspected disease, (ossification of the heart) terminated in a fatal way—and she lay in the insensibility precursive of
the grave's, when the letter written in such gladness by my poor husband & announcing the birth of his child, reached her address. "It
would have made her heart bound", said her daughter to us. Poor,
tender heart—the last throb was too near. The medical men w^d not
allow the news to be communicated. The next joy she felt, was to be
in Heaven itself. My husband has been in the deepest anguish, and
indeed, except for the courageous consideration of his sister who
wrote two letters of preparation, saying that "she was not well," & she
"was very ill" when in fact all was over, I am frightened to think what
the result would have been to him. He has loved his mother as such
passionate natures only can love, and I never saw a man so bowed
down in an extremity of sorrow—never. Even now, the depression is
great, and sometimes when I leave him alone a little & return to the
room, I find him in tears– I do earnestly wish to change the scene &
air—but where to go? England looks terrible now. He says it would
break his heart to see his mother's roses over the wall & the place
where she used to lay her scissors & gloves. Which I understand so
thoroughly that I cant say "Let us go to England". We must wait &
see what his father & sister will choose to do or choose us to do—for
of course a duty plainly seen, would draw us anywhere. My own
dearest sisters will be painfully disappointed by any change of plan—
only they are too good & kind not to understand the difficulty, . . not
to see the motive. So do *you*, I am certain. It has been very, very
painful altogether, this drawing together of life and death—Robert
was too enraptured at my safety & with his little son, . . and the sudden reaction was terrible. You see how natural that was. How kind of
you to write that note to him so full of affectionate expressions towards me! Thank you, dearest friend. He had begged my sisters to
let you know of my welfare, and I hope they did—and now it is my
turn to know of *you*, and so I do entreat you not to delay but to let
me hear exactly how you are & what your plans are for the summer.

•   •   •

Since I wrote last to you, I think we have had two revolutions here at Florence—Grand Duke out, Grand Duke in – The bells in the church opposite rang for both– They first planted a tree of liberty close to our door, and then they pulled it down. The same tune, sung under the windows, did for [']'Viva la republica" and "Viva Leopoldo". The genuine popular feeling is certainly for the Grand Duke .. ("O santissima madre di Dio,['] said our nurse, clasping her hands, "how the people do love him!["]) only nobody would run the risk of a pin's-prick to save the Ducal throne.– If the Leghornese, who put up Guerazzi on its ruins, had not refused to pay at certain Florentine caffés, we shouldn't have had revolution the second, & all this shooting in the streets. Dr. Harding who was coming to see me, had time to get behind a stable-door, just before there was a fall against it of four shot corpses; and Robert barely managed to get home across the bridges– He had been out walking in the city, apprehending nothing, when the ⟨s⟩torm gathered & broke. Sad & humiliating it all has been, and the author of 'Vanity Fair' might turn it to bitter uses for a chapter. By the way, we have just been reading 'Vanity Fair'. Very clever, very effective, but cruel to human nature– A painful book, and not the pain that purifies & exalts. Partial truths after all, & those not wholesome. But I certainly had no idea that M! Thackeray had intellectual force for such a book—the power is considerable.

•   •   •

There!—and almost I have done my paper without a single word to you of the *baby!* Ah, you wont believe that I forgot him, even if I pretend—so I wont. He is a lovely, fat, strong child, with double chins and rosy cheeks, and a great wide chest—undeniable lungs, I can assure you. D! Harding called him "a robust child", the other day, and "A more beautiful child he never saw"!– I never saw a child half as beautiful, for my part. We have had him vaccinated to everybody's satisfaction—and we are satisfied too with the wet nurse, who is immensely strong & rosy & stout, with no nerves at all, and a physique quite uninjured by intellectual cultivation—she does'nt know even *the names of the months.* I had to abdicate by force of public opinion, though my English medical adviser wished me, for his part, to nurse—but after the rapture of hearing my child's first cry, I thought of nothing but of what was best for him—and the farther from me the better surely!——— It was enough that I had not injured him so far! For myself I suffered only what was necessary– Everything was as right as could be, and I heard D! Harding say to the nurse, "that in all his practice he had never seen the functions of nature more healthfully performed". The time seemed long . . twenty one hours . . but it was less long than acquaintances of mine in Florence have had to suffer to my knowledge within the last year . . active, blooming women, . .

•   •   •

your most affectionate
Ba

Three-mile Cross
Sept., 1848. [*sic* for 1849]

How earnestly I rejoice, my beloved friend, in your continued health! and how very, very glad I shall be to see you and your baby. Remember me to Wilson, and tell her that I am quite prepared to admire him as much as will even satisfy her appetite for praise. How beautifully you describe your beautiful country! Oh! that I were with you, to lose myself in the chestnut forests, and gather grapes at the vintage! If I had but Prince Houssein's carpet,[1] I would set forth and leave Mr. May to scold and wonder, when he comes to see me tomorrow. He seems well disposed to shut me up for a month or two. Besides the chestnut woods and you, your ownselves, I should be delighted to see Mr. Lever. You know I have always had a mannish sort of fancy for those "Charles O'Malley" and "Jack Hinton" books, which always put me in good spirits and good humor (I wish he wrote so now); and I remember hearing from his illustrator, Mr. Browne, that he was exactly the "Harry Lorrequer" he describes—that is to say, full of life and glee, and all that is animating and agreeable. I remember, too, most gratefully the pleasure his books gave to my father.

"The Princess" has fine things, but would certainly not have made a reputation. It is a poem of a hundred and fifty pages, all in blank verse—inclosed within a setting of blank verse also—and the very songs introduced are of the same metre. The story is very unskillfully told, with an entire want of dramatic power, and full of the strangest words brought in after the strangest fashion. It begins in mockery, and becomes earnest as it goes on; but there are, as I said before, fine things in it.

God bless you, my beloved friend! Say every thing for me to Mr. Browning. Kiss baby for me, and pat Flush. I have written out the pain. Ever yours,

M.R.M.

I have made many inquiries about Miss Martineau; but my only answer has been from Mrs. Onory (Jane Nicholls), who lives in her circle, and says, "All I know about her is that she has brought a pipe from the East, and smokes it every day. Perhaps that may be to subdue pain or deaden irritation."

1. In the *Arabian Nights,* the magic carpet that transported its rider to any place in the world.

FLORENCE.
[SATURDAY] DEC! 1– [1849]

My ever loved friend, you will have wondered at this unusual silence; & so will my sisters to whom I wrote just now after a pause as little in my custom. It was not the fault of my head & heart . . but of this unruly body which has been laid up again in the way of all flesh of mine. In the midst of my security & vainglory in respect to health, strength, & the walking faculty, I was taken ill in the night rather more than a month ago, & miraculously escaped a miscarriage . . if the miscarriage is *really escaped,* . . which I cant help still being doubtful of, in spite of the strong opinion of the learned that everything is now going on well. My husband & I are "infatuated enough" (as we say) to *hope,* rather than to fear, that this may be the case. Pure madness . . is'nt it? We ought to groan elegiacally, or at least "make the best of it" philosophically, when we talk of a possible second baby, thirteen months after the first, . . instead of which, we are just *pleased,* like stupid people. Our wiser English friends will hold up their hands in compassion, I am sure! My late illness exhausted me more than my confinement did . . but I am well again now, . . only obliged to keep quiet, & give up my grand walking excursions, which poor Robert used to be so boastful of. If he is vain about anything in the world, it is about my improved health, . . & I used to say to him . . "But you need'nt talk so much to people, of how your wife walked here with you & there with you, as if a wife with a pair of feet was a miracle of nature". Now the poor feet have fallen into their old ways again. Ah—but if God pleases, it wont be for long.

•   •   •

The American authoress Miss Fuller, with whom we had had some slight intercourse by letter, & who has been at Rome during the siege, as a devoted friend of the republicans & a meritorious attendant on the hospitals, has taken us by surprise at Florence, . . retiring from the Roman field with a husband & child above a year old!– Nobody had even suspected a word of this underplot, & her American friends stood in mute astonishment before this apparition of them here. The husband is a Roman marquis . . appearing amiable & gentlemanly, & having fought well, they say, at the siege, but with no pretension to cope with his wife on any ground appertaining to the intellect. She talks, & he listens– I always wonder at that species of marriage; but people are so different in their matrimonial ideals, that it may answer sometimes. This Ma^dme Ossoli saw George Sand in Paris . . was at one of her soirées . . & called her "a magnificent creature". The soirée was "full of rubbish" . . in the way of its social composition, . . which George Sand likes . . Nota bene– If Ma^dme Ossoli called it *"rubbish"*, it must have been really rubbish—not expressing anything conventionally so . . she being one of the out & out *Reds*, & scorners of grades of society.

•   •   •

Oh—we have had the sight of Clough & Burbidge, at last. Clough has more thought, Burbidge more music . . but I am disappointed in the book on the whole.[1] What I like infinitely better, is Clough's 'Bothie of Topernafuosich' a "long-vacation pastoral'[']', written in loose & more-than-need-be unmusical hexameters, but full of vigour & freshness, & with passages & indeed whole scenes of great beauty & eloquence. It seems to have been written before the other poems– Try to get it, if you have not read it already. I feel certain you will like it, & think all the higher of the poet– Oh, it strikes both Robert & me as being worth twenty of the other little book, with its fragmentary, dislocated, unartistic character. Arnold's volume has two good poems in it . . 'The Sick King of Bokhara' & 'The deserted Mer-man'. I liked them both– But none of these writers are *artists* whatever they may be in future days. Have you read Shirley? & is it as good as Jane Eyre? We heard not long since that M.ʳ Chorley had discovered the author . . *the* Currer Bell![2] A woman, most certainly. We hear too that three large editions of the 'Princess' are sold – So much the happier for England & poetry!– Dearest dear Miss Mitford, mind you write to me, & dont pay me out in my own silence! *You* have not been ill, I hope & trust– Write & tell me every little thing of yourself—how you are, . . & whether there is still danger of your being uprooted from Three Mile Cross. I love & think of you always. Fancy Flush being taken in the light of a rival by Baby. Oh, Baby was quite jealous the other day, & struggled & kicked to get to me, because he saw Flush leaning his pretty head on my lap. There's a great strife for priviledges between those two. May God bless you! My husband's kind regards always—while I am

your most affectionate
EBB.

1. *Ambarvalia* (1849), a volume of poems by Arthur Hugh Clough (1819–61) and Thomas Burbidge (1816–92). Clough's *Bothie of Tober-na-Vuolich* was published in 1848.
2. *Shirley* (1849), like *Jane Eyre* (1847), appeared under Charlotte Brontë's pseudonym, Currer Bell.

Three-mile Cross
March 25, 1850.

My "Country Stories" are just coming out, to my great contentment, in the "Parlor Library," for a shilling, or perhaps ninepence—that being the price of Miss Austen's novels. I delight in this, and have no sympathy with your bemoanings over American editions. Think of the American editions of my prose. "Our Village" has been reprinted in twenty or thirty places, and "Belford Regis" in almost as many; and I like it. So do *you*, say what you may. Mr. Fields, the handsome Boston bookseller, Mr. Ticknor's partner, sent me a copy of their edition of Mr. Browning's poems, and very nicely done it is, preceded by Mr. Landor's sonnet.

After all, my dear friend, Mrs. Acton Tindal[1] was mistaken in her account of the authorship of "Jane Eyre." It was really written by a Miss Brontë, a clergyman's daughter, diminutive almost to dwarfishness—a woman of thirty, who had hardly ever left her father's parish in Yorkshire. There is great success in mystery. I think, from a thing that I have heard lately, that Sir R. Vyvyan *is* the author of the "Vestiges."[2]

Well; but was not that song[3] most sweet and harmonious, and full of grace and beauty? and what would you ask for more? A song is not necessarily an ode. For my part, I delight in such bits of melody, floating about you upon the air. I wish I dared give it to Henry Phillips, to whom I have just sent a fine translation of a German song written, words and music, by one of Prince Eugene's old troopers, and picked up by a friend of mine among the soldiers at Ehrenbreitstein.[4]

God bless you, my very dear love! K——has been very ill, but is better. Say every thing for me to Mr. Browning, and believe me ever, faithfully and most affectionately yours,

M. R. Mitford.

1. Mrs. Acton Tindal, formerly Henrietta Harrison (?–1879), minor poet and novelist.
2. *Vestiges of Creation*, published anonymously in 1844, was written by Robert Chambers (1802–71), publisher and editor.
3. Probably Tennyson's lyric "Blow, Bugle, Blow," added to *The Princess* in the 1850 edition.
4. Perhaps the popular "Prinz Eugen, der edle Ritter," commemorating the victory of Belgrade (1717) by Prince Eugene of Savoy (1663–1736). By "Phillips," MRM may have meant Henry Russell, her friend who set EBB's "The Cry of the Children" to music.

FLORENCE.
[TUESDAY] APRIL 30 [1850]

You will have seen in the papers, dearest friend, the marriage of my sister Henrietta & will have understood why I was longer silent than usual. Indeed the event has much moved me—and so much of the emotion was painful . . painfulness being inseparable from events of the sort in our family . . that I had to make an effort to realize to myself the reasonable degree of gladness & satisfaction in her release from a long, anxious transitional state, & her prospect of happiness with a man who has loved her constantly, & who is of an upright, honest, reliable & religious mind. Our father's objections were to his tractarian opinions & insufficient income. I have no sympathy myself with tractarian opinions, but I cannot under the circumstances think an objection of the kind tenable by a third person—and in truth, we all know, that if it had not been this objection, it would have been another . . there was no escape any way. An engagement of five years & an attachment still longer were to have some results; and I cannot regret, or indeed do otherwise than approve from my heart what she has done from her's— Most of her friends & relatives have considered that there was no choice, & that her step is abundantly justified. At the same time, I thank God that a letter sent to me to ask my advice, never reached me, . . (the *second* letter of my sisters, lost, since I left them! . .) because no advice *ought* to be given on any subject of the kind, and because I, especially, should have shrunk from accepting such a responsibility. So I only heard of the marriage three days before it took place . . no, four days before . . and was upset, as you may suppose, by the sudden news. Cap! Surtees Cook's sister was one of the bridesmaids, and his brother performed the ceremony. The means are very small of course—he has not much, & my sister has nothing—still it seems to me that they will have enough to live prudently on, & he looks out for a further appointment. Papa "will never again let her name be mentioned in his hearing," he *says* . . but we must hope: the dreadful business passed off better on the whole than poor Arabel expected, and things are going on as quietly as usual in Wimpole Street, now.

● ● ●

All this, you see, will throw me back with Papa . . even if I can be supposed to have gained half a step . . and I doubt it. Ah yes—dearest Miss Mitford! I have indeed again & again thought of your "Emily",[1] . . stripping the situation of "the favour & prettiness" associated with that heroine! Wiedeman might compete, though, in darlingness with the child, as the poem shows him. Still, I can accept no omen— My heart sinks when I dwell upon peculiarities difficult to analyze. I love him very deeply—. When I write to him, I lay myself at his feet—. Even if I had gained half a step, (and I doubt it, as I said) see how I must be thrown back by the indisposition to receive others!— But I cannot write of this subject—let us change it.

•   •   •

Baby correctly sings the air of "Margery Daw", and tries hard at "Viva la liberta"—he claps his hands when he approves of anything, & has various other accomplishments, with the account of which I forbear edifying you today. He looks younger than his thirteen months, little darling, through having such an infantine round face, & this contrasts the more with his great intelligence & vivacity, & quite seems to startle people sometimes. Ma^{dme} Ossoli says that 'his thoughtful eyes go to her heart.' She sails for America in a few days, with the hope of returning to Italy, and indeed I cannot believe that her Roman husband will be easily naturalized among the Yankees. A very interesting person she is, far better than her writings:—truthful, spiritual in her habitual mode of mind, . . not only exalted, but *exalteè* in her opinions, . . and yet calm in manner. We shall be sorry to lose her.

•   •   •

And, by the way, the Athenæum, since M͏ͬ Dilke left it, has grown duller & duller, colder & colder, flatter & flatter. M͏ͬ Dilke was not brilliant but he was a Brutus in criticism; & though it was his specialty to condemn his most particular friends to the hangman, the survivors thought there was something grand about it on the whole, & nobody could hold him in contempt. Now it is all different—we have not even 'public virtue' to fasten our admiration to!– You will be sure to think I am vexed at the article on my husband's new poem.[2] Why, certainly I am vexed! Who would *not* be vexed with such misunderstanding & mistating? Dear M͏ͬ Chorley writes a letter to appreciate most generously: so you see how little power he has in the paper to insert an opinion, or stop an injustice. On the same day came out a burning panegyric of six columns in the Examiner—a curious crossfire. If you read the little book . . (I wish I could send you a copy, but Chapman & Hall have not offered us copies . .) & you will catch sight of it somewhere . . I hope you will like things in it at least. It seems to me full of power. Two hundred copies went off in the first fortnight, which is a good beginning in these days. – So I am to confess to a satisfaction in the American piracies. Well—I confess, then. Only it is rather a complex smile with which one hears . . "Sir or Madam, we are selling your book at half price, as well printed as in England." "Those apples we stole from your garden, we sell at a halfpenny, instead of a penny as you do: & they are much appreciated."

Very gratifying indeed. It's worth while to rob us, that's plain—&
there's something magnificent in supplying a distant market with apples out of one's garden. Still the smile is complex in its character, &
the morality, . . simple—that's all I meant to say.–

A letter from Henrietta & her husband . . glowing with happiness, & it makes *me* happy. She says "I wonder if I shall be as happy
as you, Ba!"– God grant it. It was signified to her that she should at
once give up her engagement of five years, or leave the house. She
married directly. I do not understand how it could be otherwise, indeed. My brothers have been kind and affectionate I am happy to
say, in her case. Poor dearest Papa does injustice chiefly to his own
nature, by these severities, hard as they seem. Is K. well now? Write
soon & talk of yourself to

your ever affec.^{te}
Ba

1. In MRM's "Emily," from *Dramatic Scenes* (1827), the heroine and her father, who
   had cast her off for marrying, are reconciled when he meets her little son.
2. *Christmas-Eve and Easter-Day*, published 1 April.

Three-mile Cross,
July 1, 1850.

I can not enough thank you, my beloved friend, for your most welcome letter. The pleasure it gave me would have been unmingled but
for its delaying the hope of seeing you. But, if you come so near as
France, then we shall meet here, I hope, and there—I mean both in
France and in England; for I do still hope to get as far as Paris before
I die. At present I can not tell you where I am going. The cottage at
Swallowfield that I want to rent, belonged to a crotchety old bachelor;
he, dying, left it for her life to a sister, a rich widow, aged seventy-
seven, and after her death to another relative. It is about six miles
from Reading, on this same road, leading up from which is a short
ascending lane, terminated by this small dwelling, with a court in
front, and a garden and paddock behind. Trees overarch it like the
frame of a picture, and the cottage itself, although not pretty, yet too
unpretending to be vulgar, and abundantly snug and comfortable,
leading by different paths to all my favorite walks, and still within dis-

tance of my most valuable neighbors. It will be provoking if this woman, who has known me for forty years, and to whom my father rendered a thousand services, should, from spite to Captain Beauchamp and his excellent father, resolve rather to let the cottage tumble to pieces than admit a tenant whom they wish to see there, or indeed any tenant at all.

You are most kind in your inquiries about my health. I can not but think myself better on the whole than when I wrote last, and you will wonder to hear that I have again taken pen in hand. It reminds me of Benedick's speech—"When I said I should die a bachelor, I never thought to live to be married;" but it is our friend Henry Chorley's fault. He has taken to "The Lady's Companion," a weekly journal, belonging to Bradbury and Evans, that was going to decay (like my dwellings, present and future) under the mismanagement of Mrs. Loudon, and came to me to help him. He wanted a novel; then, finding that out of the question, he wanted something else; and, though I have refused every applicant to right and left for these eight years, this very Mrs. Loudon included, and began, of course, by refusing him, he is such a very old friend, that I really could not persist in saying No to him. So at last it ended in my undertaking to give him a series of papers to be called "Readings of Poetry, Old and New," consisting of as much prose as he can get, and extracts from favorite poets.

•   •   •

[M.R.M.]

SIENA—
[TUESDAY] SEP.ʳ 24 [1850]

To think that it is more than two months since I wrote last to you my beloved friend, make[s] the said two months seem even longer to me than otherwise they would necessarily be—a slow, heavy two months in every case, . . "with all the weights of care & death hung at them". Your letter reached me when I was confined to my bed & could scarcely read it for all the strength at my heart. So ill I have been in the old way . . miscarriage . . for the fourth time, only worse than I ever was: forced to lie with ice-applications for two days & nights together, & feeling very doubtful in my own mind, . . I, who am not easily alarmed, . . how it was likely to end. Robert was up with me all night long with Wilson, he fanning me to keep off the fainting— for the exhaustion was extreme, & indeed it is only within the last ten days that some human colour has come back to my blanched cheeks & hands. So loth I was to leave Florence—I felt so little equal to such an exertion!—yet as soon as I could be moved, & before I could walk from one room to another, D.ʳ Harding insisted on the necessity of change of air (for my part, I seemed to myself more fit to change the world than the air) and Robert carried me into the railroad like a baby, & off we came here to Siena. We took a villa a mile & a half from the town, a villa situated on a windy hill (called "poggio al vento") with magnificent views from all the windows, & set in the midst of its own vineyard & oliveground, apple trees & peach trees, not to speak of a little square flower-garden—for which we pay *eleven shillings, one penny, farthing, the week:* and at the end of these three weeks, our medical comforter's prophecy, to which I listened so incredulously, is fulfilled, and I am able to walk a mile & am really as well as ever in all essential respects. It is curious how I rally—he said that a robuster woman would find it much harder to rally from such attacks than I— but this fact does'nt console me for ever so much disappointment besides a seven weeks illness. He told my husband that he never knew *such excessive cases*—yet there is no malady,—nothing to prevent the ordinary solution . . when suddenly a sort of fury falls into the circulation & there's an end of all. How Wiedeman escaped it seems impossible to say– Ah well!—the less said the better now—it's over & I'm alive, which is considerably beyond what might have been expected. Our poor little darling too (see what disasters!) was ill four & twenty hours from a species of sun-stroke, & frightened us with a heavy, hot head, & glassy staring eyes, lying in a half stupor. Terrible, the silence that fell suddenly upon the house, without the small pattering feet, & the singing voice! But God spared us: he grew quite well directly & sang louder than ever. Since we came here his cheeks have turned into roses, . . and we have been perpetrating the cruelty of weaning him—. Poor darling! His first grief it has been. His nurse put aloes on her breast—and if you had seen him make her sit on the old seats, first on one, then on another, where everything used to go so well!– He thought the milk w.ᵈ be better there, poor darling!

What still further depressed me during our latter days at Florence was the dreadful event in America—the loss of our poor friend Ma.ᵈᵐᵉ

Ossoli . . affecting in itself, & also through association with that past, when the arrowhead of anguish was broken too deeply into my life ever to be quite drawn out. Robert wanted to keep the news from me till I was stronger, but we live too *close*, for him to keep anything from me,—& then I sh^d have known it from the first letter or visitor, so there was no use trying. The poor Ossolis spent part of their last evening in Italy with us . . he and she & their child . . and we had a note from her off Gibraltar speaking of the captain's death . . from small-pox. Afterwards it appears that her child caught the disease & lay for days between life & death—*recovered*—& then came the final agony. "Deep called unto deep" indeed. Now she is where there is no more grief & 'no more sea'—and none of the restless in this world, none of the shipwrecked in heart, ever seemed to me to want peace more than she did. We saw much of her last winter,—&, over a great gulf of differing opinion, we both felt drawn strongly to her. High & pure aspiration she had—yes, and a tender woman's heart,—& we honored the truth & courage in her, rare in woman or man. The work she was preparing upon Italy w^d probably have been more equal to her faculty than anything previously produced by her pen, (her other writing, being curiously inferior to the impressions her conversation gave you): indeed she told me it was the only production to which she had given time & labour. But if rescued, the M.S. would be but the raw material. I believe nothing was finished:—nor, if finished, could the work have been otherwise than deeply coloured by those blood-colours of social-istic views, which would have drawn the wolves on her with a still more howling enmity both in England & America. Therefore it was better for her to go. Only God and a few friends can be expected to distinguish between the pure personality of a woman & her professed opinions. She was chiefly known in America, I believe, by oral lec-tures & a connection with the newspaper-press —neither of them happy means of publicity. Was she happy in anything, I wonder? She told me that she never was. May God have made her happy in her death!

Such gloom she had in leaving Italy! So full she was of sad pre-sentiment! Do you know she gave a *bible* as a parting gift from her child to ours, writing in it "*In memory* of Angelo Eugene Ossoli" &c . . a strange, prophetical expression!– That last evening, a prophecy was talked of jestingly, . . an old prophecy made to poor Marquis Os-soli, . . "that he should shun the sea, for that it w^d be fatal to him".

I remember how she turned to me smiling & said "Our ship is called the *Elizabeth* & I accept the omen".

Now I am making you almost dull perhaps, & myself certainly duller. Rather let me tell you, dearest Miss Mitford, how delightedly I look forward to reading whatever you have written or shall write– You write "as well as twenty years ago"! Why, I should think so indeed!——Dont I know what your letters are? Have'nt I had faith in you always? Have'nt I, in fact, teazed you half to death in proof of it? . . I who was a sort of Brutus, & ought'nt to have done it, you hinted! Moreover Robert is a great admirer of yours, as I must have told you before, & has the pretension (unjustly though, as I tell *him*) to place you still higher among writers than I do . . so that we are *two* in expectancy here! May M! Chorley's periodical live a thousand years!

As my 'sea gull' wont—but you will find it in my new edition, & the 'Doves' & everything else worth a straw, of my writing. Here's a fact, which you must try to settle with your theories of simplicity & popularity— *None of these simple poems of mine have been favorites with general readers.* The unintelligible ones are always preferred, I observe, by extracters, compilers, and ladies & gentlemen who write to tell me that I'm a Muse. The very Corn Law Leaguers in the north, used to leave your 'seagulls' to fly where they could, & clap hands over mysteries of iniquity. Dearest Miss Mitford—for the rest dont mistake what I write to you sometimes,—dont fancy that I undervalue simplicity & think nothing of legitimate fame– I only mean to say that the vogue which begins with the masses, generally comes to nought . . (Berenger is an exceptional case, from the *form* of his poems, obviously) while the appreciation beginning with the few, always ends with the masses. Was'nt Wordsworth, for instance, both simple & unpopular, when he was most divine? To go from the great to the small, when I complain of the lamentable weakness of much in my Seraphim-volume, I dont complain of the Seagull & Doves & the simple verses,—but exactly of the more ambitious ones. I have had to rewrite pages upon pages of that volume– Oh, such feeble rhymes, & turns of thought! such a dingy mistiness! Even Robert could'nt say a word for much of it. I took great pains with the whole, & made considerable portions, new—only, your favorites were not touched—not a word, touched I think, in the Sea Gull—& scarcely a word in the Doves. You wont complain of me a great deal, I do hope & trust. Also I put back your "little words" into the 'House of Clouds'. The two volumes are to come out it appears, at the end of October; not before, because M! Chapman wished to inaugurate them from his new house in Piccadilly – There are some new poems, & one rather long ballad,[1] written at request of anti-slavery friends in America. I arranged that it sh^d come next to the 'Cry of the children' . . to appear impartial as to national grievances.

* * *

We stay in this villa till our month is out, and then we go for a week into Siena that I may be nearer the churches & pictures, & see something of the cathedral & Sodomas. We calculated that it was cheaper to move our quarters than to have a carriage to & fro—and then D! Harding recommended repeated change of air for me, and he has proved his ability so much, (so kindly too!) that we are bound to act on his opinions as closely as we can. Perhaps we may even go to Volterra afterwards, if the *finances* will but allow of it. If we do, it may be for another week at farthest, & then we return to Florence. You had better direct there as usual. And do write & tell me much of yourself, & set *me* down in your thoughts as quite well, & ever yours in warm & grateful affection—

EBB–

* * *

1. "The Runaway Slave at Pilgrim's Point," written for the *Liberty Bell* of Boston in 1846.

FLORENCE.
NOVEMBER [1850]

I *meant* to cross your second letter, and so, my very dear friend, you are a second time a prophetess as to my intentions, while I am still more grateful than I could have been with the literal fulfilment. Delightful it is to hear from you—do always write when you can. And though this second letter speaks of your having been unwell, still I shall continue to flatter myself that upon the whole "the better part prevails," and that if the rains dont wash you away this winter, I may have leave to think of you as strengthening and to strengthen still. Meanwhile you certainly, as you say, have roots to your feet. Never was anyone so pure as you, from the drop of gypsey blood which tingles in my veins and my husband's, and gives us every now & then a fever for roaming, strong enough to carry us to mount Caucasus if it were not for the healthy state of depletion observable in the purse. I get fond of places—so does he. We, both of us, grew rather pathetical on leaving our Sienese villa and shrank from parting with the pig. But setting out on one's travels has a great charm,—oh, I should like to be able to pay our way down the Nile, & into Greece, and into Germany, & into Spain! Every now & then we take out the road-books, calculate the expenses, & groan in the spirit when it's proved for the hundredth time that we cant do it. One must have a home, you see, to keep one's books & one's spring-sofas in; but the charm of a home is a home *to come back to* . . Do you understand? No—not you! You have as much comprehension of the pleasure of "that sort of thing" as in the peculiar taste of the three ladies who hung themselves to a French balloon the other day, operatically *nude*, in order, I conjecture, to the ultimate perfection of French delicacy in morals & manners.

But now, seriously, . . . *is* it wise of you, dearest friend, to wait in that house till the chimneys fall in? One cant . . even you cant . . live altogether in Woodcock Lane,[1] if one loves it ever so: it is necessary to have chimneys, and a roof, and dry walls & floors. Now, if you should suffer this winter from that house, I shall be very severe to the aforesaid roots in the feet, I tell you, because it does seem to me that if they wont move of themselves, somebody should dig them up with a spade—somebody . . say, your editor! or Mʳ Harness! somebody who has leave (through friendship) to be impertinent & troublesome. As for me, I can do nothing across these Alps. Paper loses the electricity of the will before it reaches you, let me charge it ever so with that kind of fire. Only tell me how you are, how you keep, . . and light fires & be warm this winter as far as the house admits of it—do!—

I long to see your papers & dare say they are charming. At the same time just because they are sure to be charming (and notwithstanding their kindness to me . . notwithstanding that I live in a glass house myself, warmed by such rare stoves!) I am a little in fear that your generosity & excess of kindliness may run the risk of lowering the ideal of poetry in England by lifting above the mark the names of some poetasters. Do you know, you take up your heart sometimes by mistake to admire with, when you ought to use it only to love with?

& this is apt to be dangerous, with your reputation & authority in matters of literature. See how impertinent I am! But we should all take care to teach the world that poetry is a divine thing, . . should we not, . . that it is not mere verse-making, though the verses be pretty in their way. Rather perish every verse *I* ever wrote, for one, than help to drag down an inch that standard of poetry which for the sake of humanity as well as literature, should be kept high. As for simplicity & clearness, did I ever deny that they were excellent qualities? Never, surely. Only, they will not *make* poetry; & absolutely vain they are, & indeed all other qualities, without the essential thing, the genius, the inspiration, the insight, . . let us call it what we please— without which, the most accomplished verse-writers had far better write prose, . . for their own sakes as for the world's—dont you think so? Which I say, because I sighed aloud over many names in your list, & now have taken pertly to write out the sigh at length. Too charmingly you are sure to have written! and see the danger! But Miss Fanshawe is well worth your writing of (let me say that I am sensible warmly of that) as one of the most witty of our wits in verse, men or women. I have only seen m.s. copies of some of her verses, & that years ago, but they struck me very much, . . & really I do not remember another female wit worthy to sit beside her, even in French literature. Motherwell is a true poet. But oh, I dont believe in your John Clares, Thomas Davises, Whittiers, Hallecks[2] . . and still less in other names which it w^d be invidious to name again. How pert I am. But you give me leave to be pert, and you know the meaning of it all, after all. Your editor quarrelled a little with me once & I with him, about the 'poetesses of the united empire', in whom I could'nt or would'nt find a poet, though there are extant two volumes of them, & Lady Winchelsea at the head. I hold that the writer of the ballad of Robin Gray was our first poetess rightly so called before Joanna Baillie.[3]

Mr Lever is in Florence I believe, now, and was at the Baths of Lucca in the summer– We never see him– It is curious. He made his way to us with the sunniest of faces & cordialest of manners at Lucca; and I who am much taken by manner was quite pleased with him, & wondered how it was that I did'nt like his books. Well—he only wanted to see if we had the right number of eyes & no odd fingers. Robert, in return for his visit, called on him three times, I think, and I left my card on Mrs Lever. But he never came again—he had seen enough of us—he could put down in his private diary that we had neither claw nor tail, . . & there an end, . . properly enough. In fact, he lives a different life from ours, . . he, in the ballroom, and we, in the cave . . nothing could be much more different, . . and perhaps there are not many subjects of common interest between us.–

I have seen extracts in the Examiner from Tennyson's "In Memoriam," which seemed to me exquisitely beautiful & pathetical. Oh— there's a poet—talking of poets! Have you read Wordsworth's last work . . the legacy? With regard to the elder Miss Jewsbury,[4] do you know, I take M.ʳ Chorley's part against you, . . because, although I know her only by her writings, the writings seem to me to imply a certain vigour & originality of mind, by no means ordinary. For instance, the fragments of her letters in his "Memorials of M.ʳˢ Hemans" are much superior to any other letters almost in the volume, . . certainly to M.ʳˢ Hemans's own. Is'nt this so? And so, you talk, you in England, of Prince Albert's "folly,"[5] do you really? Well—among the odd things we lean to in Italy . . not weaning babies till they are a year & a half old & the like . . is to an actual belief in the greatness & importance of the future exhibition. We have actually imagined it to be a noble idea,—& you take me by surprise in speaking of the general distaste to it in England. Is is really possible? For the agriculturists, I am less surprised at coldness on their part; but do you fancy that the manufacturers & free traders are cold too? Is M.ʳ Chorley against it equally? Yes, I am glad to hear of M.ʳˢ Butler's success . . or Fanny Kemble's . . ought I to say? –

Our little Wiedeman, who cant speak a word yet, waxes hotter in his ecclesiastical & musical passion. Think of that baby, (just cutting his eyeteeth), screaming in the street till he is taken into the churches . . kneeling on his knees, to the first sound of music, & folding his hands & turning up his eyes in a sort of ecstatical state. One scarcely knows how to deal with the sort of thing: it is too soon for religious controversy. He crosses himself, I assure you. Robert says it is as well to have the eyeteeth & the Puseyistical crisis over together. The child is a very curious, imaginative child, but too excitable for his age . . that's all I complain of. It is not safe to wean children early in this climate, and many are weaned later than he has been. So disappointed poor dearest Arabel was about the house, which was taken & never used. God bless you my much loved friend. Write to

Your ever affectionate
EBB.–

What books by Souliè have appeared since his death? Do you remember . . I have just got Les enfants de l'amour, by Sue. I suppose he will prove in it the illegitimacy of legitimacy, & *vice* versa. Sue is in decided decadence, for the rest, since he has taken to illustrating socialism.

I have not a wide experience yet of Chapman & Hall —our affairs are managed by others. But this I know—they have offered us not a single copy to give away—. They print for us, taking themselves all the risk, & dividing the profit—those are the terms.

1. A tree-shaded country walk in the vicinity of Reading.
2. Catherine Fanshawe (1765–1834), minor poet; William Motherwell (1797–1835), Scottish editor and poet; John Clare (1793–1864), the peasant poet; Thomas Davis (1814–45), Irish poet and politician; John Greenleaf Whittier (1807–92), American Quaker poet and editor; Fitz-Greene Halleck (1790–1867), American poet.
3. Anne Finch, Countess of Winchilsea (1661–1720), wrote *Miscellany Poems on Several Occasions* (1713); Lady Anne Lindsay (1750–1825) wrote "Auld Robin Gray" (1771); Joanna Baillie (1762–1851), dramatist and poet, wrote *Metrical Legends* (1821).
4. Maria Jewsbury Fletcher (1800–33), minor poet, sister of the novelist Geraldine Jewsbury, wrote *Letters to the Young* (1828).
5. The Crystal Palace, site of the first international industrial exhibit held in London in 1851.

FLORENCE.
[FRIDAY] DEC. 13. [1850]

•   •   •

Let me tell you what I have heard of Mrs Gaskell for fear I should forget it later. She is connected by marriage with Mrs A. T. Thompson,[1] & from a friend of Mrs Thompson's it came to me, & really seems to exonerate Chapman & Hall from the charge advanced against them. Mary Barton was shown in M.S. to Mrs Thompson & failed to please her; and in deference to her judgement certain alterations were made. Subsequently it was offered to all or nearly all the publishers in London, & rejected. Chapman & Hall accepted & gave a hundred pounds, as you heard, for the copyright of the work: and though the success did not perhaps (that is quite possible) induce any liberality with regard to copies, they gave *another hundred pounds* upon printing the second edition, and it was not in the bond to do so. I am told that the liberality of the proceeding was appreciated by the author & her friends accordingly—& there's the end of my story. Two hundred pounds is a good price . . is'nt it? . . for a novel, as times go– Miss Lynn[2] had only a hundred & fifty for her Ægyptian novel— or perhaps for the Greek one. Taking the long run of poetry (if it runs at all) I am half given to think that it pays better than the novel does, in spite of everything. Not that we speak out of golden experience— alas, no! we have had not a sous from our books for a year past, the booksellers being bound of course to cover their own expenses first. Then this Christmas account has not yet reached us. But the former editions paid us regularly so much a year, & so will the present ones I hope– Only I was not thinking of *them*, in preferring what may strike you as an extravagant paradox, . . but of Tennyson's returns from Moxon last year which I understand amounted to five hundred pounds. To be sure 'In Memoriam' was a new success—which should not prevent our considering the fact of a regular income proceeding from the previous books. A novel flashes up for a season & does not often outlast it. For Mary Barton, I am a little, little disappointed, do you know. I have just done reading it. There is power & truth—she can shape & she can pierce—but I wish half the book away, it is so tedious every now & then,—and besides I want more beauty, more air from the universal world—these class-books must always be defective as works of art. How could I help being disappointed a little when Mrs Jameson told me that "since the Bride of Lammermoor, nothing had appeared equal to Mary Barton"? Then the style of the book is slovenly, & given to a kind of phraseology which would be vulgar even as colloquial English. Oh—it is a powerful book in many ways– You are not to set me down as hypercritical. Probably the author will write herself clear of many of her faults: she has strength enough. As to [']'In Memoriam," I have seen it, I have read it, . . dear Mr Kenyon had the goodness to send it to me by an American traveller . . & now, I really do disagree with you, for the book has gone to my heart & soul . . I think it full of deep pathos & beauty. All I wish away, is the marriage hymn at the end, & *that*, for every reason I wish away—it's a discord in the music. The monotony is a part of the position—the sea is monotonous, so is lasting grief: your complaint is against fate & humanity rather than against the poet Tennyson. Who that has suffered, has not felt wave after wave break dully against one rock, till brain & heart with all their radiances seemed lost in a single shadow? So the effect of the book is artistic &

true, I think—& indeed I do not wonder at the opinion which has reached us from various quarters that Tennyson stands higher through having written it. You see what he appeared to want according to the view of many, was an earnest personality & direct purpose. In this last book, though of course there is not room in it for that exercise of creative faculty which elsewhere established his fame, he appeals, heart to heart, directly as from his own to the universal heart, & we all feel him nearer to us—*I* do . .

· · ·

We know very few residents in Florence—& these, with chance visitors, chiefly Americans, are all that keep us from solitude: every now & then in the evening somebody drops in to tea. Would indeed you were near! but should I be satisfied with you "once a week," do you fancy? Ah—you would soon love Robert. You could'nt possibly help it, I am sure. *I* should be soon turned down to an underplace, &, under the circumstances, would not struggle. Do you remember once telling me that "all men are tyrants" . . as sweeping an opinion as the apostle's, that "all men are liars." Well—if you knew Robert, you would make an exception certainly.–

· · ·

your ever affec.^{te}
Ba

1. Catherine Byerley Thomson (1797–1862), minor novelist under the pseudonym Grace Wharton, and wife of a prominent Scottish physician whose sister was step-mother to the novelist Elizabeth Gaskell.
2. Elizabeth Lynn, later Linton (1822–98), author of *Azeth, the Egyptian* (1847) and *Amymone* (1848).

LONDON AND PARIS

Reunion and French Politics

1851–52

For EBB, 1851 meant her first trip to England since leaving it five years before. With Robert, Pen, and Wilson she left Florence in May and after stops in Venice and Paris arrived in July in London where MRM, despite her lameness, journeyed to see her (for what proved to be their last meeting). MRM also managed a visit to the Crystal Palace, and in September moved her "four tons of books" from Three Mile Cross to a more comfortable cottage at nearby Swallowfield. From here she saw her *Recollections of a Literary Life, or Books, Places, and People* (1852) published to great popular success. In Paris, where the Brownings moved for the winter, EBB—still brooding about her father's refusal to see her—was further pained by the revelations about Bro's death that MRM, with all good intentions, had included in *Recollections*. Nevertheless, EBB shared with her old friend in minute detail in 15–[16] February [1852] the circumstances of her long-dreamed-of meeting with their idol George Sand, as well as her high hopes (shared by neither Browning nor MRM) for the liberalism of Louis Napoleon, whose December coup d'état had made him Emperor Napoleon III. When the Brownings returned to London in July of 1852 for three months, MRM was bedridden and they failed to meet. EBB did meet, however, the Italian patriot Giuseppe Mazzini, indulged her interest in the occult at a crystal-ball demonstration, and was entertained by old friends like Chorley and John Kenyon and new friends like the poet Alfred Tennyson and his wife.

LONDON:
[WEDNESDAY] SEPTEMBER 24. [1851]

My dear dearest Miss Mitford, although I have behaved to you like a savage (who can't read or write) it's impossible for me to leave England without saying one 'goodbye, God bless you!' One thing that kept my conscience still, was hearing from Mrs. Dupuy that you had'nt a moment in which to read letters, just now, because you were absorbed in a third volume . . which is sure to absorb other people presently.

I have been, for my part, trodden down & crushed with engagements, visits, & heaps upon heaps of things necessary to do. For a fortnight I was sole nurserymaid to my child. Oh, not in play, but in a good earnest. Wilson went into the country to see her family, & the child w^d let no human being do anything except myself. I had to sleep with him, dress & wash him, feed him . . I was not let out of his sight a moment. So, I missed the Royal academy, the national Gallery, all, worth seeing—and Robert would not go alone—we have really seen nothing in London,—except *faces*, & the new Houses of Parliament & the zoological gardens where our child went with us – Then, two or three times I have been quite unwell . . suffering from cough . . it is better now, but still, it seems wise not to linger among these nascent fogs, but to get settled in Paris while there's a shred of sunshine in the season to hold by.

Ah—dearest friend—you are not a prophetess—which is strange! There has been no mutiny, no accident, no happy result in any way. I wrote to say that I was *here* . . to beseech my father at least to kiss my child—and my husband wrote a letter which I fondly thought, would be irresistible. There was a violent reply to Robert, together with two packets enclosing *all* the letters I had written in the course of five years, *seals unbroken* . . several of them written in black edged paper, suggesting the death of my child, perhaps. The doubt had not moved my father to break a seal. They all came back to me. So now, I cannot write again! I must leave all in God's hands & wait. It was a great blow to me, the sight of those poor letters! He had cast me off for ever, he said, as a child! & *that*, indeed, proved it.

May God bless you, dearest friend. Write to me poste restante, at Paris, & tell me how you are, how you have managed about your house, & book . . all about yourself, in fact. I love you & pray God to bless you, & am ever & ever,

Your attached
Ba–

Robert's warm regards to you—always. We had tea with Mr Rogers yesterday evening. He is wonderfully well, & most benignant.

138 AVENUE DES CH. ELYSÉES.
[WEDNESDAY] CHRISTMAS EVE– [1851]

What can you have thought of me? That I was shot or deserved to be? Forgive in the first instance, dearest friend, & believe that I wont behave so any more if in any way I can help it.

Tell me your thought now about L. Napoleon. He rode under our windows on the second of December through an immense shout from the Carrousel to the Arc de l'Etoile—there was the army & the sun of Austerlitz, & even I thought it one of the grandest of sights,—for he rode there in the name of the people after all.

The parties of every colour are frantic with rage, and I hear so much passion from the french & so much nonsense from the English, that it is difficult to keep one's own thoughts upright & at work. But from the beginning my own opinion has been favorable to the movement– The position as it was, was perfectly untenable, the wheel at a dead-lock. The only question was by whose hand the law was to be shattered at last. I cant pretend to put on looks of horror, at the violence done to an impossible constitution & an impracticable assembly, though, as Englishmen, people are necessarily pedantic about such things: it seems to me that I am a purer democrat in admitting of an appeal to the universal suffrage of the people over the heads of their unrepresenting representatives. For the rest, one cannot answer. He is justified so far, I think,—yet in another month he may be unjustifiable. I cant pretend to answer for his abnegation & patriotism– Can *you?* Only, if he attempts absolutism, it wont do in France—the prestige will die away & he will go down to the dust, and deservedly. The French are the most democratical of people; but the American forms are repugnant to them, & they will insist on having individualities rather than officialties, always,—they have too much "sentiment" (use the french word) to bear with your committee-men. The unanimity rather than the majority of the election will be wonderful therefore: notwithstanding which, he will not *stand* except through standing fast by the people as well as appealing to them—& I think & hope that he is too able a man not to perceive this, himself. I have faith in the people at all events—& none in the Times Newspaper, which, pray read backwards upon most occasions, when it speaks about France. We have suffered no alarm whatever– Wiedeman was carried out to walk as usual on the worst day– Still, I sate up that thursday night in my dressing-gown till one in the morning, because we could hear the firing & I could not escape the emotion of the situation. Nothing could exceed the vigour & promptitude of that coup d'etat. Pure or impure, he is a man of incontestable courage & ability—that's certain.

But we know men, most opposed to him, . . writers of the old 'Presse' & 'National'—and Orleanists & Legitimists . . & the fury of all such, I can scarcely express to you after the life. Emile de Girardin and his friends had a sublime scheme of going over in a body to England & establishing a socialist periodical . . inscribing on their new habitation "Içi c'est la France". He actually advertised for sale his beautiful house close by, in the Champs Elysées—asked ten thousand pounds, English, for it,—& would have been "rather disappointed," as one of his sympathizing friends confessed to us, if the offer had been accepted. I heard a good story the other day– A lady visitor was groaning politically to Madame de Girardin, over the desperateness of the situation. "Il n'y a que Celui qui est en haut, qui peut nous en tirer" said she, casting up her eyes. "Oui, . . c'est vrai,"—replied Madame, "il le pourrait, lui", . . glancing towards the second floor, where Emile was at work upon feuilletons. Not that she mistakes him habitually for her deity, by any manner of means, . . if scandal is to be listened to.

•   •   •

Louis Napoleon is said to say (a bitter foe of his told me this) that "there will be four phases of his life. The first was all rashness & imprudence . . but it was necessary to make him known: the second, the struggle with & triumph over anarchy: the third, the settlement of France & the pacification of Europe: the fourth . . . a *"coup de pisto-*

let"." Se non é vero, ben trovato. Nothing is more likely than the catastrophe in any case: & the violence of the passions excited in the minority, makes me wonder at his surviving a day even. Do you know, I heard your idol of a Napoleon (the antique hero) called the other evening through a black beard & gnashing teeth, "le plus grand scelerat du monde", & his empire, "le regne du Satan", & his "marshalls," "des coquins". After that, I wont tell you that "le neveu" is reproached with every iniquity possible to anybody's public & private life. Perhaps he is not 'sans reproche' in respect to the latter—not altogether—he has a mistress & debts undeniably: but one cant believe, & ought'nt, even infinitesimally the things which are talked on the subject.

On the 6th of December, the temperature being very mild, I & Robert went in a close carriage to the scene of the fighting—but the barricades had vanished & nothing was to be seen except the bullet-holes in the walls, & the staring horror of the windows dashed in. The pavement was black with men, but the repose had already become absolute. Believe no exaggerations. He had Paris with him from the beginning. All our tradespeople for instance applauded him from the first word spoken to the last step taken– "Ah, Madame . . mais c'est le vrai neveu de son oncle! il est admirable".

Ah—I am so vexed about George Sand– She came, she has gone, & we have'nt met! There was a M. François who pretended to be her very, very particular friend, & who managed the business so particularly ill, from some motive or some incapacity, that he did not give us an opportunity of presenting our letter. He did not 'DARE' to present it for us, he said. She is shy—she distrusts book-making strangers, & she intended to be incognita while in Paris. He proposed that we should leave it at the theatre—& Robert refused– Robert said he would'nt have our letter mixed up with the love-letters of the actresses, or perhaps given to the"premier comique" to read aloud in the green room, as a relief to the "Chère adorable" which had produced so much laughter. Robert was a little proud—& M. François very stupid—& I, between the two, in a furious state of dissent from either. Robert tries to smooth down my ruffled plumage now, by promising to look out for some other opportunity—but the late one is gone. She is said to have appeared in Paris, in a bloom of recovered beauty & brilliancy of eyes—& the success of her play, 'le mariage de Victorine' was complete. A strange, wild, wonderful woman, certainly!– While she was here, she used a bedroom, which belonged to

her son . . a mere 'chambre de garçon', . . and for the rest, saw whatever friends she chose to see, only at the 'café,' where she breakfasted & dined. She has just finished a romance, we hear, and took
fifty two nights to write it. She writes only at night. People call her
Ma^dme Sand: there seems to be no other name for her, in society or
letters.

•   •   •

   I heard of Eugene Sue, too, yesterday. Our child is invited to a
Christmas tree & party . . & Robert says he is too young to go, but I
persist in sending him for half an hour with Wilson . . oh, really I
must—though he will be by far the youngest of the thirty children
invited⟨.⟩ The lady of the house, Miss Fitton, an English resident in
Paris, an elderly woman, shrewd & kind, said to Robert that she had
a great mind to have Eugene Sue . . only he was so . . scampish—I
think that was the word . . or something alarmingly equivalent. Now
I should like to see Eugene Sue with my little innocent child in his
arms—the idea of the combination pleases me somehow. But I shant
see it in any case. We had three cold days last week which brought
back my cough & took away my voice—I am dumb for the present &
cant go out any more.

•   •   •

Love your ever affectionate & grateful
Ba–

138. Avenue des Ch. Elysées.
[Sunday–Monday] Feb. 15 [–16 1852].

Thank you thank you my beloved friend. Yes—I do understand in my
heart all your kindness. Yes, I do believe that on some points I am
full of disease—and this has exposed me several times to shocks of
pain in the ordinary intercourse of the world, which, for bystanders,
were hard, I dare say, to make out. Once at the Baths of Lucca I was
literally nearly struck down to the ground by a single word said in all
kindness by a friend whom I had not seen for ten years. The blue sky
reeled over me, & I caught at something, not to fall. Well—there is
no use dwelling on this subject. I understand your affectionateness &

tender consideration I repeat, and thank you—& love you, which is better. Now let us talk of reasonable things.

Berenger lives close to us, & Robert has seen him in his white hat wandering along the asphalte. I had a notion somehow that he was very old—but he is only elderly—not much indeed above sixty (which is the prime of life now a days) and he lives quietly & keeps out of scrapes poetical & political, and if Robert & I had but a little less modesty we are assured that we should find access to him easy. But we cant make up our minds to go to his door & introduce ourselves as vagrant minstrels, when he may probably not know our names. We never *could* follow the fashion of certain authors who send their books about without intimations of their being likely to be acceptable or not . . of which practice poor Tennyson knows too much for his peace. If indeed a letter of introduction to Berenger were vouchsafed to us from any benign quarter, we should both be delighted, but we must wait patiently for the influence of the stars. Meanwhile, we have at last sent our letter (Mazzini's) to George Sand, accompanied with a little note signed by both of us, though written by me, as seemed right, being the woman. We half despaired in doing this—for it is most difficult it appears, to get at her, she having taken vows against seeing strangers, in consequence of various annoyances & persecutions in & out of print, which it's the mere instinct of a woman to avoid– I can understand it perfectly. Also, she is in Paris for only a few days, & under a new name, to escape from the plague of her notoriety. People said to us . . "She will never see you—you have no chance, I am afraid." But we determined to try. At least I pricked Robert up to the leap—for he was really inclined to sit in his chair & be proud a little– 'No', said I, 'you *shant* be proud . . and I *wont* be proud—and we *will* see her—I wont die, if I can help it, without seeing George Sand'. So we gave our letter to a friend who was to give it to a friend who was to place it in her hands—her abode being a mystery, & the name she used, unknown. The next day, came by the post, this answer . .

Madame
　　J'aurai l'honneur de vous recevoir dimanche prochain rue Racine 3. C'est le seul jour que je puisse passer chez moi, et encore je n'en suis pas absolument certaine. Mais j'y ferai tellement mon possible, que ma bonne ètoile m'y aidera peutêtre un peu.

Agreez mille remerciment de cœur ainsi que Monsieur Browning, que j'espére voir avec vous, pour la sympathie que vous m'accordez.

George Sand.

Paris. 12 fevríer. 52.

This is graceful & kind—is it not?—and we are, going tomorrow, . . I, rather at the risk of my life . . but I shall roll myself up head & all in a thick shawl, & we shall go in a close carriage, & I hope I shall be able to tell you about the result before shutting up this letter.

One of her objects in coming to Paris this time was to get a commutation of the sentence upon her friend Marc Dufraisse who was ordered to Cayenne. She had an interview accordingly with the President. He shook hands with her & granted her request—and in the course of conversation pointed to a great heap of "Decrees" on the table, being hatched 'for the good of France'. I have heard scarcely anything of him, except from his professed enemies; and it is really a good deal the simple recoil from manifest falsehoods & gross exaggerations, which has thrown me on the ground of his defenders. For the rest, it remains to be *proved*, I think, whether he is a mere ambitious man, or better—whether his personality or his country stands highest with him as an object. I thought & still think that a Washington might have dissolved the assembly as he did, & appealed to the people. Which is not saying however that he is a Washington. We must wait, I think, to judge the man. Only it is right to bear in mind one fact . . that admitting the lawfulness of the coup d'état, you must not object to the dictatorship– And admitting the temporary necessity of the dictatorship, it is absolute folly to expect under it the liberty & ease of a regular government.

What has saved him with me from the beginning was his appeal to the people—and what makes his government respectable in my eyes, is the answer of the people to that appeal. Being a democrat, I dare to be so *consequently*. There never was a more legitimate chief of a state than Louis Napoleon is now,—elected by seven millions & a half—and I do maintain that ape or demigod, to insult him where he is, is to insult the people who placed him there. As to the stupid outcry in England about forced votes, voters pricked forward by bayonets, . . why, nothing can be more stupid. Nobody, not blinded by passion, could maintain such a thing for a moment. No frenchman, however blinded by passion, has maintained it in my presence.

A very philosophically minded man (french) was talking of these things the other day—one of the most thoughtful, liberal men, I ever knew of any country, & high & pure in his moral views—also (let me add) more *anglomane* in general than I am. He was talking of the English press. He said, he "did it justice for good & noble intentions" . .

(more than I do!)

"but marvelled at its extraordinary ignorance. Those writers did not know the A B C of France. Then, as to Louis Napoleon, whether he was right or wrong, they erred in supposing him not to be in earnest with his constitution & other remedies for France. The fact was . . he not only was in earnest—he was even *fanatical*."

There is of course much to deplore in the present state of affairs—much that is very melancholy. The constitution is not a model one, & no prospect of even comparative liberty of the press has been offered. At the same time, I hope still. As tranquility is established, there will be certain modifications—this indeed has been intimated,—and I think the press will by degrees attain to its emancipation. Meanwhile the Athenæum & other English periodicals say wrongly that there is a censure established on books. There is a censure on pamphlets & newspapers—on *books*, no. Cormenin is said to have been the adviser of the Orleans confiscation.

Monday– I have seen George Sand. She received us in a room with a bed in it, . . the only room she has to occupy, I suppose, during her short stay in Paris. She came forward to us very cordially with her hand held out, which I, in the emotion of the moment, stooped & kissed, . . upon which she exclaimed, "Mais, non! je ne veux pas . ." & kissed my lips. I dont think she is a great deal taller than I am . . yes, taller, but not a great deal . . and a little over-stout for that height. The upper part of the face is fine, the forehead, eyebrows & eyes, . . dark glowing eyes as they should be . . the lower part not so good. The beautiful teeth project a little, flashing out the smile of the large characteristic mouth; & the chin recedes. It never could have been a beautiful face, Robert & I agree, but noble & expressive it has been & is. The complexion is olive, quite without colour, . . the hair, black & glossy, divided with evident care & twisted back into a knot behind the head, & she wore no covering to it. Some of the portraits represent her in ringlets—& ringlets would be much more becoming to the style of face, I fancy, for the cheeks are rather over-full. She was dressed in a sort of woollen grey gown, with a jacket of the same material, (according to the ruling fashion)—the gown fastened up to the throat, with a small linen collarette, & plain white muslin sleeves buttoned round the wrists. The hands appeared to me small & well-shaped. Her manners were quite as simple as her costume. I never saw a simpler woman. Not a shade of affectation or consciousness even—not a suffusion of coquetry,—-& not a cigarette to be seen!– Two or three young men were sitting with her, & I observed the profound respect with which they listened to every word she said– She speaks rapidly, with a low, unemphatic voice– Repose of manner is much more her characteristic than animation is—only, under all the quietness, & perhaps by means of it, you are aware of an intense burning soul.

She kissed me again when we went away[.]

•   •   •

your most affec^{te} & grateful
Ba–

[LONDON] 58. WELBECK STREET.
FRIDAY– [30 JULY 1852]

•   •   •

I mean to go down to see you one day, but certainly we must account it right not to tire you while you are weak, & not to spoil our enjoyment by forestalling it. Two months are full of days—we can afford to wait. Meantime let us have a little gossip such as the gods allow of.

Dear Mr Kenyon has not yet gone to Scotland, though his intentions still stand north. He passed an evening with us some evenings ago, & was brilliant & charming, (the two things together), & good & affectionate at the same time. Mr Landor was staying with him—(perhaps I told you that) & went away into Worcestershire . . assuring me, when he took leave of me, that he never would enter London again. A week passes . . and lo! Mr Kenyon expects him again. Resolutions are not always irrevocable, you observe.

I must tell you what Landor said about Louis Napoleon. You are aware that he loathed the first Napoleon & that he hates the French nation—also, he detests the present state of French affairs, & has foamed over in the Examiner "in prose & rhyme" on the subject of them. Nevertheless, he who calls 'the Emperor' "an infernal fool" expresses himself to this effect about the president. "I always knew him to be a man of wonderful genius. I knew him intimately, & I was persuaded of what was in him. When people have said to me, 'How can you like to waste your time with so trifling a man' I have answered, 'If all your Houses of Parliament, putting their heads together, could make a head equal to this trifling man's head, it would be well for England' ".

It was quite unexpected to me to hear M.ʳ Landor talk so.

He . . M.ʳ Landor . . is looking as young as ever, as full of life & passionate energy.

Did M.ʳ Horne write to you before he went to Australia? Did I speak to you about his going? Did you see the letter which he put into the papers as a farewell to England? I think of it all sadly.

Mazzini came to see us the other day, with that pale spiritual face of his, & those intense eyes, full of melancholy illusions. I was thinking while he sate there, on what Italian turf he would lie at last, with a bullet in his heart——or perhaps with a knife in his back—for to one of those ends it will surely come. M.ʳˢ Carlyle came with him—She is a great favorite of mine—full of thought & feeling & character, it seems to me.

London is emptying itself, & the relief will be great in a certain way,— for one gets exhausted sometimes. Let me remember whom I have seen—M.ʳˢ Newton Crosland, who spoke of you very warmly —Miss Mulock, who wrote the "Ogilvies" (that series of novels) & is interesting, gentle & young, & seems to have worked half her life away in spite of youth. M.ʳ Field, we have not seen—only heard of. Miss Clarke . . no . . but I am to see her, I understand, & that she is an American Corinna in yellow silk, but pretty.[1] We drove out to Kensington with Monkton Milnes & his wife, and I like her . . she is quiet & kind, & seems to have accomplishments—and we are to meet Fanny Kemble at the Procters some day next week. Many good faces . . but the best wanting! Ah—I wish, Lord Stanhope who shows the spirits of the sun in a Chrystal ball, could show us *that*? Have you heard of the chrystal ball? We went to meet it & the seer, the other morning, with sundry of the believers & unbelievers . . among the latter, chief among the latter, M⸍ Chorley, who was highly indignant & greatly scandalized, particularly on account of the combination sought to be established by the Lady of the house, between lobster salad & Oremus spirit of the sun. For my part, I endured both luncheon & spiritual phenomena, with great equanimity. It was very curious altogether to my mind, as a sign of the times, if in no other respect of philosophy. But I love the marvellous. Write my word to me, I beseech you, & love me & think of me, as I love & think of you. God bless you. Robert's love.

Your ever affec⸍ᵗᵉ
Ba–

Yes—Henrietta expects her second child[—]she is gone to Taunton—but Arabel sends her warm regards to you. I shall try & go to see your picture.[2]

1. Camilla Toulmin Crosland (1812–95), minor poet and essayist; Dinah Mulock (1826–87), later Craik, novelist, author of *The Ogilvies* (1851); James T. Fields (1817–81), American publisher and editor, and friend of MRM; Sara Jane Clarke (1823–1904), later Lippincott, poet and essayist under the pseudonym Grace Greenwood, author of *Greenwood Leaves* (1850).

2. A new portrait of MRM by her friend John Lucas, being completed in the artist's London studio. See frontispiece.

LONDON.
FRIDAY [–SATURDAY]. [8–9 OCTOBER 1852]

My dearest Miss Mitford I am quite in pain to have to write a farewell to you after all. As soon as Wilson had returned—& she stayed away much longer than last year . . we found ourselves pushed to the edge of our time for remaining in England,—& the accumulation of business to be done before we could go, pressed on us. I am almost mad with the amount of things to be done, as it is—but I should have put the visit to you at the head of them & swept all the rest on one side for a day, if it had'nt been for the detestable weather, & my horrible cough which combines with it. When Wilson came back, she found me coughing in my old way, & it has been without intermission up to now, or rather waxing worse & worse. To have gone down to you & inflicted the noise of it on you, would have simply made you nervous, while the risk to myself would have been very great indeed– Still, I have waited & waited—feeling it scarcely possible to write to you & say "I am not coming this year". Ah—I am so very sorry & disappointed! I hoped against hope for a break in the weather, & an improvement in myself—now, we must go, & there is no hope. For about a fortnight I have been a prisoner in the house– This climate wont let me live—there's the truth. So we are going on monday – We go to Paris for a week or two, & then to Florence, & then to Rome, & then to Naples, . . but we shall be back next year, if God pleases, and then I shall sieze on an early summer-day to run down straight to you & find you stronger, if God blesses me so far– Think of me & love me a little meanwhile. I shall do it by you– And do, *do* . . since there is no time to hear from you in London, . . send a fragment of a note to Arabel for me that I may have it in Paris before we set out on our long Italian journey– Let me have the comfort of knowing exactly how you are before we set out. As for me I expect to be better on crossing the channel. How people manage to live & enjoy life in this fog & cold is inexplicable to me. I understand the system of the American rapping spirits considerably better –

Henrietta has a little girl – She was ill only three hours & is doing excellently now, thank God– My heart will ache at leaving England, for Arabel's sake—but it has ached in it too– I tried another letter — which was sent back again—with an intimation that there should be an end for the future to such "pestering" applications. No throb of natural tenderness– Well!–

The Tennysons in the kindest words pressed us to be present at their child's christening which took place last tuesday, but I could not go—it was not possible– Robert went alone therefore, & nursed the baby for ten or twelve minutes to its obvious contentment he flatters himself– It was christened Hallam Tennyson. M.ʳ Hallam was the godfather & present in his vocation. That was touching—was'nt it? I hear that the Laureate talks vehemently against the French president & the French —but for the rest, he is genial & good, & has been quite affectionate to us–

Here are the autographs . . .

Saturday morning

I wrote so far last night, & this morning I have your letter. You will undestand now why I did not send the autographs directly. I was waiting & waiting in the hope of being able to carry them to you– They are enclosed–

I am delighted to see our dearest M! Kenyon looking so well this time & seeming in such happy spirits. By the way he promises to send you his own autograph.

Ah—I know you would'nt have done such a thing as print a letter of mine, you knowing how I hate such publicities. You did it to frighten me– You would'nt either print or give. I know you would'nt. We send the three autographs you ask for.

So I go without seeing you! Grieved I am. Love me to make amends– Robert's love goes with me *[sic]*.

Your ever most affectionate
Ba–

.　　.　　.

FLORENCE,

BAGNI DI LUCCA, AND ROME

Conclusion—
Late Successes
and Last Words
1853–54

In November 1852 the Brownings returned to Casa Guidi to stay until they went to Bagni di Lucca the following summer. Both were busy with work: he on poems for *Men and Women* (1855) and she on the novel-poem *Aurora Leigh* (1856) and revisions for another edition of *Poems* (1844) published in October 1853. Among the latest publications EBB read were the immensely popular *Uncle Tom's Cabin* (1852) by the American Harriet Beecher Stowe (1811–96) and Alfred Tennyson's first major work as laureate, "Ode on the Death of the Duke of Wellington." "Our play" mentioned in 15 March and in 20 May [1853] was Robert's *Colombe's Birthday* (1844) which the actress Helen Faucit (1820–98) had just produced, with only modest success, in London. New friends included the minor poet Frederick Tennyson (1807–98), older brother of Alfred, and the American lawyer and sculptor William Wetmore Story (1819–95) and his wife whom they knew at Bagni di Lucca and later in Rome, to which the Brownings moved for six months in November 1853. The Storys' five-year-old child died there on 23 November, poisoning the atmosphere for EBB despite the pleasant society of the novelist Thackeray and their old acquaintances, the Kemble sisters. For her part, MRM, although weakened by a carriage accident late in 1852, managed to publish *Atherton and Other Tales* which enjoyed some success on its appearance in May 1854 and was followed in July by a new edition of her plays. She, too, followed, although more skeptically than EBB, the spiritualist

phenomenon and the course of Empire under Louis Napoleon. Her
last days were brightened by the friendship of the novelist Charles
Kingsley (1819–75), who had a living at nearby Eversley, and of Lady
Marie Clotilde Russell, wife of Sir Henry Russell (1783–1852), second
Baronet, whose seat was at Swallowfield. Attended by Lady Russell
and the long-time servants K and Sam Sweetman, MRM died peace-
fully, apparently of heart failure, on 10 January 1855.

FLORENCE.

[TUESDAY] MARCH 15– [1853]

•   •   •

The spring has surprised us here just as we were beginning to
murmur at the cold. Think of somebody advising me the other day
not to send out my child without a double-lined parasol! There's a
precaution for March. The sun is powerful—we are rejoicing in our
Italian climate. Oh, that I could cut out just a mantle of it to wrap
myself in, & so go and see you!—— Your house is dry you say– Is the
room you occupy airy as well as warm? Because being confined to a
small room, with you who are so used to liberty & out of door life,
must be depressing to the vital energies. Do you read much? No,
no—you ought not to think of the press of course, till you are strong.
Ah—if you should get to London to see our play, how glad I should
be! We, too, talk of London . . but somewhat mistily, and not so
early in the summer. M.ʳ & M.ʳˢ Marsh . . he is the american minister
at Constantinople . . have been staying in Florence, & passing some
evenings with us. They tempt us with an invitation to Constantinople
this summer, which would be irresistible if we had the money for the
voyage, perhaps . . so perhaps it is as well that we have not. Enough
for us that we are going to Rome & to Naples—then northward. I am
busy in the meanwhile with various things—a new poem, . . and re-
vising for a third edition which is called for by the gracious public.
Robert too is busy with another book. Then I am helping to make
frocks for my child, reading Proudhon (& Swedenborg) and in deep
meditation on the nature of the rapping spirits, upon whom, I understand, a fellow dramatist of yours, Henry Spicer, (I think you once
mentioned him to me as such) has just written a book entitled "The
Mystery of the Age".[1] A happy winter it has been to me altogether–
We have had so much repose, & at the same time, so much interest

in life, . . also I have been so well, . . that I shall be sorry when we go out of harbour again with the spring breezes. We like M.͏ʳ Tennyson extremely, & he is a constant visitor of ours:—the poet's elder brother. By the way, the new edition of the Ode on the Duke of Wellington, seems to contain wonderful strokes of improvement. Have you seen it?– As to Alexandre Dumas, fils, I hope it is not true that he is in any scrape from the cause you mention. He is very clever— & I have a feeling for him for his father's sake as well as because he presents a rare instance of intellectual heirship. Did'nt I tell you of the prodigious success of his drama of the "Dame aux Camelias," which ran above a hundred nights last year, & is running again? how there were caricatures on the boulevards, showing the public of the pit holding up umbrellas to protect themselves from the tears rained down by the public of the boxes? how the President of the republic went to see, & sent a bracelet to the first actress, & how the English newspapers called him immoral for it?—how I went to see, myself, & cried so that I was ill for two days, & how my aunt called *me* immoral for it? I was properly lectured, I assure you. She "quite wondered how M.͏ʳ Browning could allow such a thing," . . not comprehending that M.͏ʳ Browning never, or scarcely ever, does think of restraining his wife from anything she much pleases to do. The play was too painful . . that was the worst of it . . but I maintain it is a highly moral play, rightly considered . . & the acting was certainly most exquisite on the part of all the performers. Not that Alexandre Dumas, fils, excels generally in morals (in his books, I mean) but he is really a promising writer as to cleverness, & when he has learnt a little more art, he will take no low rank as a novelist. Robert has just been reading a tale of his called 'Diane de Lys,' & throws it down with . . "You must read that, Ba—it is clever—only, outrageous as to morals." Just what I should expect from Alexandre Dumas, fils. I have a tenderness for the whole family, you see!

You dont say a word to me of M.͏ʳˢ Beecher Stowe. How did her book impress you? No woman ever had such a success, such a fame! No man ever had, in a single book. For my part I rejoice greatly in it. It is an individual glory full of healthy influence & benediction to the world.

•   •   •

[EBB]

1. *Sights and Sounds: The Mystery of the Day* (1853) by the minor dramatist Henry Spicer (?–1891).

FLORENCE.
[FRIDAY] MAY 20. [1853]

I am so disappointed, my dearest Miss Mitford, so grieved at this new account of you. May the evil be turned aside before my lamentation over it can reach you! In the meanwhile I shall be perforce very anxious. The weather must be warmer even with you at the present depth in May, and you will be receiving & reviving under, I pray God, its happy influences— Do let me hear without delay— A short letter, if a long letter tires—but a letter in any case!—— I throw myself on your proved kindness for this.

We dont go to Rome till later—we could'nt help ourselves—& the only vexation of it is, that we shant *probably* get to England till next spring— So looks the probability at least. I have strong faith— credulity, say my friends, . . Mr Chorley, for instance, who is "fretted" about my tenderness towards the "rapping spirits". (After all it's an open question whether the man who affirms most or the man who denies most, arrives at most of truth.) Well—I have strong credulity, say my friends—and among other figments, I have an undeniable tendency to believing in the falling of skies & catching of larks. So we *may* get to England this summer—who knows? Only the probability is against it certainly as far as we can see yet.

You dont like the restoration of the punishment of death for political offences in France, do you? I dont. Your hero does'nt do all things well. He has however great & intelligent care for the poorer classes; & what the provisional government attempted to do, & failed, in this way, he has compassed & is compassing— Paris will be transfigured under his hand. Always beautiful, it will become wonderfully beautiful as by the stroke of a wand. Were you not sorry for the Empress's misfortune?[1] He has taken it much to heart, I understand. Also she seems to suffer in general health. She was always weak in the chest: & it was on that account, that she went yearly to the Pyrenees. Previous to the accident, the castle at Pau (Henri quâtre's) was being prepared for her; & courtly etiquette was likely enough to disagree with a woman spontaneous in her nature & ways to the verge of what is called wildness.

Yes, the moving of tables is an incontestable fact. A phenomenon of a magnetic character, involved in the curious history of the American manifestations, & from which other phenomena will probably be evolved if we have patience to wait. A year ago when the subject was talked of in Paris (where it was much talked of) I have heard sceptics say . . "Yes, let me see a table move, & I will believe anything". Now the table moves, all Europe witnessing—"E pur si muove" . . being the motto to an Italian pamphlet on the subject which has just come out! People never meet now-a-days in Florence, except to move tables. And I must turn the tables on unbelievers in general. As to the "rappings", . . the wonderful things narrated to me by persons who have "mediums" in their families, or who have been "mediums" themselves . . tears running from the eyes of the speakers—(intelligent eyes, too) I do not dare to tell you. We have a number of American visitors, & of the more cultivated order of Americans—& nearly everybody is more or less a believer. Then I always believed in a spirit-world & in the possibility of communications, & I believed long ago in the fact of such communications having taken place in Germany & elsewhere; (what is peculiar in the actual movement is the universality of it—) so I have less to get over than persons of a less speculative tendency. Somebody came to us the other day straight from Mrs Trollope where they have been trying table-experiments . . he is an Englishman, & a Chinese & Japanese scholar, & a cutter out in black paper of characteristic profiles. After testifying to the moving tables, he insisted on cutting out me & Robert. I am in a dreadful state of humiliation after the operation . . which is natural enough . . for why should people without features (like me) allow themselves to be agonized into a black profile? why, I wonder. I resisted as long as was decent—that's all that can be said for me. Mrs Trollope is better again.

•   •   •

Do you know Whittier's poems? Yes. Some extracts, I have seen, are direct & noble, I think—but I dont care for Dr Parson's stanzas on the bust of Dante. Then the view of Dante's soul is wrong & contracted, . . and the engraving of the portrait, a thing most unlike. Emerson & Lowell are the best poets in America, according to my creed. Emerson would be great if he had the musical faculty which he wants. As it is he is the *torso* of a poet. Lowell is completer, & really fine in some of his later poems, . . for he is vital & grows– Also he is one of the wittiest of writers when he pleases– I think highly of him—& I liked him personally & his interesting wife, when we met in London. As for yourself, may your laurels flower more & more– I like to hear about your letters —about everything relating to you–

• • •

Yes—Robert's play succeeded, but there could be no "run" for a play of that kind—it was a "success d'estime" & something more, which is surprising perhaps, considering the miserable acting of the men—Miss Faucit was alone in doing us justice – God bless you & keep you & love you, dearest friend. Do write, & believe that I think of you tenderly–

Your ever affec^te
Ba.

• • •

1. The Empress Eugénie had suffered a miscarriage from a fall in April.

CASA TOLOMEI, ALLA VILLA, BAGNI DI LUCCA.
[SATURDAY–SUNDAY] AUGUST 20th–21– [1853]

It is a comfort, my much loved friend, that you are making advances, however slow they may be. The horrible summer in England must have been much against you, and when you begin to improve decidedly, the progress will quicken itself probably. Tell me—are you able to move—unassisted, say, . . from one side of a bed to another? Can you stand for a moment? Is it weakness in the limbs or stiffness? And does not Mr May think that warm sea baths would be useful to you? Ask him, for my sake. You were longer than usual in writing to me, & I was on the point of sending you a dunning letter because it is natural for me to get anxious while you are not well. How is it with your appetite & sleep? and does it weary you now to read as much as you used to do? oh, I could ask a thousand questions & have more to ask–

Write to me, do, as soon as you can. I observe with satisfaction that your handwriting has not a trace of weakness in it—the old characteristic lines, with all the energetic twitches in them, just as they always were!– God bless & keep you dear, dear friend!–

We are enjoying the mountains here, riding the donkeys in the footsteps of the sheep, & eating strawberries & milk by basinsfull. The strawberries succeed one another, generation after generation, throughout the summer, through growing on different aspects of the hills. If a tree is felled in the forests, strawberries spring up, just as mushrooms might, . . & the peasants sell them for just nothing. Our little Penini is wild with happiness . . he asks in his prayers that God would "mate him dood and tate him on a dontey" . . (make him good & take him on a donkey) so resuming all aspiration for spiritual & worldly prosperity.

Then our friends M.ͬ & M.ͬˢ Story help the mountains to please us a good deal– He is the son of Judge Story, the biographer of his father, & for himself sculptor & poet—& she a sympathetic, graceful woman, fresh & innocent in face & thought. We go backwards & forwards to tea & talk at one another's houses. Last night they were our visitors, & your name came in among the Household Gods to make us as agreeable as might be– We were considering your expectations about M.ͬ Hawthorne—"All right", says M.ͬ Story, . . *"except the rare half hours."* (of eloquence.) He represents M.ͬ Hawthorne as not silent only by shyness but by nature & inaptitude. He is a man, it seems, who talks wholly & exclusively with the pen, & who does not open out vocally with his most intimate friends any more than with strangers. It is'nt his *way* to converse– That has been a characteristic of some men of genius before him, you know—but you will be nevertheless disappointed, very surely. Also, M.ͬ Story does not imagine that you will get anything from him on the subject of the "manifestations"– You have read the 'Blithesdale Romance' & are aware of his opinion expressed there? He evidently recognized them as a sort of scurvy spirits, good to be slighted because of their disreputableness–

•   •   •

Oh yes—I like M.ͬ Kingsley. I am glad he spoke kindly of *us*, because really I like him & admire him. Few people have struck me as much as he did last year in England. "Manly", do you say? But I am not very fond of praising men by calling them *manly*. I hate & detest a masculine man. *Humanly* bold, brave, true, direct, M.ͬ Kingsley is,—a moral cordiality and an original intellect uniting in him. I did not see *her* & the children, but I hope we shall be in better fortune next time.

Since I began this letter the Storys & ourselves have had a grand donkey-excursion to a village called Benabbia & the cross above it on the mountain peak. We returned in the dark & were in some danger of tumbling down various precipices . . but the scenery was exquisite, past speaking of for beauty– Oh those jagged mountains, rolled together like pre-Adamite beasts & setting their teeth against the sky!

It was wonderful– You may as well guess at a lion by a lady's lapdog, as at nature by what you see in England . . all honour to England, lanes & meadowland, notwithstanding! to the great trees, above all. Will you write to me sooner? Will you give me the details of yourself? Will you love me?

Your most affec^{te}
Ba.

Robert's love with mine.

Swallowfield
Nov. 10, 1853.

My very dear Friend,—I can not enough thank you for your most affectionate letter. I am still just as I was; but I have no sort of faith either in homœopathy or mesmerism. Indeed my friend, Dr. Spencer Hall, the great mesmerist, gave up the one, which had nearly killed him, and has taken to the other, which, I suppose, does less harm to the physician if not to the patient; so that I have got to believe them grown-up toys, the skipping-ropes and battledores of elderly people; and I now cling obstinately enough to the quiet rational ways of established practitioners. My present ailment is rheumatism, which has been long coming on—"a highly rheumatic condition," to use the medical phrase, upon which that terrible overturn, just at the beginning of a wet winter, fell like a spark among gunpowder. I don't think there is the slightest chance of any improvement, and must be content with what remains to me—the use of my intellect, and to a certain extent of my right hand, a comfortable cottage, excellent servants, kind neighbors, and most dear friends. And this is much. We must not forget, in thinking of my case, that for above thirty years I had perpetual anxieties to encounter—my parents to support and for a long time to nurse—and generally an amount of labor and of worry and of care of every sort, such as has seldom fallen to the lot of woman. I had not time to take care of myself, or of my health; and that, beyond a doubt, laid the foundation of my complaints. When I see you in the summer, my own beloved friend, if it please God to spare me so long, you will perhaps find me sitting under my acacia-tree; and I hope to get a garden chair and be wheeled about in the open air. It is a great thing to have a man like Sam, at once so strong and so gentle, who can bear me along by putting his hands under my arms, and even lift me down stairs step by step—only that that is so painful a process that I avoid it whenever I can, and see as few strangers or mere acquaintances as possible.

I have had a most interesting account of Miss Brontë and a charming letter from her. She is a little, quiet, gentle person; the upper part of the face good, but something amiss in the formation of the mouth; her conversation full of power and charm. She lives with her father—the only child remaining out of six—in a most secluded Yorkshire village amongst the moors. He is a gentlemanly and amiable man. I suppose the living is very small, for Miss Brontë went to France for two years; and the *début* of Lucy Stowe (*vide* "Villette")[1] in Brussels was literally her own. She also speaks to me of coming to London without necessity, as a thing hardly warrantable; and seems to me exceedingly unaffected and unspoiled. I like both "Shirley" and "Villette."

Remember me to your dear Robert and Mrs. Trollope. Ever most affectionately yours,

M. R. MITFORD

1. Lucy Snowe was the young teacher and heroine of Charlotte Brontë's novel *Villette* (1853), which, with *Shirley* (1849), was based on the author's memories of her life as a student in Brussels.

ROME—— 43. VIA BOCCA DI LEONE. 3.º *PIANO.*
[WEDNESDAY] JAN.ʸ 18– [1854]

It is long my ever dearest Miss Mitford since I wrote to you last—but since we came to Rome we have had troubles, out of the deep pit of which I was unwilling to write to you lest the shadows of it should cleave as blots to my pen. Then one day followed another, & one day's work was laid on another's shoulders. Well—we are all well, to begin with, & have been well—our troubles came to us through sympathy entirely. A most exquisite journey of eight days we had from Florence to Rome, seeing the great monastery & triple church of Assissi & the wonderful Terni by the way . . that passion of the waters which makes the human heart seem so still. In the highest spirits we entered Rome, Robert & Penini singing actually . . for the child was radiant & flushed with the continual change of air & scene, & he had an excellent scheme about "tissing the pope's foot" to prevent his taking away "mine gun" . . somebody having told him that such dangerous weapons were not allowed by the Roman police. You remember my telling you of our friends the Storys . . how they & their two children helped to make the summer go pleasantly at the Baths of Lucca. They had taken an apartment for us in Rome, so that we arrived in comfort to lighted fires & lamps as if coming home . . & we had a glimpse of their smiling faces that evening– In the morning before breakfast, little Edith was brought over to us by the manservant with a message—"The boy was in convulsions . . there was danger". We hurried to the house of course, leaving Edith with Wilson. Too true!—all that first day was spent beside a deathbed . . for the child never rallied . . never opened his eyes in consciousness, & by eight in the evening, he was gone. In the meanwhile, Edith was taken ill at our house . . could not be moved, said the physicians. We had no room for her, but a friend of the Storys' on the floor immediately below, M.ʳ Page,[1] the artist, took her in & put her to bed. Gastric fever, with a tendency to the brain—& within two days her life was almost despaired of—exactly the same malady as her brother's. Also, the English nurse, was apparently dying at the Storys' house—and Emma Page, the artist's youngest daughter, sickened with the same symptoms. Now you will not wonder that after the first absorbing flow of sympathy I fell into a selfish human panic about my child. Oh, I "lost my head," said Robert,—and if I COULD have caught him up in my arms & run to the ends of the world, the hooting after me of all Rome would not have stopped me. I wished—how I wished . . for the wings of a dove . . or any unclean bird . . to fly away with him & be at peace. But there was no possibility but to stay—also the physicians assured me solemnly that there was no contagion possible . . otherwise I would have at least sent him from us to another house. To pass over this dreary time I will tell you at once that the three patients recovered . . only in poor little Edith's case Roman fever followed the Gastric & has persisted so, ever since in periodical recurrence that she is very pale & thin– Roman fever is not dangerous to life . . simple fever & ague . . but it is exhausting if not cut off . . and the quinine fails sometimes– For three or four days now she has been free from the symptoms, & we are beginning to hope.——

Now you will understand at once what ghastly flakes of death have changed the sense of Rome to me. The first day, by a deathbed! The first drive out, to the cemetery,—where poor little Joe is laid close to Shelley's heart (*cor cordium* says the epitaph) & where the mother insisted on going when she & I went out in the carriage together. I am horribly weak about such things. I cant look on the earth-side of death . . I flinch from corpses & graves, & never meet a common funeral without a sort of horror. When I look death-wards I look OVER death—& upwards . . or I cant look that way at all. So that it was a struggle with me to sit upright in that carriage in which the poor stricken mother sate so calmly———not to drop from the seat . . which would have been worse than absurd of me. Well—all this has blackened Rome to me. I cant think about the Cæsars in the old strain of thought—the antique words get muddled & blurred with warm dashes of modern, everyday tears & fresh grave-clay. Rome is spoiled to me—there's the truth– Still, one lives through one's associations when not too strong . . & I have arrived at almost enjoying some things . . the climate for instance, which though perilous to the general health, agrees particularly with me . . and the sight of the blue sky floating like a sea-tide through the great gaps & rifts of ruins. We read in the papers of a tremendously cold winter in England & elsewhere, while I am able on most days to walk out as in an English summer, & while we are all forced to take precautions against the sun. Also Robert is well—and our child has not dropped a single rose-leaf from his radiant cheeks. We are very comfortably settled in rooms turned to the sun, and do work & play by turns . . having almost too many visitors . . hear excellent music at Mrs Sartoris's (Adelaide Kemble) once or twice a week, & have Fanny Kemble to come & talk to us with the doors shut, we three together. This is pleasant– I like her decidedly– If anybody wants small talk by handfulls of glittering dust swept out of salons, here's Mr Thackeray besides!—and if anybody wants a snow-man to match Southey's snow-woman (see 'Thalaba') here's Mr Lockhart,[2] who in complexion, hair, conversation & manners, might have been made out of one of your English *"drifts"* . . "sixteen feet deep in some places" says Galignani.

●   ●   ●

I go out very little in the evening both from fear of the night air & from disinclination to stir. Mr Page, our neighbour down stairs, pleases me much—and you ought to know more of him in England, for his portraits are like Titian's, flesh, blood & soul . . I never saw such portraits from a living hand. He professes to have discovered se-crets, & plainly *knows* them, from his wonderful effects of colour on canvass . . not merely in words. His portrait of Miss Cushman[3] is a miracle. Gibson's famous painted Venus[4] is very pretty—that's my criticism. Yes, I will say beside that I have seldom, if ever, seen so indecent a statue. The colouring with an approximation to flesh-tints, produces that effect to my apprehension—— I dont like this statue-colouring—no, not at all.

•   •   •

How is the book getting on? To have anything like a novel from you will be delightful. The dramas are not out, are they? I hunt the advertisements for the name. God bless you–

Ever your most affectionate
Ba.

1. William Page (1811–85), American portrait painter, whose experiments with pig-ments caused his paintings to blacken rapidly, as was the case with his portrait of Browning.
2. John Gibson Lockhart (1794–1854), critic, journalist, and biographer of Sir Walter Scott.
3. Charlotte Cushman (1816–76), American actress who had appeared in MRM's *Rienzi*.
4. "The Tinted Venus," a polychromed sculpture by John Gibson (1790–1866), Eng-lish sculptor who worked in Rome.

ROME. 43. VIA BOCCA DI LEONE.
[SUNDAY] MARCH 19. [1854]

My dearest Miss Mitford, your letter made my heart ache. It is sad sad indeed that you should have had this renewed cold just as you appeared to be rallying a little from previous shocks, and I know how depressing & enfeebling a malady this influenza is. It's the vulture finishing the work of the wolf. I pray God that, having battled through this last attack, you may be gradually strengthened & relieved by the incoming of the spring—(though an English spring makes one shiver to think of generally—) & with the summer come out into the garden, to sit in a chair & be shone upon, dear, dear friend. I shall be in England then, & get down to see you this time, & I tenderly hold to the dear hope of seeing you smile again & having you talk in the old way– About mesmerism I hold you to be wrong. Even unbelievers in the spiritual phenomena will admit the good done physically by such means—and, as M.ʳ May seems to have exhausted his resources & to promise nothing very confidently, I cant conceive why you should not make an experiment *attended with no risk to you* . . for, observe, if you fail to get benefit from mesmerism, you at least can get no injury.

•   •   •

For our own parts I have scarcely much heart to write to you of ourselves while thinking of you so sadly—but we are well in this air of miasma, I thank God– Those poor friends of ours, the Storys, have been forced to take away their remaining child at last (I wonder they did'nt do it months ago) by the persistent fever & ague, & have been interrupted on their journey to Naples, at Velletri, through an access of illness which I fear is threatening to life– They write in great distress, & I am anxious for the post today. A continued residence at Rome is perilous for children, to say nothing of men & women,—& I would'nt for California spend another winter here; in spite of my little Penini's ruddy checks hitherto. As to myself the climate agrees with me of course, because of the mildness of it. But let me cough, so that my husband & child run no risk– I choose Cheapside rather than anxiety for *them*!

We see a good deal of the Kembles here, & like them both, especially the Fanny who is looking magnificent still, with her black hair & radiant smile– A very noble creature, indeed. Somewhat unelastic, unpliant to the age . . attached to the old modes of thought & convention . . but noble in qualities & defects – I like her much– She thinks me credulous & full of dreams, but does not despise me for that reason . . which is good & tolerant of her . . & pleasant too, for I should not be quite easy under her contempt—M.ʳˢ Sartoris is genial & generous—her milk has had time to stand to cream, in her happy family relations, which poor Fanny Kemble's has not had. The Sartoris house has the best society at Rome, & exquisite music of course. We met Lockhart there, & my husband sees a good deal of him . . more than I do . . because of the access of cold weather lately which has kept me at home chiefly. Robert went down to the seaside in a day's excursion with him & the Sartoris[e]s, &, I hear, found favour in his sight – Said the critic, "I like Browning—he is'nt at all like a damned literary man". That's a compliment I believe, according to your dictionary– It made me laugh & think of you directly. I am afraid Lockhart's health is in a bad state—he looks very ill, & every now & then his strength seems to fail –

Robert has been sitting for his picture to Fisher the English artist,[1] who painted M! Kenyon & Landor—you remember those pictures in M! Kenyon's house? Landor's was praised much by Southey. Well—he has painted Robert, & it is an admirable likeness. The expression is an exceptional expression but highly characteristic—it is one of Fisher's best works– Now he is about our Wiedeman,—and if he succeeds as well in painting angels as men, will do something beautiful with that seraphic face – You are to understand that these works are done by the artist *for* the artist. Oh—we could'nt afford to have such a luxury as a portrait done for us. But I am pleased to have a good likeness of each of my treasures *extant*––in the possession of somebody.

•   •   •

To see those two works through the press must be a fatigue to you in your present weak state, dearest friend, and I keep wishing vainly I could be of use to you in the matter of the proof sheets—I might, you know, if I were in England. I do some work myself, but doubt much whether I shall be ready for the printers by July—no indeed—it is clear I shall not. If Robert is, it will be well.

•   •   •

Oh—I have been reading poor Haydon's biography[2] – There is tragedy! The pain of it one can hardly shake off. Surely, surely, wrong was done somewhere, when the worst is admitted of Haydon. For himself, . . looking forward beyond the grave, . . I seem to understand that all things when most bitter, worked ultimate good to him —for that sublime arrogance of his would have been fatal perhaps to the moral nature, if developped further by success. But for the nation, we had our duties—& we should not suffer our teachers & originators to sink thus– It is a book written in blood of the heart– Poor Haydon!

May God bless you my ever dear friend. I think of you & love
you dearly. Robert's love, put to mine, & Penini's love put to Robert's. I give away *Penini's* love as I please just now.

> Your ever attached
> EBB.

Send me my *bulletins*—only *two lines* if you will!–

1. William Fisher (?–1895), English portrait painter who did portraits of Landor and
   Kenyon in Bath in 1838.
2. *The Life of Benjamin Robert Haydon* (1853), edited by Tom Taylor, included
   Haydon's memoirs and journals.

> Swallowfield
> March 29, 1854.

Weaker and weaker, dearest friend, and worse and worse; and writing
brings on such agony that you would not ask for it if you knew the
consequences. It seems that in that overturn the spine was seriously
injured. There was hope that it might have got better; but last summer destroyed all chance. This accounts for the loss of power in the
limbs, and the anguish in the nerves of the back, and more especially
in those over the chest and under the arms. Visitors bring on such
exhaustion, and such increase of pain, that Mr. May forbids all but
Lady Russell. Perhaps by the time you arrive in England I may be a
little better. If so, it would be a great happiness to see you, if only
for half an hour.
   May God bless you, my beloved friend, and all whom you love!

> M.R. MITFORD.

> FLORENCE.
> [TUESDAY] JUNE 6.th [1854]

Yes, dearest friend, I had your few lines which Arabel sent to me – I
had them on the very day I had posted my letter to you, and I need
not say how deeply it moved me that you should have thought of giv-

ing me that pleasure of M.r Ruskin's kind word[1] at the expense of what I know to be so much pain to yourself. This last letter of your's brings me altogether a more pleasant emotion—there's a little improvement, a little ease, thank God. Now as the summer sets in . . if the summer ever sets in, in England . . we may hope for something like general amelioration surely. Here is your friend M.rs Trollope who ebbs & flows like the sea—has attacks affecting vital organs, and recovers, and takes long walks again and writes half a dozen more romances –

• • •

I left Rome with joy. If I had been thirsty I w.d not have drunken of the fountain of Trevi. My darling Penini was more unwell there than I ever saw him—he had three separate fits of diarrhœa & feverishness, & his roses faded, & blue marks fixed themselves under his languid eyes, & his dimples dropped away– That climate is pestilential, I do hold. Scarcely had we left it when he began to revive, & a week at Florence has produced a great change for the better–

• • •

We mean to stay at Florence a week or two longer & then go northward– I love Florence—the place looks exquisitely beautiful in its garden-ground of vineyards & olive-trees, sung round by the nightingales day & night, . . nay, sung *into* by the nightingales, for as you walk along the streets in the evening, the song trickles down into them till you stop to listen. Such nights we have between starlight & fire-fly-light, & the nightingales singing! I would willingly stay here, if it were not that we are constrained by duty & love to go—& at some day not distant, I dare say we shall come back 'for good & all' as people say,—seeing that, if you take one thing with another, there's no place in the world like Florence I am persuaded, for a place to live in. Cheap, tranquil, cheerful, beautiful, within the limit of civilization yet out of the crush of it. I have not seen the Trollopes yet—but we have spent two delicious evenings at villas on the outside the gates . . one with young Lytton,[2] Sir Edward's son, of whom I have told you ⟨I th⟩ink. I like him . . we both do . . from the bottom of our hearts. Then our friend Frederick Tennyson, the new poet, we are delighted to see again – Have you caught sight of his poems? If you have, tell me your thought. M.rs Howe's[3] I have read since I wrote last. Some of them are good—many of the thoughts striking, & all of a certain elevation. Of poetry however, strictly speaking, there is not much; and there's a large proportion of conventional stuff in the volume. She must be a clever woman. Of the ordinary impotencies & prettinesses of female poets she does not partake, but she cant take rank with poets in the good meaning of the word, I think, so as to stand without leaning– Also, there is some bad taste & affectation in the draping of her personality – I dare say M! Fields will bring you her book. Talking of American literature, with the publishers on the back of it, we think of offering the proofs of our new works to any publisher over the water who will pay us properly for the advantage of bringing out a v⟨o⟩lume in America simultaneously with the publication in England – We have heard that such a proposal will be acceptable, & mean to try it. The words you sent to me from M! Ruskin gave me great pleasure indeed, as how should they not from such a man? I like him personally too, besides my admiration for him as a writer, & I was deeply gratified in every way to have his approbation. His 'Seven Lamps' I have not read yet – Books come out slowly to Italy– It's our disadvantage, as you know. Ruskin & Art go together– I must tell you how Rome made me some amends after all– Page the American artist, painted a picture of Robert, like a Titian, & then presented it to me like a prince. It is a wonderful picture, the colouring so absolutely VENETIAN that artists cant (for the most part) keep their temper when they look at it, and the truth of the likeness is literal. M! Page has *secrets* in the art—certainly nobody else paints like him— & his nature, I must say, is equal to his genius & worthy of it.

•   •   •

Atherton, meanwhile, wants nobody to praise it, I am sure– How glad I shall be to sieze & read it, & how I thank you for the gift! May God bless & keep you. I may hear again if you write soon to Florence, but dont pain yourself for the world, I entreat you– I shall see you before long I think.

Your ever affectionate
EBB.

Robert's love.

1. Ruskin had written that some of EBB's poems, like "The Dead Pan," moved him to tears. His *Seven Lamps of Architecture*, mentioned below, appeared in 1849.

2. Edward Robert Bulwer (1831–91), a diplomat known by choice as "Robert Lytton," wrote poetry under the pseudonym Owen Meredith.

3. Julia Ward Howe (1819–1910), American poet and reformer, published *Passion Flowers* (1854).

FLORENCE.
[THURSDAY] OCT. 19 [1854]

I will not try to be overjoyed my dear dearest Miss Mitford, but indeed it is difficult to refrain from catching at hope with both hands. If the general health will but rally, there is nothing fatal about a spine disease– May God bless you—give you the best blessing in earth & heaven, as the God of the *living* in both places. We ought not to be selfish, nor stupid, so as to be afraid of leaving you in His hands. What is beautiful & joyful to observe, is, the patience & selfpossession with which you endure even the most painful manifestation of His will, & that while you lose none of that interest in the things of our mortal life which is characteristic of your sympathetic nature, you are content, just as if you felt none, to let the world go, according to the decision of God. May you be more & more confirmed & elevated & at rest—being the Lord's, whether absent from the body or present in it. For my own part I have been long convinced that what we call death is a mere incident in life—perhaps scarcely a greater one than the occurrence of puberty, or the revolution which comes with any new emotion or influx of new knowledge. I am heterodox about sepulchres & believe that no *part of us* will ever lie in a grave. I dont think much of my nail-parings . . do you?—not even of the nail of my thumb when I cut off what Penini calls the "gift-mark" on it. I believe that the body of flesh is a mere husk which drops off at death, while the spiritual body (see St Paul) emerges in glorious resurrection at once. Swedenborg says, some persons do not immediately realize that they have passed death—& this seems to me highly probable. It is curious that Maurice,[1] M.ʳ Kingsley's friend about whom so much lately has been written & quarrelled (& who *has* made certain great mistakes I think) takes this precise view of the resurrection, with an apparent unconsciousness of what Swedenborg has stated upon the subject, & that I, too, long before I knew Swedenborg, or heard the name of Maurice, came to the same conclusions. I wonder if M.ʳ King[s]ley agrees with us—I dare say he does, upon the whole—for the ordinary doctrine seems to me as little taught by Scripture as it can be reconciled to philosophical probabilities. I believe in an active, HUMAN life, beyond death as before it, an uninterrupted human life. I believe in no waiting in the grave, & in no vague effluence of spirit in a formless vapour. But you'll be tired with "what I believe".

I have been to the other side of Florence to call on Mrs Trollope on purpose that I might talk to her of you, but she was not at home though she has returned from the Baths of Lucca. From what I hear, she appears to be well, & has recommenced her "public mornings" which we shrink away from. She 'receives' every saturday morning in the most heterogeneous way possible. It must be amusing to anybody not overwhelmed ⟨by⟩ it, & people say that she snatches up 'characters' for her "so many volumes a year" out of the diversities of masks presented to her on these occasions. Oh—our Florence! In vain do I cry out for "Atherton". The most active circulating library has'nt "got it yet," they say. I must still wait. Meanwhile of course I am delighted with all your successes—and your books wont spoil by keeping like certain other books. So I may wait.

How young children unfold like flowers, & how pleasant it is to watch them! I congratulate you upon yours—your baby-girl must be a dear forward little thing.[2] But I wish I could show you my Penini with his drooping golden ringlets & seraphic smile, and his talk about angels—you would like him I know. Your girl-baby has avenged my name for me . . and now, if you heard my Penini say in the midst of a coaxing fit . . "O my sweetest little mama—my darling, dear*lest* little *Ba*", you would admit that "Ba" must have a music in it, to my ears at least. The love of two generations is poured out to me in that name—and the stream seems to run (in one instance) when alas! the fountain is dry – I do not refer to the Dead, who love still.

Ah—dearest friend, you feel how I must have felt about the accident in Wimpole Street.[3] I can scarcely talk to you about it. There will be permanent lameness, Arabel says, according to the medical opinion, though the general health was not for a moment affected. But . . permanent lameness! That is sad, for a person of active habits. I ventured to write a little note . . which was not returned . . I thank God—or read . . I dare say!—but of course there was no result– I never even expected it as matters have been.

I must tell you that our pecuniary affairs are promising better results for next year, & that we shall not in all probability be tied up from going to England. For the rest . . if I understand you . . . Oh no—! My husband has a family likeness to Lucifer in being proud.

Besides it's not necessary. When literary people are treated in England as in some other countries . . in that case & that time, we may come in for our share in the pensions given by the people, without holding out our hands. Now . . think of Carlyle, unpensioned!!! ——— Why, if we sate here in rags, we would'nt press in for an obolus before Belisarius—! ———

Mrs Sartoris has been here on her way to Rome, spending most of her time with us—singing passionately & talking eloquently. She is really charming. May God bless you, keep you, & love you, beloved friend.

Love your ever affec.^te
Ba!

May it be? Robert's love.

1. Frederick Denison Maurice (1805–72), Christian Socialist clergyman and author of *Theological Essays* (1853), which rejected the idea of eternal punishment.
2. The child of MRM's servants K and Sam Sweetman.
3. EBB's father had been confined after suffering a fall.

APPENDIX A

Elizabeth Barrett Browning
Chronology

1806	Born 6 March at Coxhoe Hall near Durham, eldest of eleven surviving children of Edward Moulton-Barrett and Mary Graham-Clarke.
1809–10	Family moved to palatial estate of Hope End in Herefordshire.
1815	October–November, visited France.
1817–18	Wrote *The Battle of Marathon*, which was privately printed in 1820.
1821	Published two poems in *New Monthly Magazine* on the loss of freedom in Greece. First signs of lifelong disease of the lungs.
1823–24	Spent seven months with her family in Boulogne.
1826	Published *An Essay on Mind with Other Poems;* began study of Greek under tutelage of the blind scholar Hugh Stuart Boyd.
1828	Mother died.
1832	Hope End sold because of financial difficulties; family moved to Sidmouth where EBB met Independent minister George Barrett Hunter who later became a regular visitor at Wimpole Street.
1833	Published translation of *Prometheus Bound*.
1835	Moved with family to Gloucester Place, London.
1836	May, introduced by John Kenyon to MRM and began correspondence.
1837	Contributed to *Findens' Tableaux*.
1838	Moved to 50 Wimpole Street. Published *The Seraphim, and Other Poems* to favorable notice. In September, went to Torquay to recuperate from a lung hemorrhage.
1840	Suffered a near-fatal illness after her eldest brother ("Bro") drowned in a sailing accident in Tor Bay.
1841	Acquired the spaniel Flush, a gift from MRM; September, returned to Wimpole Street.

1842	Wrote critical series on the Greek Christian poets for the *Athenæum*. Collaborated with MRM on *Bijou Almanack*.
1843	Collaborated with R. H. Horne on *A New Spirit of the Age*.
1844	Published *Poems*.
1845	January, began correspondence with Robert Browning; May, began receiving him.
1846	12 September, married to Robert Browning; moved to Italy.
1847	April, moved to Florence from Pisa.
1848	Settled in Casa Guidi as permanent residence.
1849	9 March, gave birth to son, Robert Wiedemann Barrett Browning (Pen).
1850	Published *Poems*.
1851	May, to London via Venice and Paris; July, saw MRM in London. Published *Casa Guidi Windows*. Autumn and winter in Paris; July–October, London.
1852	Winter in Paris.
1853	November, to Rome.
1854	May, returned to Florence. June, Flush died.
1855	January, MRM died.
1856	June, to London; October, returned to Florence; November, *Aurora Leigh* published (dated 1857); December, John Kenyon died.
1857	April, Edward Moulton-Barrett died.
1858	July, to Paris; October, returned to Florence; November, to Rome.
1859	May, returned to Florence.
1860	Published *Poems before Congress*.
1861	Returned from Rome to Casa Guidi 5 June; died 29 June; buried 1 July in Protestant Cemetery, Florence.

Mary Russell Mitford
Chronology

1787	Born 16 December at Alresford, Hampshire, only surviving child of Mary Russell and Dr. George Mitford.
1797	Won £20,000 lottery; moved to Reading.
1802	Moved to Bertram House, built by Dr. Mitford three miles out of Reading.

1806	Visited London and toured father's home in Northumberland.
1810	Published *Miscellaneous Poems;* met Sir William Elford with whom she corresponded for several years.
1820	Moved to cottage at Three Mile Cross near Reading.
1824	Her drama *Julian* performed; *Our Village,* vol. I, published.
1826	Published her tragedy *Foscari.*
1827	Published *Inez de Castro* and *Dramatic Scenes, Sonnets, and Other Poems.*
1828	Published tragedy *Rienzi.*
1830	Mother died.
1833	Published *Julian.*
1834	*Charles the First, an Historical Tragedy* produced in London.
1835	Published *Belford Regis, or Sketches of a Country Town.*
1836	May, introduced by John Kenyon to EBB and began correspondence.
1837	Received pension of £100; published *Country Stories;* began editing *Findens' Tableaux.*
1841	Injured in a fall; beginning of lameness.
1842	Edited *Bijou Almanack;* December, Dr. Mitford died.
1843	Friends raised subscription; trip to Bath.
1851	Week in London to see EBB; moved to Swallowfield in September.
1852	Published *Recollections of a Literary Life.*
1854	Published *Atherton and Other Tales* and *Dramatic Works.*
1855	Died 10 January; buried in Swallowfield churchyard.

APPENDIX B

Principal Works of
Elizabeth Barrett Browning

POETRY

Aurora Leigh. London: Chapman and Hall, 1857.

The Battle of Marathon: A Poem. London: Linsell, 1820.

Casa Guidi Windows: A Poem, in Two Parts. London: Chapman and Hall, 1851.

Elizabeth Barrett Browning: Hitherto Unpublished Poems and Stories with an Inedited Autobiography. Edited by H. Buxton Forman. 2 vols. Boston: The Bibliophile Society, 1914.

An Essay on Mind, with Other Poems. London: James Duncan, 1826.

Last Poems. London: Chapman and Hall, 1862.

New Poems by Robert and Elizabeth Barrett Browning. Edited by Frederic G. Kenyon. London: Smith, Elder & Co., 1914.

Poems. 2 vols. London: Edward Moxon, 1844.

Poems. New edition. 2 vols. London: Chapman and Hall, 1850.

Poems. 3d ed. 2 vols. London: Chapman and Hall, 1853.

Poems. 4th ed. 3 vols. London: Chapman and Hall, 1856.

Poems. 5th ed. 3 vols. London: Chapman and Hall, 1862. [Reprint of 4th ed.]

Poems before Congress. London: Chapman and Hall, 1860.

The Poet's Enchiridion. Edited by H. Buxton Forman. Boston: The Bibliophile Society, 1914.

Prometheus Bound. Translated from the Greek of Æschylus. And Miscellaneous Poems. London: Valpy, 1833.

The Seraphim, and Other Poems. London: Saunders and Otley, 1838.

Two Poems by Elizabeth Barrett and Robert Browning. London: Chapman and Hall, 1854. "A Plea for the Ragged Schools of London" was EBB's contribution.

PROSE

The Greek Christian Poets and the English Poets. London: Chapman and Hall, 1863. Appeared originally as two series in the *Athenæum*, 1842. "The English Poets" was a review of an anthology entitled *The Book of the Poets*.

In Collaboration with
R. H. Horne

A New Spirit of the Age. Edited by R. H. Horne. 2 vols. London: Smith, Elder & Co., 1844. Several essays by EBB.

Psyche Apocalypté: A Lyrical Drama. Projected drama in collaboration with R. H. Horne. *St. James Magazine and United Empire Review,* February 1876. Reprinted for private circulation: London: Hazell, Watson and Viney, 1876.

"Queen Annelida and False Arcite" and "The Complaint of Annelida to False Arcite," contributed to *The Poems of Geoffrey Chaucer, Modernized* [introduction by R. H. Horne]. London: Whittaker and Co., 1841.

A detailed list of EBB's contributions to annuals, periodicals, and series may be found in Gardner B. Taplin, *The Life of Elizabeth Barrett Browning* (New Haven: Yale University Press, 1957), 458–64.

Principal Works of
Mary Russell Mitford

American Stories for Little Boys and Girls, Intended for Children under Ten Years of Age. London: Whittaker, Treacher, 1831.

Atherton and Other Tales. London: Hurst and Blackett, 1854.

Belford Regis, or Sketches of a Country Town. London: R. Bentley, 1835.

Charles the First, an Historical Tragedy. In five acts [and in verse]. London: J. Duncombe and Co., 1834.

Christina, the Maid of the South Seas: A Poem. London: Printed by A. J. Valpy for F. C. and J. Rivington, 1811.

Country Stories. London: Saunders and Otley, 1837.

Dramatic Scenes, Sonnets, and Other Poems. London: G. B. Whittaker, 1827.

Dramatic Works. 2 vols. London: Hurst and Blackett, 1854.

Findens' Tableaux. Edited. London: C. Tilt, 1838–41.

Foscari: A Tragedy [in five acts and in verse]. London: G. B. Whittaker, 1826.

Fragments des œuvres d' Alexandre Dumas choisis à l'usage de la jeunesse par Miss M. R. Mitford. Brussels: Pierre Rolandi, 1846.

Inez de Castro. London, 1827. (Original complete edition, London: J. Dicks [1885].)

The Iris of Prose, Poetry, Art for MDCCCXL. Edited. London: C. Tilt, 1840.

Julian: A Tragedy in Five Acts. London: G. and W. B. Whittaker, 1833.

Lights and Shadows of American Life. Edited. London: H. Colburn and R. Bentley, 1832.

Match-making and Other Tales. London, n.d.

Our Village. 5 vols. London: G. and B. Whittaker, 1824–32.

Poems. London: Printed by A. J. Valpy for Longman, Hurst, Reese, and Orme, 1810.

Recollections of a Literary Life. London: R. Bentley, 1852.

Rienzi: A Tragedy in Five Acts [and in verse]. London: J. Cumberland, 1828.

Sadak and Kalasrade; or the Waters of Oblivion. A Romantic Opera, in Two Acts. London: Fairbrother, 1836.

Schloss's English Bijou Almanack for 1843. Poetically illustrated by Miss Mitford. London: Schloss, 1843.

Stories of American Life, by American Writers. Edited. London: H. Colburn and R. Bentley, 1830.

Tales for Young People . . . Selected from American Writers. Edited. London: Whittaker and Co., 1835.

APPENDIX C

Listing of Wellesley Letters From the English Poetry Collection, Wellesley College, Wellesley, Massachusetts

Kelley, Philip and Ronald Hudson, *The Brownings' Correspondence: A Checklist* (Winfield, Kansas), 1978.

KELLEY/ HUDSON NUMBER	DATE
36.14	[3 June 1836]
36.23	[24? August 1836]
36.25	[29 September 1836]
37.16	[Late February or Early March 1837] (Date correction)
37.26	29 June [1837]
37.41	26 October 1837
37.49	[19? December 1837]
38.27	[Early April 1838] (Date correction)
38.57	[10–11 August 1838]
38.63	30 October [1838]
38.64	[7 November 1838]
39.7 39.8	7 [–12] March [1839]
39.16	[16 May 1839] ERM-B & W (Date correction)
39.24	17 June [1839]
39.28	3 August 1839
40.2	[Late January 1840]
40.10	6 March 1840
40.43	[October or November 1840]

41.5	[21? January 1841] ERM-B & W
41.27	30 May [1841]
41.30	14 June 1841
41.38	17 July 1841
41.43	25 July 1841 ERM-B Folger & W
41.51	5 August 1841 ERM-B & W
41.62	13 September [1841]
41.71	[13] October 1841
41.77	2 November 1841
42.33	[5] March 1842
42.41	[27-28] March 1842 Folger & W
42.49	1 April 1842 ERM-B & W
42.62	14 May 1842
42.71	[4? June 1842] Fitz. Folger & W
42.79	4 July 1842 Folger & W
42.86	26 July 1842
42.89	1 August 1842
42.92	30 August 1842 Fitz. & Folger
42.98	14 September 1842
42.115	19 October 1842
42.117	21 October 1842 Folger & W
42.121	27 [–28] October 1842
42.124	31 October 1842
42.167	[12] December 1842 (Date correction)
42.172	14 December 1842
43.12	2 January [1843]
44.285	[February ? 1843] Folger & W (Date correction)
43.129	26 April 1843
43.144	4 May [1843]
43.167	24 May 1843
43.199	19 June 1843 Folger & W
43.284	[16] September 1843 ERM-B, Fitz. & W
43.378	27 December 1843
44.139	7 May 1844
44.206	6 August 1844
44.259	28 September 1844
45.28	28 January 1845
45.35	8 February 1845

45.38	11 February 1845
45.46	[19] February 1845
45.69	18 March 1845
45.124	[26 May 1845]
45.129	[4 June 1845]
45.141	[21 June 1845] ERM-B & W
45.162	[10 July 1845]
45.210	[13? September 1845]
45.267	[27 October 1845]
45.307	[1 December 1845]
46.71	[21 February 1846]
46.80	[Early March 1846]
46.284	[30 June 1846]
46.447	[18 September 1846]
47.26	[30 April 1847]
48.17	28 May [1848]
48.27	24 August [1848]
48.31	10 October [1848]
49.9	30 January [1849]
49.26	30 April [1849]
49.56	1 December [1849]
50.25	30 April [1850]
50.54	24 September [1850]
50.59	November [1850]
50.66	13 December [1850]
51.86	24 December [1851]
52.23	15 [–16] February [1852]
52.78	[30 July 1852]
52.125	[8–9 October 1852]
53.21	15 March [1853]
53.47	20 May [1853]
53.86	20–21 August [1853]
54.24	18 January [1854]
54.43	19 March [1854]
54.75	6 June [1854]
54.114	19 October [1854]

INDEX

Index

Bayley, Sarah, 90, 97, 100n4
Beacon Hill, 26
Beacon Terrace, 26
Beauchamp, Captain, 228
Beaumont, Francis, 76
Bedfords, vi
Beinecke Rare Book and Manuscript
    Library, xvii
Belisarius, 272
Bell, Currer. *See* Brontë, Charlotte
Ben (MRM's manservant). *See* Kirby, Ben
Bentham, Jeremy, 32, 33n1
Bentley, Richard, 131
Béranger, Pierre-Jean de, 207, 245
Bernard, Charles du Grail de la Villette,
    160, 162n2, 171, 172n1, 200
Bertram House, vi
Beulah Spa, The Royal, 3, 3n1, 5
Bezzi, Giovanni Aubrey, 27, 27n3, 47, 97
Bishop of Oxford Street (dog-stealer),
    136, 137
Black Mountains, 97
Blackstone, Rev. F. C., 181, 182n2
Blackwood's Edinburgh Magazine, 22,
    23n2, 33, 37, 72n1, 106, 106n1,
    107n2, 125n3
Bokhara, Kings of, 165
Bolingbroke, John, 75
Bowles, Caroline. *See* Southey, Caroline
    Bowles
Box tunnel, 125
Boyd, Hugh Stuart, 13, 14n1, 16, 181
"Boz." *See* Dickens, Charles
Bradbury and Evans, 228
Braddons, The, 25
Brand, Barbarina. *See* Dacre, Lady
Bremer, Frederika, x, 89, 89n1, 156; *See
    also* Howitt, Mary
Brissot, Jean Pierre de Warville, 215
British Library, xvi-xvii
British Museum, 123n1
Brontë, Charlotte, 210, 217, 223, 223n2,
    224, 261, 261n1
Brooke, Lord (Fulke Greville), 119,
    120n1
Brougham, Henry Peter, First Baron
    Brougham and Vaux, 94, 95n3

Brougham, Miss, 94, 95
Browne, Mr., 220
Browning, Elizabeth Barrett Moulton-
    Barrett
  Birth, vii
  Death, viii
  Family, vii, viii, 1
  Health
    Lung disease, viii, 16, 20, 21-22, 25,
      28, 38, 44, 45-46, 64, 101, 106, 109,
      115, 158, 182-83, 185-87, 188
    Miscarriages, 194, 198-99, 213-14,
      216, 221-22, 228-29
  Marriage, viii, 192, 195-98
  Opinions on
    America, 94, 123-24, 135, 144, 175,
      179, 189, 226, 229, 241, 269
    Art, 35, 66, 170, 214
    Death and after-life, 116, 263,
      270-71
    Letters, xiii, 40, 58, 63, 71, 78, 89,
      129, 130, 152, 153, 201
    Nature, 35, 84, 85, 88, 128, 202-03,
      209
    Poetics, 4, 7, 17, 18, 30, 36, 42,
      53-54, 55, 57, 75, 234
    Religion, x, 14, 20, 36, 37, 38, 69,
      73, 74, 102, 106, 110, 117, 118, 217
    Theater-going, 76, 92, 255
    Women's Role, 31, 77, 90, 95, 96,
      98, 99, 160, 173, 202
  Pet-name, 8, 271
  Reviews of, 22, 24, 56, 174
  Works—Poetry
    Aurora Leigh, v, viii, x, 159, 253
    Casa Guidi Windows, 211
    "Cry of the Children, The," 168,
      179, 224n4, 232
    "Dead Pan, The," 269n1
    "Doves, My," 231
    "Drama of Exile, A," 143, 145n1,
      146
    Essay on Mind, An, 42n1
    "House of Clouds, The," 64, 67,
      231
    "Lady Geraldine's Courtship," x,
      158

Index

Index

Index

Queen's visit, 158, 162–65
Subscription, 115, 123
Translations, 156, 157n3
Works—Poetry
  Blanche and the Rival Sisters, 83
  Miscellaneous Poems, 83
  Readings of Poetry, Old and New
  (poetry and prose), 228
Works—Prose
  American editions, 223
  Atherton and Other Tales, vi, 253, 269, 271
  "Baron's Daughter," 24
  Belford Regis, 155, 223
  "Buccaneer, The," 24
  "Cartel, The," 24
  Country Stories, vi, 223
  "Cristina, the Maid of the South Seas," 83
  Dramatic Scenes, 227
  "Emily," 225, 227n1
  "Exile, The," 18
  Findens' Tableaux
  "Tales," 24
  Foscari, 3n3
  "Marion Campbell," 18
  Otto, 2, 10n1
  Our Village, 94, 97, 223
  Recollections of a Literary Life, vi, 115, 212, 239
  Rienzi, vi, 148, 148n2
Monkey heat, 58
Montague, Eleanora Louisa, 124, 125n2
Montgomery, Rev. Robert, 131, 132n1
Morpeth, Lord, George William Frederick, 167
Moscheles, Ignaz, 128
"Mother-Age, the wondrous," 151
Motherwell, William, 234, 236n2
Moxon, Edward (publisher), 121, 140, 144, 146, 167, 237
Mulock, Dinah (Mrs. Craik), xii, 249, 250n1
Murphy, Patrick, 19n1
Murray, John, 207, 208
Murray, John, Publishers, xvii

Naples, 214

Napoleon I, 57, 93, 133, 151–52, 156, 164, 167, 167n1, 215n2, 216, 243, 249
Napoleon III. *See* Louis Napoleon
National, La, 242
National Gallery, 240
Nazianzen, St. Gregory, 70
New Monthly Magazine, The, 4, 8, 91, 93n2, 128, 174
New Spirit of the Age, A, 64, 144, 147
Newman, Francis William, 122–23, 123n3
Newman, John Henry, 122, 123n2
Norreys, 206
North American Review, The, 105, 105n3, 106
North, Christopher. *See* Wilson, John
Nugent, Major, 86

O'Connell, Daniel, xv, 133–34, 134n2, 151
Oedipus, 18
"Ogilvies." *See* Mulock, Dinah
Onory, Jane Nicholls, 221
Opium, xi, 135, 145
Orkney, Lord, 206
Orkwells, 206
Orleanists, 242
Orléans, 194, 196, 197, 247
Orme, Mrs., 20, 34
Ossoli, Angelo Eugene, 230
Ossoli, Margaret Fuller. *See* Fuller, Margaret
Ossoli, Marquis Angelo, 211, 212, 222, 230
Otley. *See* Saunders and Otley
Otto of Wittelsbach, 2, 10, 10n1
Our Village, vi, 41, 94, 97
Oxford, 122, 133
Oxford Movement, 123n2
Oxford student. *See* Ruskin, John

"P's, Miss," 90, 95–97, 126
Page, Emma, 262
Page, William, 262, 263–64, 264n1, 269
Pailleterie, Marquis de la, 200n1
Palmer, Lady Madalina, 82
Palmer, Mr., 82

290

Index

Shelley, Percy Bysshe, 54, 263
Shepherd, Henry J., 14n3
Shepherd, Lady Mary, 14n3
Shepherd, Mary, 14, 14n3
Shrewsbury, Lady, 206
Sidmouth, viii, 84n1, 122, 127
Sidney, Sir Philip, 120n1
Siena, 212, 229, 232, 233
Sigourney, Lydia, 50, 51n1
Silchester, 84
Simmons, Bartholomew, 106, 106n1
Sindbad the Sailor, 17
Sinigaglia, 208
Skerrett, Marianne, 44, 58, 95n4
Smith, Charlotte, 85, 85n1
Smith, Dora, 104
Smith, Sydney, 144, 145n2, 175
Smith, Thomas Southwood, 144, 145n4
Smollett, Tobias, 126
Sodoma, (Giovanni de Bazzi), 232
Soulié, Frederic, 171, 181, 182n3, 215, 236
Southey, Caroline Bowles, 142, 143n1
Southey, Robert, 23, 32, 39, 85, 97, 142, 263, 266
Southsea, 147
Spicer, Henry, 254, 255n1
Spiritualism, xi, 140, 249–50, 251, 253–54, 256–57, 259, 265; See also mesmerism
Staël, Mme de, 42
Stanhope, Lord, 249
Stephens, George, 63, 65, 105n2
Stephens, John Lloyd, 93, 95n2
Sterling, John, 105, 105n3, 106
Sterling, Mrs., 105
Story, Edith, 262
Story, Emelyn Eldredge, 253, 259, 262, 265
Story, Joseph, xv, 253, 263
Story, Judge Joseph, 259
Story, William Wetmore, 253, 259, 262, 265
Stowe, Harriet Beecher, 253, 255
Strathfieldsaye, 158, 162, 163
Stratton, Charles Sherwood ("General Tom Thumb"), 180, 193
Sue, Eugène, 171, 236, 244

Sunbeam, The, 24, 27, 27n2
Surrey, 101
Swallowfield, vii, viii, 162, 227, 239, 254
Swedenborg, 40, 42n2, 254, 270
Sweetman, Mary, 271, 272n2
Sweetman, Sam, 254, 261

Tait's Edinburgh Magazine, 33
Talfourd, Thomas Noon, 34, 34n2, 40, 155, 177, 181
Taylor (dogstealer), 136–38
Taylor, Tom, 267n2
Tennent, Sir James Emerson, 213
Tennyson, Alfred Lord, x, 4, 20, 32, 87, 96, 106, 118, 119, 121, 144, 151, 167n2, 178, 180, 182n1, 189, 194, 201, 202, 205, 220–21, 223, 235, 237, 238, 240, 245, 251, 253, 255
Tennyson, Emily Sellwood, 182, 240, 251
Tennyson, Frederick, 253, 255, 268
Tennyson, Hallam, 251
Terni, 261
Thackeray, William Makepeace, 210, 219, 253, 263
Thackwray, William (William T. Walworth), 15, 15n3
Thames, 195, 206
Thomson, Mrs. A. T. (Catherine Byerley), 236, 238n1
Three Mile Cross, vi, xv, 1, 37, 44, 90, 150, 194, 223, 237
Ticknor, W. D., 223
Tilt, Charles, 1, 11, 11n1, 32
Times, The, 242
Tindal, Mrs. Acton (Henrietta Harrison), xii, 224, 224n1
Tiny Tim, 143
Titian, 264, 269
Tom Thumb, General. See Stratton, Charles Sherwood
Tom Thumb (MRM's horse), 130
Tonna, Charlotte Elizabeth, 102, 103, 104n2
Torquay, viii, x, 20, 21, 26, 44
Tours, 217
Toussaint L'Ouverture, Pierre, 49, 49n1
Townsend, Richard E. A., 106

292